The Reformers on War, Peace, and Justice

# The Reformers on War, Peace, and Justice

Timothy J. Demy

Mark J. Larson

AND

J. Daryl Charles

PICKWICK *Publications* · Eugene, Oregon

THE REFORMERS ON WAR, PEACE, AND JUSTICE

Copyright © 2019 Timothy J. Demy, Mark J. Larson, and J. Daryl Charles. All rights reserved. Except for brief quotations in critical publications or reviews, no part of this book may be reproduced in any manner without prior written permission from the publisher. Write: Permissions, Wipf and Stock Publishers, 199 W. 8th Ave., Suite 3, Eugene, OR 97401.

Pickwick Publications
An Imprint of Wipf and Stock Publishers
199 W. 8th Ave., Suite 3
Eugene, OR 97401

www.wipfandstock.com

PAPERBACK ISBN: 978-1-4982-0697-6
HARDCOVER ISBN: 978-1-4982-0699-0
EBOOK ISBN: 978-1-4982-0698-3

## *Cataloguing-in-Publication data:*

Names: Demy, Timothy J., author | Larson, Mark J., author | Charles, J. Daryl., author

Title: The reformers on war, peace, and justice / Timothy J. Demy, Mark J. Larson, and J. Daryl Charles.

Description: Eugene, OR: Pickwick Publications, 2019 | Includes bibliographical references.

Identifiers: ISBN 978-1-4982-0697-6 (paperback) | ISBN 978-1-4982-0699-0 (hardcover) | ISBN 978-1-4982-0698-3 (ebook)

Subjects: LCSH: Reformation | Theology, Doctrinal—History—16th century | Theology, Doctrinal—16th century | Church history—16th century | War—Religious aspects—Christianity | Just war doctrine | Peace—Religious aspects—Christianity

Classification: BR305.3 D46 2019 (print) | BR305.3 (ebook)

The views represented in this book are solely those of the individual authors and do not represent those of the US Naval War College, the US Navy, or any governmental agency or department.

Manufactured in the U.S.A.                                                     08/28/19

# Contents

# Introduction

No idea—or doctrine—arises in a vacuum. There is always a context, and frequently that context is shaped by current events. Ideas, like people, have genealogies—intellectual ones. These intellectual genealogies can be traced through proponents and developers of the ideas, through events affecting the ideas, and through statements, declarations, and writings regarding the ideas. Such is certainly true of the subject of this book.

Issues of war and peace during the era of the Reformation were considered, articulated, and experienced against the larger backdrop of doctrines of the church and political authority. For example, what were the beliefs regarding the role of government with respect to Christians, individually and collectively? Ideas about war and peace can be studied as a subset of either political theory or theology, and the overlapping of the two categories was quite prominent during the Reformation. No ideas were static, and there was as much development in the realm of political theory and legal theory as there was in theology.

This book is not comprehensive. Rather, the material presented in this volume should be viewed as a beginning rather than an ending. The work is the result of the collaboration of the three authors with the hope that the effort gives those interested in the subject a place to begin study on the subject. With some of the individuals studied, there are portions of their writings that relate to war and peace. These are not the totality of what these people wrote about the subject, but it does provide a starting point. The authors are grateful for the permissions given by the respective publishers and copyright holders to reprint material where applicable.

# Part 1

# Czech and German Reformers

## CHAPTER I

# Jan Hus (1369–1415)

MORE THAN A CENTURY before Martin Luther's rebellious and reforming acts against the prevailing religious dogmas and structures of his day,
Jan Hus, Czech (Bohemian) priest and Master at Charles University in
Prague, lit the theological fuse that would ignite and lead to a religious
explosion with Luther's act of defiance in 1517. The theological flames
would then spread through the efforts of leaders such as Calvin, Zwingli,
Knox, and others. Because of his efforts, Hus frequently is labeled as the
first Protestant reformer.

Jan Hus (also known in English as John Hus or John Huss) was a
central figure in the Bohemian (Czech) Reformation who was martyred
because of his beliefs. His martyrdom on July 6, 1415 fueled the later Hussite Wars of 1419–1436.

Hus was born in 1369 in Husinec in southern Bohemia and at an early
age traveled to Prague, where he supported himself by singing in churches.
He earned the bachelor of arts degree (1393) and the master of arts degree
(1396) from Charles University (University of Prague). Hus was ordained
in 1400 and became a popular preacher at the non-parochial Bethlehem
Chapel in Prague (preaching in Czech). He soon came under the influence of the Englishman John Wycliffe (also Wyclif, 1320–1384), who was
deemed a heretic by the Roman church, and translated one of Wycliffe's
works into Czech. Hus also was influenced by native Czech reformers Jan
Milič (d. 1374) and Matěj of Janov (d. 1393). Hus's sermons were thoroughly orthodox and called for moral and spiritual reform, but he also
denounced some popular religious superstitions.

As a result of the Council of Pisa (1409) that elected Alexander V
(1339–1410) as the third pontiff competing for legitimacy as pope in what
is known as the Great Schism or the Western Schism, Hus supported King

Václav IV. In turn, this king supported the Pisan Alexander V, and Hus became embroiled in the fallout of papal politics and divisions as they affected Bohemia. Dissent also was fueled by rising Czech nationalism, and Hus had a large popular following because his preaching spoke to the common person.

In 1410, Alexander V died and was succeeded by antipope John XXIII (ca. 1370–1419). John XXIII proclaimed a crusade against King Ladislaus of Naples in 1411 and authorized the sale of indulgences to fund the war. Hus opposed the sale of indulgences and was especially vocal against them for the purposes of funding warfare. Hus believed that no bishop or pope had the right to make war. In 1412, Prague was placed under papal interdict and Hus, by then a very popular and prominent figure, went from Prague into voluntary exile in southern Bohemia for two years. During this period he wrote fifteen treatises on ecclesiastical reform and church practices and tied all of the writings to social concerns as well.

In the fall of 1414, Hus was invited to appear at the Council of Constance, which had been called by emperor-elect Sigismund and Pope John XXIII to deal with the papal schism. Once there, Hus was arrested, imprisoned, and, in June 1415, tried for heresy. Found guilty and refusing to recant, Hus was executed by burning at the stake.

The death of Hus further inflamed the already growing Czech nationalism and opposition to papal authority, creating a national movement that many understand to be the forerunner of the sixteenth-century Protestant Reformation (although there are distinct theological differences between the two movements). Hus scholar Thomas A. Fudge notes:

> During the sixteenth century Hus was perceived as being in the vanguard of Protestantism. While Hus has frequently been regarded as a precursor or forerunner to the Protestant movements, this notion has also been called into question. Hus challenged the structure and authority of the medieval church, denounced abuses, and approved the practice of Utraquism but held the soteriological principle of *fides caritate formata* [faith formed by charity/good works], retained the Eucharistic dogma of transubstantiation, and delineated his paradigm of authority in terms of scripture, conscience, and tradition, not *sola scriptura*. He neither replaced the altar with the pulpit (Calvin, Zwingli) nor preached justification by faith (Luther).[1]

---

1. Fudge, "Hus, Jan," 277.

Unquestionably, Hus was a martyr, and later generations in Bohemia and elsewhere rallied around him as such. However, as Fudge notes above, there is disagreement as to the extent of Hus's ideas being identical to the ideas of those who came after him. "The reform movement and revolutionary outburst that took his name had little in common with Hus himself. After all, Hus approved of the lay chalice with considerable unease, though it later became the symbol of Hussite Bohemia."[2]

Unlike later reformers who spoke about and at times participated in war and conflict, Hus is remembered as a martyr, and it is in this regard that his life and work are best understood with respect to war and peace. The martyrdom of Hus became a rallying symbol for many Bohemians who had theological, political, and social complaints against religious and political authorities.

Fighting eventually erupted in 1419, and, during the course of the next seventeen years, five crusades were called against the Hussites and factions among them. The wars finally came to an end in 1439 when royal Polish troops defeated the Hussites at the Battle of Lipany. Throughout the era, the memory and martyrdom of Jan Hus provided a motivation for fighting and created a legacy that other reformers would look back to in the sixteenth century.

In 1537, Martin Luther wrote an extensive introduction to the letters of Hus and had it published. In that work, Luther stated that as a divinity student he read a volume of Hus's sermons in the monastery library in Erfurt that had escaped destruction. Luther wrote: "If such a man is to be regarded as a heretic, no person under the sun can be looked on as a true Christian."[3]

## Political Thought of Czech Reformers in the Era of Hus

Hus and the Bohemian religious reformers of his era in the decades before his death were neither political thinkers nor political reformers. They were looking for spiritual reform rather than political reform or revolution. Although Hus is the most well-known, there were other like-minded reformers in Bohemia: Jan Milič (d. 1374), Matěj z Janova (ca. 1350–55–1393), Tomáš Štítný ze Štítnéeho (c. 1333–1401/09), Stanislov ze Znojma (ca.

2. Smahel, *Companion to Jan Hus,* 5.

3. Luther, "Preliminary Notice," 4, 9.

1351–1414), Jeroným Pražský (Jerome of Prague, 1379–1416), Štěpán Páleč (c. 1370–1424), and Jacoubek ze Stříba (Jacob of Miles, 1372–1429).

Unlike the reformers who would come after them in the sixteenth century, Hus and the writings of other Bohemians touch on political matters only incidentally.[4] However, what few statements were made were used by the followers of Hus after his death. R. R. Betts has observed regarding the roots of later militant Hussites: "On the political philosophy of the early Czech reformers, occasional and unsystematic as it was, was built the first nation in Western Europe to proclaim and practice the doctrine of the supremacy of the State in all things, spiritual as well as temporal, or, perhaps one should say, the doctrine of the identity of the nation State and the national Church."[5] In many ways, this was a precursor of what would occur throughout Europe in later centuries.

These Hus-era reformers were wide-ranging in the sources from which they drew their sparse statements, relying on the Bible, Church Fathers, Thomists, Scotists, popes, and others. However, their preference was for biblical authority, especially pronouncements as expressed in the Gospels and the Epistles of Paul and Peter. Thus, they contended that the Bible teaches that political authority is of divine origin and that civil obedience is a duty and obligation of all Christians.[6] Biblical admonitions such as those of Matthew 22:21 and Romans 13:1 were upheld by the Czech reformers as remaining valid in fifteenth-century Bohemia. In addition to the biblical text, some of the Czech reformers followed the political (and theological) thought of Augustine. In following Augustine, they could see the state as the "Beast" of the Apocalypse but also believe that the state was part of God's divine plan.

Some of what the Czech reformers articulated with respect to politics and the state was commonly accepted medieval political thought, and for these reformers the primary concerns were individual spiritual vitality and moral uprightness rather than political considerations. However, there were differences among the Czech reformers. Pre-fifteenth-century reformers such as Jan Milič did not view the king (state) as an instrument of reformation. In part, this was due to Milič's eschatology wherein he saw the end of the world as imminent.[7] The earliest of the Czech reformers to begin bringing

4. Betts, "Some Political Ideas," 20.
5. Betts, "Some Political Ideas," 20.
6. Betts, "Some Political Ideas," 21.
7. Betts, "Some Political Ideas," 24.

political precision into their thought was Matěj z Janova (1350–1393). He viewed the state as the "Beast" of the Apocalypse and believed that the state was too corrupt or tyrannical to reform the Church.

However, in the first decade of the fifteenth-century copies of John Wycliffe's polemical writings came to Bohemia through the travels of men such as Jerome of Prague, Mikulás Faulfis, and Jiri z Knehnic.[8] The political thought of early English reformers such as John Wycliffe (d. 1384) and the Irishman Richard FitzRalph, Archbishop of Armagh (d. 1360), created a linkage between the spiritual life and political life of an individual and came to be accepted. Betts writes:

> These writings . . . attracted the interest of the Czechs because the corner-stone . . . was the principle that moral rectitude is a condition of civil and ecclesiastical authority. This principle of dominion founded on grace, with its corollary that no priest or magistrate has either the power or right to exercise the functions of his office if he is in a state of mortal sin, was eagerly accepted by the Czech reformers because it provided a theoretical rationalization for their crusade against the immorality of office holders in Church and State.[9]

A second political principle accepted by the Czechs and inherited from the English reformers such as Wycliffe was that it was the right and the duty of the state to reform the Church. If such reforming required force, that was acceptable, as was the confiscation of ecclesiastical property.[10]

The Reformation did not occur in a social, cultural, or political vacuum. In every geographic region of the Reformation, local history affected political thought and actions of the reformers in those areas. Similar biblical interpretations played out differently in various regions based on the local and regional circumstances. For example, in Bohemia, many of the higher clergy were German by origin and speech, and this exacerbated Hussite nationalism and ecclesiastical antagonism.[11]

Political differences between England and Bohemia also created hesitations on Hus's part in completely following the political ideas of Wycliffe. Because of England's long tradition of a strong monarchy, Wycliffe, as expressed in his work *Tractatus de Officio Regis* (*Tractate on the Office of the*

---

8. See Hudson, "From Oxford to Prague"; Van Dussen, *From England to Bohemia,* 84.

9. Betts, "Some Political Ideas," 23.

10. Betts, "Some Political Ideas," 23–24.

11. Betts, "Some Political Ideas," 28.

*King),* was more willing to trust the state and hope for it to be a reforming power for the Church than was Hus, who did not put his trust in princes and political leaders. Betts observes: "All in all, the mechanism of the executive instruments of the Czech State was still far too inadequate and ineffective to be the instrument for the reformation and government of the Church before the revolution of 1419."[12] Yet, even though Hus favored the Church over the state, he was also wary of the power of the Church.

The most important idea that Hus accepted from the writings and thought of Wycliffe was that of *dominum ex gracia* that Wycliffe articulated in *Tractatus de Civili Domino (Tractate on Civil Dominion).* Of the importance of this idea Betts observes:

> In modern terms, this means that the exercise of office or authority and the enjoyment of property should be conditional on a subjective qualification. If this principle were accepted, nobody, be he pope, bishop, priest, or friar, king, judge, landlord or merchant, has any right to exercise the functions of his office or trade in the virtue of any act of consecration, election, ordination, or by right of inheritance, purchase, conquest, gift or charter. It was a doctrine to unmake popes, trample the bishops underfoot, cripple monasticism, and provoke political and social revolution.[13]

Such revolution would not come in Hus's day or those of the later reformers (though the idea of Wycliffe, accepted by Hus, is linked to Luther's doctrine of the priesthood of every Christian), but the ideological and theological seeds were being planted and would be harvested by other religious and political thinkers in the seventeenth and eighteenth centuries in the thinking of people such as John Locke.

12. Betts, "Some Political Ideas," 29.

13. Betts, "Some Political Ideas," 32.

CHAPTER 2

# Martin Luther (1483–1546)

MARTIN LUTHER, THE PROTESTANT reformer and the dominant figure of the sixteenth century, was born in Eisleben in eastern Germany in 1483. He grew up in Mansfeld, where his father Hans Luther was a prosperous copper miner. Luther earned a master's degree at the University of Erfurt in 1505 and immediately began legal studies in preparation for a career as a lawyer. He abandoned law school after only a few weeks after he made a vow in the midst of a thunderstorm to become a monk. He soon joined the large monastery of the Observant Augustinian friars in Erfurt. After he was awarded the doctorate in theology at the University of Wittenberg in 1512, he became a professor in Bible at the same university. He then added to his professorial labors the responsibility of preaching in the town church in Wittenberg. For the rest of his life Luther served in Wittenberg as both professor and pastor, developing a theology that emphasized the authority of scripture, the priesthood of believers, the two kingdoms, law and gospel, and the theology of the cross. In his teaching on theological ethics, he espoused classical just war doctrine even as he dissented from holy war practices in the sixteenth century—wars initiated by popes and wars prosecuted without restraint by Turkish sultans.[1]

Holy war advocates believed that the church had the authority to declare war. Pope Innocent IV had authorized prelates to declare and lead wars.[2] The First Crusade had been proclaimed by Pope Urban II in 1095 to liberate Jerusalem from Muslim control and oppression. The crusade mentality continued into the sixteenth century, even though Thomas Aquinas had reasserted the classic just war doctrine of Augustine in the thirteenth

1. Corey, "Luther and the Just War," 305–28.
2. Miller, "Fighting Like a Christian," 47.

9

century. A crusade league, which included the Papacy, defeated the Turks in the Battle of Lepanto on October 7, 1571.

Luther spoke against the medieval holy war tradition in his treatise *On War against the Turk* (1529). He declared that it is not right for the pope to lead a church army. He insisted that the civil magistrate alone is authorized by God to make war. On this issue Luther stood in continuity with the position articulated by Augustine of Hippo in his *Reply to Faustus the Manichaean*.[3]

Luther agreed with Augustine's perspective that "the natural order which seeks the peace of mankind, ordains that the monarch should have the power of undertaking war if he thinks it advisable."[4] At the same time, he dissented from the Reformed view that parliamentary bodies may take up arms against tyrannical monarchs. The Reformed theologian Peter Martyr Vermigli, for example, approved of the deposition of King Christian II by the parliamentary body in Denmark. Luther in contrast repudiated the deposition. He based his position on his interpretation of Romans 13 and set forth this contention: "No one shall fight or make war against his overlord, for a man owes his overlord obedience, honor, fear." He went on to say that he intended his remarks to apply to "peasants, citizens of the cities, nobles, counts, and princes as well." In fact, he maintained, "A rebellious noble, count, or prince should have his head cut off the same as a rebellious peasant."[5]

It should be pointed out, however, that there was a point of overlap between Luther and Reformed theologians on the matter of who had the authority to resist tyranny. Theodore Beza, for example, asserted that the inferior magistrates had the right to engage in a defensive war against a tyrannical monarch. They were authorized to take up arms against the armies of the prince who would seek to exterminate them. This was the same position that Luther had articulated in his *Warning to His Dear German People*.[6] Both Beza and Luther took the position that although the inferior

---

3. Miller, "Fighting Like a Christian," 44, properly notes that Luther drew heavily on Augustine's views of the just war. Hendrix, "Luther," 41, makes the observation concerning Luther that "next to the Bible the most important influence in his early theology was Augustine of Hippo."

4. Augustine, "Reply to Faustus the Manichaean" 22.75.

5. Luther, "Whether Soldiers, Too," 116.

6. Edwards, *Luther's Last Battles,* 20–37, provides a nuanced discussion on Luther's resistance theory and a careful analysis of his *Warning to His Dear German People*.

magistrates did not have the authority to depose and execute a king, they could defend themselves against a king who moved against them.[7]

The second constituent of classical just war doctrine related to the matter of just cause. A legitimate war assumes that wrongdoing has been committed. Luther embraced this perspective by raising the question: "What else is war but the punishment of wrong and evil?"[8] Luther at this point reflected a long-standing position in the church. Augustine had maintained that "the real evils in war are love of violence, revengeful cruelty, fierce and implacable enmity, wild resistance, and the lust of power." He then added that "it is generally to punish these things" that "good men undertake wars."[9]

Luther denounced Islam for its lack of a commitment to a just cause in its waging of war. Its commitment to *jihad* or military striving meant that countries were attacked that had committed no wrong. Their wars in the view of Luther were nothing more than "robbing and murdering, devouring more and more of those that are around them."[10]

Luther also believed that Israel had gone to war against the Canaanites without a just cause. He did not condemn them, however, for what they had done. He maintained that "God's hands are not bound so that he cannot bid us make war against those who have not given us just cause, as he did when he commanded the children of Israel to go to war against the Canaanites." He asserted, "In such cases God's command is necessity enough."[11]

A just war according to Augustine had to have a third requirement, namely, a right intention. Soldiers in the view of Augustine "should perform their military duties in behalf of the peace and safety of the community."[12] Medieval teaching continued with the same perspective, which was

---

7. Whitford, "Luther's Political Encounters," 190, identifies Luther's position as one of "limited acceptance of resistance to tyranny."

8. Luther, "Whether Soldiers, Too," 95.

9. Augustine, "Reply to Faustus the Manichaean" 22.74.

10. Luther, "On War against the Turk," 179.

11. Luther, "Whether Soldiers, Too," 125. In this interpretation, Luther differed from John Calvin who embraced the view that the Jews first offered mercy and peace to the Canaanites before they initiated war against them. Calvin had stated, "The Israelites were ordered to offer peace to all, that they might thereafter have a just and legitimate cause for declaring war." Thus, while Luther affirmed that the Jewish wars under Moses were initiated without just cause, Calvin insisted that there was just cause. "The blinded nations," he wrote, "obstinately refused the peace thus offered" (Calvin, *Commentaries*, 4:99).

12. Augustine, "Reply to Faustus the Manichaean" 22.74).

embraced by Luther as well. "Why does anyone go to war," he contended, "except he desires peace and obedience."[13]

Luther clearly maintained the traditional position that a just war has three constituents—the proper authority, a just cause, and a right intention. Although Luther did not offer an elaborate treatment of the subject, he also believed that war ought to be a last resort. He exhorted the European princes of his day not to think of themselves as if they were the Turkish sultan. He counseled, "Wait until the situation compels you to fight when you have no desire to do so." He then added, "You will still have more than enough wars to fight."[14]

Luther stood in continuity with the medieval teaching on the justice of war, *jus ad bellum*. Medieval writers, though, were not oblivious to the distinction between the *justice of war* and *justice in war*. While the justice of war category focuses upon the preliminary issues that lead to war, the matter of justice in war concerns whether or not the war is being fought justly or unjustly.

One of the customary restraints that medieval theologians insisted upon related to the extent of harm that could be done in battle. An example of this is seen in the Peace of God movement in the thirteenth century. Eight kinds of people enjoyed noncombatant immunity—the list included religious figures, travelers, merchants, and peasants.

Luther fundamentally embraced the medieval tradition with its restraint upon the amount of harm to be administered. His humanitarian commitment is seen in his repudiation of Turkish warfare, which disregarded this aspect of the justice in war tradition. Ottoman disdain for the justice in war practice of restraint in battle was reflected at Mohacs in 1526. Suleyman's policy of taking no prisoners resulted in the annihilation of some 30,000 soldiers. The captives that he temporarily held were put to death.

Such conduct impelled Luther to identify the Turks as "the army of the devil."[15] The Turks, he said, were a "wild and barbarous people."[16] They were a people who regarded women as being "immeasurably cheap," to be "bought and sold like cattle."[17] Their wars entailed murder and a lack of

13. Luther, "Whether Soldiers, Too," 95.
14. Luther, "Whether Soldiers, Too," 118.
15. Luther, "On War against the Turk," 193.
16. Luther, "On War against the Turk," 175.
17. Luther, "On War against the Turk," 181.

restraint.[18] If and when they did take prisoners, there was no humanitarian impulse in their treatment of captives. "How cruelly the Turk treats those whom he takes captive," Luther wrote. "He treats them like cattle, dragging, towing, driving those who can move, and killing on the spot those that cannot move, whether they are young or old."[19]

Luther broke with the teaching of faith plus works on the doctrine of salvation that was widely espoused in the late medieval church. He renounced semi-Pelagian theologians such as Gabriel Biel. His biblical exegesis led him to espouse what he regarded as the foundational doctrine of the Christian church, justification by grace through faith alone. In his moral theology on the subject of war he was less innovative, standing in continuity with the medieval tradition on just war doctrine. His opposition to holy war doctrine, however, was an important contribution in the period.[20]

## Martin Luther, "Whether Soldiers, Too, Can Be Saved."

From *Luther's Works*, edited by Jaroslav Pelikan, et al., 94–98. Vol. 46. St Louis: Concordia; Philadelphia: Fortress, 1967. Used by permission.

In the first place, we must distinguish between an occupation and the man who holds it, between a work and the man who does it. An occupation or a work can be good and right in itself and yet be bad and wrong if the man who does the work is evil or wrong or does not do his work properly. The occupation of a judge is a valuable divine office. This is true both of the office of the trial judge who declares the verdict and the executioner who carries out the sentence. But when the office is assumed by one to whom it has not been committed or when one who holds it rightly uses it to gain riches or popularity, then it is no longer right or good. The married state is also precious and godly, but there are many rascals and scoundrels in it. It is the same with the profession or work of the soldier; in itself it is right and godly, but we must see to it that the persons who are in this profession and who do the work are the right kind of persons, that is, godly and upright, as we shall hear.

18. Luther, "On War against the Turk," 178.
19. Luther, "On War against the Turk," 200.
20. Miller, "Fighting Like a Christian," 48.

In the second place, I want you to understand that here I am not speaking about the righteousness that makes men good in the sight of God. Only faith in Jesus Christ can do that; and it is granted and given us by the grace of God alone, without any works or merits of our own, as I have written and taught so often and so much in other places. Rather, I am speaking here about external righteousness which is to be sought in offices and works. In other words, to put it plainly, I am dealing here with such questions as these: whether the Christian faith, by which we are accounted righteous before God, is compatible with being a soldier, going to war, stabbing and killing, robbing and burning, as military law requires us to do to our enemies in wartime. Is this work sinful or unjust? Should it give us a bad conscience before God? Must a Christian only do good and love, and kill no one, nor do anyone any harm? I say that this office or work, even though it is godly and right, can nevertheless become evil and unjust if the person engaged in it is evil and unjust.

In the third place, it is not my intention to explain here at length how the occupation and work of a soldier is in itself right and godly because I have written quite enough about that in my book *Temporal Authority: To What Extent It Should be Obeyed.* Indeed, I might boast here that not since the time of the apostles have the temporal sword and temporal government been so clearly described or so highly praised as by me. Even my enemies must admit this, but the reward, honor, and thanks that I have earned by it are to have my doctrine called seditious and condemned as resistance to rulers. God be praised for that! For the very fact that the sword has been instituted by God to punish the evil, protect the good, and preserve peace is powerful and sufficient proof that war and killing along with all the things that accompany wartime and martial law have been instituted by God. What else is war but the punishment of wrong and evil? Why does anyone go to war, except because he desires peace and obedience?

Now slaying and robbing do not seem to be works of love. A simple man therefore does not think it is a Christian thing to do. In truth, however, even this is a work of love. For example, a good doctor sometimes finds so serious and terrible a sickness that he must amputate or destroy a hand, foot, ear, eye, to save the body. Looking at it from the point of view of the body, which the doctor wants to save, he is a fine and true man and does a good and Christian work, as far as the work itself is concerned. In the same way, when I think of a soldier fulfilling his office by punishing the wicked, killing the wicked, and creating so much misery, it seems an un-Christian work completely contrary to Christian love. But when I think of how it protects the good and keeps and preserves wife and child, house and farm, property, and honor and peace, then I see how precious and godly the work is; and I observe that it amputates a leg or a hand, so that the whole body may not perish. For if the sword were not on guard to preserve peace, everything in the world would be ruined because of lack of peace. Therefore, such a war is only a very brief lack of peace that prevents an everlasting and immeasurable lack of peace, a small misfortune that prevents a great misfortune.

What men write about war, saying that it is a great plague, is all true. But they should also consider how great the plague is that war prevents. If people were good and wanted to keep peace, war would be the greatest plague on earth. But what are you going to do about the fact that people will not keep the peace, but rob, steal, kill, outrage women and children, and take away property and honor? The small lack of peace called war or the sword must set a limit to this universal, world-wide lack of peace which would destroy everyone.

This is why God honors the sword so highly that he says that he himself has instituted it and does not want men to say or think that they have invented it or instituted it. For the hand that wields this sword and kills with it is not man's hand, but God's; and it is not man, but God, who hangs, tortures, beheads, kills, and fights. All these are God's works and judgments.

To sum it up, we must, in thinking about a soldier's office, not concentrate on the killing, burning, striking, hitting, seizing, etc. This is what children with their limited and restricted vision see when they regard a doctor as a sawbones who amputates, but do not see that he does this only to save the whole body. So, too, we must look at the office of the soldier, or the sword, with the eyes of an adult and see why this office slays and acts so cruelly. Then it will prove itself to be an office which, in itself, is godly and as needful and useful to the world as eating and drinking or any other work.

There are some who abuse this office, and strike and kill people needlessly simply because they want to. But that is the fault of the persons, not of the office, for where is there an office or a work or anything else so good that self-willed, wicked people do not abuse it? They are like mad physicians who would needlessly amputate a healthy hand just because they wanted to. Indeed, they themselves are a part of that universal lack of peace which must be prevented by just wars and the sword and be forced into peace. It always happens and always has happened that those who begin a war unnecessarily are beaten. Ultimately, they cannot escape God's judgment and sword. In the end God's justice finds them and strikes, as happened to the peasants in the revolt.

As proof, I quote John the Baptist, who, except for Christ, was the greatest teacher and preacher of all. When soldiers came to him and asked him what they should do, he did not condemn their office or advise them to stop doing their work; rather, according to Luke 3, he approved it by saying, "Rob no one by violence or by false accusation, and be content with your wages." Thus he praised the military profession, but at the same time forbade its abuse. Now the abuse does not affect the office. When Christ stood before Pilate he admitted that war was not wrong when he said, "If my kingship were of this world, then my servants would fight that I might not be handed over to the Jews." Here, too, belong all the stories of war in the Old Testament, the stories of Abraham, Moses, Joshua, the Judges, Samuel, David, and the kings of Israel. If the waging of war and the military profession were in themselves wrong and displeasing to God, we should have to condemn Abraham, Moses, Joshua, David, and all the rest of the holy fathers, kings, and princes, who served God as soldiers and are highly praised in Scripture because of this service, as all of us who have read even a little in Holy Scripture know well, and there is no need to offer further proof of it here.

## The Peasants' War

Peasants in Germany occupied the lowest stratum in society. In 1524 and 1525, they rebelled in the largest uprising in the history of Germany involving as many as 300,000 common people.[21] A contributing factor was the Lutheran revolt against Rome, which had social and political implications.[22] Anti-authoritarian ideas, articulated by Luther and his supporters in the ecclesiastical realm, spread widely. In addition, Luther's teaching on the priesthood of all believers could be applied to the issues of social equality and economic justice.[23]

The rebellion began on June 24, 1524 in the Black Forest region of Germany in the county of Stühlingen near the Swiss border. It would spread to the central and eastern parts of Germany. Initially it was merely a public

21. Blickle, *Revolution of 1525*; Preus, "Political Function of Luther's *Doctrina*," 591–99.

22. Dickens and Tonkin, *Reformation in Historical Thought*, 7–57.

23. Kirchner, *Luther and the Peasants' War*.

demonstration. The peasants felt crushed by the dues and services that had been imposed upon them by their manorial lords.

The peasants set forth their demands in the *Twelve Articles of Upper Swabia* in March of 1525, incorporating rhetoric from the Lutheran reformation in the call to freedom.[24] The rights that they affirmed included the privilege of calling their own pastors who were to receive a decent salary, a restoration of the freedom to gather wood in the forests and to fish in the streams, and justice in the courts.[25] Luther expressed sympathy for their desires in his essay *Admonition to Peace* (April 1525). He even blamed the princes for not treating the peasants with justice.[26] The political powers responded to the peasants in Swabia, however, by dismissing their request for milder treatment.

It seems clear that the turn to violence on the part of the peasants occurred when they became convinced that they would never receive a fair hearing of their grievances by recourse to legal procedures. When the peasants captured the castle of Wemsberg, they slaughtered the landlords. They forced the Count of Helfenstein and other nobles to run the gauntlet of pikes, a form of military execution. The massacre of Wemsberg on Easter Sunday, April 16, 1525 outraged Luther. The attacks upon lords and rulers, the plundering and destruction of churches, monasteries, and castles were too much to bear.[27] Luther responded in the first week of May with his little treatise *Against the Robbing and Murdering Hordes of Peasants*.

Luther began by indicting the peasants for their actions.[28] He called attention to their insubordination, rebellion, murder, and robbery. He reminded the peasants of the biblical duty of submission, quoting from Romans 13:1: "Let every person by subject to the governing authorities."[29] He also referred to 1 Peter 2:13: "Be subject to every ordinance of man."[30]

Luther also expressed his belief that the devil was behind the uprising. "See what a mighty prince the devil is," he wrote, "how he has the world in his hands and can throw everything into confusion, when he can so quickly

---

24. "Twelve Articles of Upper Swabia," 252–57.

25. Oberman, "Gospel of Social Unrest," 111.

26. Kolb, "Luther on the Peasants and Princes," 131.

27. Kolb, "Luther on the Peasants and Princes," 131. Kolb draws attention to Luther's "profound fear of disorder in society" (128).

28. Luther, "Against Robbing and Murdering," 49.

29. Luther, "Against Robbing and Murdering," 50.

30. Luther, "Against Robbing and Murdering," 51.

catch so many thousands of peasants, deceive them, blind them, harden them, and throw them into revolt, and do with them whatever his raging fury undertakes."[31] He conjectured that there was no longer "a devil in hell; they have all gone into the peasants."[32]

Luther's treatise was addressed to the governing authorities as well. He exhorted them to seek a peaceful resolution of the dispute, if possible. "We must go beyond our duty," he asserted, "and offer the mad peasants an opportunity to come to terms, even though they are not worthy of it."[33] If that did not work, the rebellion was to be put down by force. "Let everyone who can," he implored, "smite, slay, and stab, secretly or openly, remembering that nothing can be more poisonous, hurtful, or devilish than a rebel."[34]

Luther was not urging an indiscriminate slaughter at this point. This was simply Luther—colorful and dramatic, captivating and emphatic. He distinguished between the peasants who instigated and initiated the rebellion and the people who were coerced by the peasants to join the rebellion. With regard to the participants who had been forced to join the rebellion, Luther admonished, "The rulers ought to have mercy on these prisoners of the peasants."[35] Luther was urging discrimination in the putting down of the rebellion, rather than an indiscriminate slaughter of everyone connected with it.

The peasants had prevailed in the massacre at Wemsberg in April of 1525. The tide began to change for the governing authorities a month later at a battle in Frankenhausen. On May 15 peasant forces led by Thomas Müntzer were decimated by Count Ernst of Mansfeld.[36] Six thousand peasants were killed. Müntzer was executed, and the princes rallied and crushed the poorly armed peasants within the year. The Peasants' War was a disaster in which the peasants lost 100,000 men in the rebellion.

31. Luther, "Against Robbing and Murdering," 51.

32. Luther, "Against Robbing and Murdering," 51–52.

33. Luther, "Against Robbing and Murdering," 52.

34. Luther, "Against Robbing and Murdering," 50.

35. Luther, "Against Robbing and Murdering," 54.

36. Josipovic and McNiel, "Thomas Müntzer as 'Disturber of the Godless,'" 446.

# Martin Luther, "Against the Robbing and Murdering Hordes of Peasants."

From *Luther's Works*, edited by Jaroslav Pelikan, et al., 49–54. Vol. 46. St. Louis: Concordia; Philadelphia: Fortress, 1967. Used by permission.

The peasants have taken upon themselves the burden of three terrible sins against God and man; by this they have abundantly merited death in body and soul. In the first place, they have sworn to be true and faithful, submissive and obedient, to their rulers, as Christ commands when he says, "Render to Caesar the things that are Caesar's." And Romans 13 says, "Let every person be subject to the governing authorities." Since they are now deliberately and violently breaking this oath of obedience and setting themselves in opposition to their masters, they have forfeited body and soul, as faithless, perjured, lying, disobedient rascals and scoundrels usually do. St. Paul passed this judgment on them in Romans 13 when he said that those who resist the authorities will bring a judgment upon themselves. This saying will smite the peasants sooner or later, for God wants people to be loyal and to do their duty.

In the second place, they are starting a rebellion, and are violently robbing and plundering monasteries and castles which are not theirs; by this they have doubly deserved death in body and soul as highwaymen and murderers. Furthermore, anyone who can be proved to be a seditious person is an outlaw before God and the emperor; and whoever is the first to put him to death does right and well. For if a man is in open rebellion, everyone is both his judge and his executioner; just as when a fire starts, the first man who can put it out is the best man to do the job. For rebellion is not just simple murder; it is like a great fire, which attacks and devastates a whole land. Thus rebellion brings with it a land filled with murder and bloodshed; it makes widows and orphans, and turns everything upside down, like the worst disaster. Therefore let everyone who can, smite, slay, and stab, secretly or openly, remembering that nothing can be more poisonous, hurtful, or devilish than a rebel. It is just as when one must kill a mad dog; if you do not strike him, he will strike you, and a whole land with you.

In the third place, they cloak this terrible and horrible sin with the gospel, call themselves "Christian brethren," take oaths and submit to them, and compel people to go along with them in these abominations. Thus they become the worst blasphemers of God and slanderers of his holy name.

19

Under the outward appearance of the gospel, they honor and serve the devil, thus deserving death in body and soul ten times over. I have never heard of a more hideous sin. I suspect that the devil feels that the Last Day is coming and therefore he undertakes such an unheard-of act, as though saying to himself, "This is the end, therefore it shall be the worst; I will stir up the dregs and knock out the bottom." God will guard us against him! See what a mighty prince the devil is, how he has the world in his hands and can throw everything into confusion, when he can so quickly catch so many thousands of peasants, deceive them, blind them, harden them, and throw them into revolt, and do with them whatever his raging fury undertakes.

It does not help the peasants when they pretend that according to Genesis 1 and 2 all things were created free and common and that all of us alike have been baptized. For under the New Testament, Moses does not count; for there stands our Master, Christ, and subjects us, along with our bodies and our property, to the emperor and the law of this world, when he says, "Render to Caesar the things that are Caesar's." Paul, too, speaking in Romans 13 to all baptized Christians, says, "Let every person be subject to the governing authorities." And Peter says, "Be subject to every ordinance of man." We are bound to live according to this teaching of Christ, as the Father commands from heaven, saying, "This is my beloved Son, listen to him."

For baptism does not make men free in body and property, but in soul; and the gospel does not make goods common, except in the case of those who, of their own free will, do what the apostles and disciples did in Acts 4. They did not demand, as do our insane peasants in their raging, that the goods of others—of Pilate and Herod—should be common, but only their own goods. Our peasants, however, want to make the goods of other men common, and keep their own for themselves. Fine Christians they are! I think there is not a devil left in hell; they have all gone into the peasants. Their raving has gone beyond all measure.

Now since the peasants have brought [the wrath of] both God and man down upon themselves and are already many times guilty of death in body and soul, and since they submit to no court and wait for no verdict, but only rage on, I must instruct the temporal authorities on how they may act with a clear conscience in this matter.

First, I will not oppose a ruler who, even though he does not tolerate the gospel, will smite and punish these peasants without first offering to submit the case to judgment. He is within his rights, since the peasants are not contending any longer for the gospel, but have become faithless, perjured, disobedient, rebellious murderers, robbers, and blasphemers, whom even a heathen ruler has the right and authority to punish. Indeed, it is his duty to punish such scoundrels, for this is why he bears the sword and is "the servant of God to execute his wrath on the wrongdoer" (Rom 13).

But if a ruler is a Christian and tolerates the gospel, so that the peasants have no appearance of a case against him, he should proceed with fear. First he must take the matter to God, confessing that we have deserved these things, and remembering that God may, perhaps, have thus aroused the devil as a punishment upon all Germany. Then he should humbly pray for help against the devil, for we are contending not only "against flesh and blood," but "against the spiritual hosts of wickedness in the air," which must be attacked with prayer. Then, when our hearts are so turned to God that we are ready to let his divine will be done, whether he will or will not have us to be princes or lords, we must go beyond our duty, and offer the mad peasants an opportunity to come to terms, even though they are not worthy of it. Finally, if that does not help, then swiftly take to the sword.

For in this case a prince and lord must remember that according to Romans 13 he is God's minister and the servant of his wrath and that the sword has been given him to use against such people. If he does not fulfill the duties of his office by punishing some and protecting others, he commits as great a sin before God as when someone who has not been given the sword commits murder. If he is able to punish and does not do it—even though he would have had to kill someone or shed blood—he becomes guilty of all the murder and evil that these people commit. For by deliberately disregarding God's command he permits such rascals to go about their wicked business, even though he was able to prevent it and it was his duty to do so. This is not a time to sleep. And there is no place for patience or mercy. This is the time of the sword, not the day of grace.

The rulers, then, should press on and take action in this matter with a good conscience as long as their hearts still beat. It is to the rulers' advantage that the peasants have a bad conscience and an unjust cause, and that any peasant who is killed is lost in body and soul and is eternally the devil's. But the rulers have a good conscience and a just cause; they can, therefore, say to God with all confidence of heart, "Behold, my God, you have appointed me prince or lord, of this I can have no doubt; and you have given me the sword to use against evildoers (Rom 13). It is your word, and it cannot lie, so I must fulfill the duties of my office, or forfeit your grace. It is also plain that these peasants have deserved death many times over, in your eyes and in the eyes of the world, and have been committed to me for punishment. If you will me to be slain by them, and let my authority be taken from me and destroyed, so be it: let your will be done. I shall be defeated and die because of your divine command and word and shall die while obeying your command and fulfilling the duties of my office. Therefore I will punish and smite as long as my heart beats. You will be the judge and make things right."

Thus, anyone who is killed fighting on the side of the rulers may be a true martyr in the eyes of God, if he fights with the kind of conscience I have just described, for he acts in obedience to God's word. On the other hand, anyone who perishes on the peasants' side is an eternal firebrand of hell, for he bears the sword against God's word and is disobedient to him, and is a member of the devil. And even if the peasants happen to gain the upper hand (God forbid!)—for to God all things are possible, and we do not know whether it may be his will, through the devil, to destroy all rule and order and cast the world upon a desolate heap, as a prelude to the Last Day, which cannot be far off—nevertheless, those who are found exercising the duties of their office can die without worry and go to the scaffold with a good conscience, and leave the kingdom of this world to the devil and take in exchange the everlasting kingdom. These are strange times, when a prince can win heaven with bloodshed better than other men with prayer!

Finally, there is another thing that ought to motivate the rulers. The peasants are not content with belonging to the devil themselves; they force and compel many good people to join their devilish league against their wills, and so make them partakers of all of their own wickedness and damnation. Anyone who consorts with them goes to the devil with them and is guilty of all the evil deeds that they commit, even though he has to do this because he is so weak in faith that he could not resist them. A pious Christian ought to suffer a hundred deaths rather than give a hairs-breadth of consent to the peasants' cause. O how many martyrs could now be made by the bloodthirsty peasants and the prophets of murder! Now the rulers ought to have mercy on these prisoners of the peasants, and if they had no other reason to use the sword with a good conscience against the peasants, and to risk their own lives and property in fighting them, this would be reason enough, and more than enough: they would be rescuing and helping these souls whom the peasants have forced into their devilish league and who, without willing it, are sinning so horribly and must be damned. For truly these souls are in purgatory; indeed, they are in the bonds of hell and the devil.

## The Ottoman Turks and the Siege of Vienna

The Ottoman Empire was the world's leading power in the sixteenth century. It had been expanding since its beginning in the fourteenth century, conquering in the name of Allah. It had put an end to the Byzantine Empire, which had endured for a millennium, capturing Constantinople in 1453. The empire reached the apex of its power under Sultan Suleyman (also spelled Suleiman), who ruled from 1520–1566. The Turks controlled the Balkans. On May 10, 1529, Suleyman began his campaign to take Vienna, setting out with a force of at least 75,000 consisting of cavalry and elite janissary foot soldiers.[37]

When Martin Luther published his 1529 treatise *On War against the Turk,* he understood that the future territorial integrity of the heartland of Europe looked ominous.[38] No one had been able to stop the Turkish military. Before the forces of Suleyman, two citadels had fallen in succession, Belgrade (1520) and Rhodes (1521). The Hungarians had been massacred at Mohacs (1526).[39] When Luther penned his treatise, Suleyman was poised to strike again. Luther wrote, "It is a fact that the Turk is at our throat."[40]

Luther maintained that the Turks were invincible due to the fact that they were energized by the devil. He stated, "I believe that the Turk's Allah does more in war than they themselves. He gives them courage and wiles; he guides sword and fist, horse and man."[41] It would take a miracle, Luther contended, to defeat them.[42]

From Luther's perspective, the Turks were "the army of the devil."[43] Much of their power, though, resided in their overwhelming size. Luther differentiated the strength of the Sultan from that of other powers in Europe. "Fighting against the Turk," he insisted, "is not like fighting against the king of France, or the Venetians, or the pope; he is a different kind of warrior." At this point, Luther drew attention to the size of his army: "The Turk has people and money in abundance." He then conjectured,

37. Miller, "Luther on the Turks and Islam," 193.

38. Smith, "Luther, the Turks, and Islam," 352.

39. Hantsch, "Zum ungarisch-türkischen Problem," 58.

40. Luther, "On War against the Turk," 204.

41. Luther, "On War against the Turk," 183.

42. Luther, "On War against the Turk," 184.

43. Luther, "On War against the Turk," 193.

"His people are always under arms so that he can quickly muster three or four hundred thousand men."[44]

To the Christian community, Luther gave spiritual counsel, providing the exhortation that it must "fight against" the Turk "with repentance, tears, and prayer."[45] Repentance must be the starting point. "We must reform our lives," he warned, "or we shall fight in vain."[46] Prayer was to be continuous, offered during the everyday activities of life. Each Christian ought to raise to Christ, Luther wrote, "at least a sigh of the heart for grace to lead a better life and for help against the Turk."[47] The Christian's prayer was to be directed against the Ottoman army that was on the verge of conquering all of Europe: "We must pray against the Turk as against other enemies of our salvation and of all good, indeed, as we pray against the devil himself."[48] Luther exhorted his readers, "Let everyone pray who can that this abomination not become lord over us."[49]

Luther also advised the political and military elite of his time. He began by urging the princes of Europe to unite so that they would confront Suleyman with a massive force, rather than engaging him single-handedly, "yesterday the king of Hungary, today the king of Poland, and tomorrow the king of Bohemia—until the Turk devours them one after another."[50] He also set forth his opinion regarding the composition of the fighting force that needed to be assembled against Suleyman. "The pope and his bishops," he asserted, "would be deserting their calling and office to fight with the sword against flesh and blood. They are not commanded to do this; it is forbidden."[51] He referred to the military activities of Pope Julius and Clement, "who people think is almost a god of war."[52] As to the bishops who engaged in combat upon the field, he asked, "How many wars . . . have there

44. Luther, "On War against the Turk," 202.

45. Luther, "On War against the Turk," 184.

46. Luther, "On War against the Turk," 171.

47. Luther, "On War against the Turk," 173.

48. Luther, "On War against the Turk," 175.

49. Luther, "On War against the Turk," 178.

50. Luther, "On War against the Turk," 202. Luther here was referring to the disaster at Mohacs on August 29, 1526—in which Suleyman obliterated the army of King Louis II, wiping out the Christian kingdom of Hungary. The fundamental problem at Mohacs was that the Hungarians were outnumbered three to one. Suleyman had at least 70,000 men, while Louis fielded a much smaller force of some 24,000 men.

51. Luther, "On War against the Turk," 165.

52. Luther, "On War against the Turk," 169.

been against the Turk in which we would not have suffered heavy losses if the bishops and clergy had not been there?"[53]

Bishops had a spiritual work to do, to give themselves as shepherds of the flock of Christ, to preach the Word of God.[54] While they were to stay at home attending to their pastoral duties, Emperor Charles V and the princes were to take the initiative, to unfurl the banner upon which was written: "Protect the good; punish the wicked." If the emperor had done what he was called to do, Luther contended, the princes would have followed his leadership, and "the Turk would not have become so mighty."[55]

By way of historical notation, it should be observed that Suleyman never got past Vienna in his attempt to conquer the European heartland. Although he had left Constantinople in May of 1529 with a large invading force, he was not able to launch an attack upon the fortified city of Vienna until September 30. Bombardments and efforts to mine the walls followed. The walls withstood everything that was thrown at them. A couple of weeks later he had to withdraw. What happened? The summer of 1529 brought torrential rains of a kind that had not been seen for many years. The deluge meant that Suleyman was not able to move his massive cannons, the kind of artillery that were useful in knocking holes in massive walls of cities. The rain kept coming, and the Turks were slowed in their advance. Vienna was reinforced with German *Landsknechte* pikemen and Spanish musketeers. Suleyman had neither the time nor the artillery that he needed. The snow fell early. The food supply dwindled. Casualties mounted. Soldiers fell with illness. The mighty Sultan gave up the siege. Central Europe was spared.[56]

## Martin Luther, "On War against the Turk."

From *Luther's Works*, edited by Jaroslav Pelikan, et al., 184–89. Vol. 46. St. Louis: Concordia; Philadelphia: Fortress, 1967. Used by permission.

53. Luther, "On War against the Turk," 167. It could be that Luther had in mind the slaughter at Mohacs of not only the king of Hungary, but also two archbishops and five bishops.

54. Luther, "On War against the Turk," 165–67.

55. Luther, "On War against the Turk," 190.

56. Davis, *Encyclopedia of Invasions and Conquests*, 150; Rice and Grafton, *Foundations of Early Modern Europe*, 11; Anderson, *Origins of the Modern European State*, 227.

The second man who ought to fight against the Turk is Emperor Charles, or whoever may be the emperor; for the Turk is attacking his subjects and his empire, and it is his duty, as a regular ruler appointed by God, to defend his own. I repeat it here: I would not urge or bid anyone to fight against the Turk unless the first method, mentioned above, that men had first repented and been reconciled to God, etc., had been followed. If anyone wants to go to war in another way, let him take his chances. It is not proper for me to say anything more about it other than to point out everyone's duty and to instruct his conscience.

I see clearly that kings and princes are taking such a foolish and careless attitude toward the Turk that I fear they underestimate God and the Turk too greatly, or perhaps they do not know that the Turk is such a mighty lord that no kingdom or land, whatever it is, is strong enough to resist him alone, unless God performs a miracle. Now I cannot expect any miracle or special grace of God for Germany unless men amend their ways and honor the word of God differently than they have before. But enough has been said about that for those who will listen. Now we want to speak of the emperor.

In the first place, if there is to be war against the Turk, it should be fought at the emperor's command, under his banner, and in his name. Then everyone can be sure in his conscience that he is obeying the ordinance of God, since we know that the emperor is our true overlord and head and that whoever obeys him in such a case obeys God also, whereas he who disobeys him also disobeys God. If he dies in this obedience, he dies in a good state, and if he has previously repented and believes in Christ, he will be saved. I suppose everyone knows these things better than I can teach him, and would to God they knew them as well as they think they do. Yet we will say something more about them.

In the second place, this fighting under the emperor's banner and obedience to him ought to be true and simple. The emperor should seek nothing else than simply to perform the work and duty of his office, which is to protect his subjects, and those under his banner should seek simply to do the work and duty of obedience. By this simplicity you should understand that you are not fighting the Turk for the reasons the emperor and princes have been urged to go to war for, such as the winning of great honor, glory, and wealth, the extension of territory, or wrath and revenge and other such reasons. By waging war for these reasons men seek only their own self-interest, not what is right or to obey, and so we have had no good fortune up to now, either in fighting or planning to fight against the Turk.

Therefore the urging and inciting with which the emperor and the princes have been stirred up to fight against the Turk ought to cease. He has been urged, as head of Christendom and as protector of the church and defender of the faith, to wipe out the Turk's religion, and the urging and exhorting have been based on the wickedness and vice of the Turks. Not so! The emperor is not the head of Christendom or defender of the gospel or the faith. The church and the faith must have a defender other than emperor and kings. They are usually the worst enemies of Christendom and of the faith, as Psalm 2 says and as the church constantly laments. That kind of urging and exhorting only makes things worse and angers God deeply because it interferes with his honor and his work, and would ascribe it to men, which is idolatry and blasphemy.

And if the emperor were supposed to destroy the unbelievers and non-Christians, he would have to begin with the pope, bishops, and clergy, and perhaps not spare us or himself, for there is enough horrible idolatry in his own empire to make it unnecessary for him to fight the Turks for this reason. There are entirely too many Turks, Jews, heathen, and non-Christians among us with open false doctrine and with offensive, shameful lives. Let the Turk believe and live as he will, just as one lets the papacy and other false Christians live. The emperor's sword has nothing to do with the faith; it belongs to physical, worldly things, if God is not to become angry with us. If we pervert his order and throw it into confusion, he too becomes perverse and throws us into confusion and all kinds of misfortune, as it is written, "With the crooked thou dost show thyself perverse." We can perceive and grasp this through the fortune we have had up to now against the Turk. Think of all the heartbreak and misery that have been caused by the *cruciata*, by the indulgences, and by crusade taxes. With these Christians have been stirred up to take the sword and fight the Turk when they ought to have been fighting the devil and unbelief with the word and with prayer.

Here is what should be done. The emperor and the princes should be exhorted concerning their office and their bounden duty to give serious and constant thought to governing their subjects in peace and to protecting them against the Turk. This would be their duty whether they themselves were Christians or not, though it would be very good if they were Christians. But since it is and remains uncertain whether they are Christians, and it is certain that they are emperors and princes, that is, that they have God's command to protect their subjects and are duty bound to do so, we must let the uncertain go and hold to the certain, urge them with continual preaching and exhortation, and lay it heavily upon their consciences that it is their duty to God not to let their subjects perish so terribly, and that they commit serious sin when they are not mindful of their office and do not use all their power to bring counsel and help to those who should live, with body and goods, under their protection and who are bound to them by oaths of homage.

For I think (so far as I have observed the matter in our diets) that neither emperor nor princes themselves believe that they are emperor and princes. They act as though it were up to them whether to rescue and protect their subjects from the power of the Turk or not; and the princes neither care nor think that they are bound and obligated before God to counsel and help the emperor in this matter with body and goods. Each of them passes it by as though it were no concern of his and though he were forced neither by command nor necessity, but as though it were left up to him to do it or not. They are just like the common people who do not think they have a responsibility to God and the world when they have bright sons, to send them to school and have them study; but everyone thinks he has the right to raise his son as he pleases regardless of God's word and ordinance. Indeed, the councilmen in the cities and almost all the rulers act in the same way and let the schools go to ruin, as though they had no responsibility for them, and had an indulgence besides. No one remembers that God earnestly commands and desires bright children to be reared to his praise and for his work. This cannot be done without the schools. On the contrary, everyone is in a hurry to have his children make a living, as though God and Christendom needed no pastors, preachers, physicians of souls, and as though the worldly rulers needed no chancellors, counselors, or secretaries—but more of this another time. The pen must remain empress, or God will show us something else.

Emperor, kings, and princes act the same way. They do not stop to think that God's commandment requires them to protect their subjects; they think it is a matter for them to decide if they get the notion or if they have leisure for it. Dear fellow, let us all do that! Let none of us attend to that which is commanded him and which God orders him to do; let all our actions and duties depend on our own free will, and God will give us good grace and fortune, and we shall be plagued by the Turk here and by the devil yonder in eternity.

Perhaps, then, some worthless prattler—I should say a legate—will come from Rome and exhort the estates of the empire and stir them up against the Turk by telling them how the enemy of the Christian faith has done such great harm to Christendom, and that the emperor, as guardian of the church and defender of the faith, should do this and that; as though they themselves were great friends of the Christian faith! But I say to him: You are a baseborn scoundrel, you impotent chatterer! All you accomplish is to make the emperor feel that he should do a good Christian work, one that he is not commanded to do, and one that is a matter of his own free choice. His conscience is not touched at all by that, and he is not reminded of the duty laid upon him by God, but the whole thing is left to his free choice.

This is how a legate ought to deal with the estates of the empire at the diet. He should hold God's commandment before them and make it an unavoidable issue, and say, "Dear lords, emperor, and princes, if you want to be emperor and princes, then act as emperor and princes, or the Turk will teach you with God's wrath and disfavor. Germany, or the empire, is given and committed to you by God for you to protect, rule, counsel, and help, and you not only should but must do this at the risk of losing your soul's salvation and God's favor and grace. But now it is evident that none of you believes or takes this seriously; you take your office as a jest, as though it were a Shrove Tuesday mummery. You abandon the subjects God has committed to you to wretched harassment, to being taken captive, put to shame, plundered, slain, and sold by the Turk. Are you not aware that since God has committed this office to you, and has even given you money and people for you to do good to them, he will hold you accountable for all the subjects whom you so shamefully deserted while you danced, reveled in pomp, and gambled? If you seriously believed that God appointed and ordained you to be emperor and princes, you would leave your banqueting and rivalry for seats of honor and other unprofitable displays for a while, and give conscientious consideration to how to discharge your office, fulfill God's commandment, and rescue your consciences from all the blood and misery which the Turk inflicts upon your subjects.

## CHAPTER 3

# Philip Melanchthon (1497–1560)

PHILIP MELANCHTHON WAS BORN in 1497 in Bretten, a city in the electoral Palatinate. His father, Georg Schwartzerdt, made armor for princes, including a suit of armor for the Emperor Maximillian; he was also skilled in the making and firing of ordnance. His uncle Johannes Reuchlin was the greatest Christian Hebrew scholar of the time and also served as a judge in the duchy of Württemberg. It was Reuchlin who gave young Philip a Greek grammar in which he had written his humanist name, Melanchthon—the Greek version of the German "Schwartzerdt," meaning black earth. This was the last name that Philip embraced for himself.

After studying at the Pforzheim Latin School with Reuchlin, Melanchthon then proceeded to his university studies, taking the BA at Heidelberg and the MA at Tübingen. On the recommendation of Reuchlin, he was called in 1518 to teach Greek as part of the liberal arts faculty at the University of Wittenberg. He immediately came under the influence of Luther, earning the baccalaureate in theology in 1519 and joining the theological faculty as well.[1] He soon produced the first Protestant theology text entitled the *Commonplaces* (*Loci Communes*) in 1521, which was followed by many expanded editions in the ensuing years. Each edition presented important topics (*loci*) that arise out of the biblical text, including teaching on government and war.[2]

Melanchthon placed the doctrine of war within the overall context of the distinction between two kingdoms, i.e., the kingdom of Christ and the kingdom of the world. In his biblical commentary on Colossians, he stressed the necessity of distinguishing between these two kingdoms. "Let

1. Wartenberg, "Philip Melanchthon," 374, draws attention to the fact that "Melanchthon acknowledged that he had learned the gospel from Luther."

2. Kusukawa, "Melanchthon," 58–59.

us carefully discern these two kingdoms," he said, "the kingdom of this world and the kingdom of Christ." Melanchthon identified the kingdom of Christ in this way: "The kingdom of Christ is found in the hearts of the saints who according to the gospel believe that they have been received into grace on account of Christ, who are renewed and made holy by the Holy Spirit and taste of eternal life, who show forth their faith in good works and, on account of God's glory, do good to all, so that they invite many to knowledge of the gospel." He then asserted that the saints within the kingdom of Christ "tolerate all things, nor do they allow themselves to take up arms in a desire for vengeance against those who have injured them."[3]

In the context of the kingdom of Christ, believers do not take up arms. Melanchthon was not in this statement advocating the Anabaptist position of pacifism. Christians may fight in military engagements in the context of their place in the kingdom of the world. Indeed, "they obey the magistrates with great care, they hold public office (if such are entrusted to them) with vigilance and courage." He then added, "If duty demands, they punish the guilty and fight in battle." All of these assertions regarding the propriety of the saints involving themselves in governmental affairs were based on Melanchthon's fundamental perspective that "the kingdom of this world" is "a legitimate order that defends public peace with the authority of magistrates, with laws, judgments, punishments and war."[4] This is a position that he also maintained in his biblical commentary on Romans. "Government, that is, the order of rules or the form of the state, is a good thing, which God by his own work both instituted and preserves."[5]

Melanchthon similarly distinguished between ecclesiastical and civil magistrates in the first edition of the *Loci*. Ecclesiastical magistrates have one fundamental responsibility, being "enjoined only to preach the Word of God." The civil magistrate, conversely, "is one who bears the sword and watches over the civil peace." "The fact that the magistrate wields the sword is pleasing to God."[6] In fact, he noted in the 1543 edition of the *Loci* that the apex of power that is exercised by a government is seen in its capacity

3. Melanchthon, cited in Wengert, "Philip Melanchthon and a Christian Politics," 50.
4. Melanchthon, cited in Wengert, "Philip Melanchthon and a Christian Politics," 50.
5. Melanchthon, *Commentary on Romans*, 217.
6. Melanchthon, "1521 *Loci Communes*," 148–49. In his *Commentary on Romans*, Melanchthon stated that we must remember "the difference of authorities. God committed to magistrates that they should lay down just laws. . . . But to pastors he gave his sure Word; he does not want us to be over and above lawgivers, or to add other laws" (Melanchthon, *Commentary on Romans*, 222).

to wage war. He contended, "War is the highest degree of political power," although he had to admit that such political power "is the most abused, and just and lawful wars are very rare." He nevertheless could refer to specific examples of just wars, "as when Constantine repressed the savagery of Licinius by force of arms."[7]

Melanchthon embraced the three classical constituents of justice of war doctrine that had been espoused by Augustine and Aquinas.[8] A given war could only be just if it were authorized by the proper authority on the basis of a just cause with a right intention. He agreed with Luther that "certain men are given" the "right to wage war." "Christ permits a ruler to carry out his work" regarding "bearing arms" and "waging lawful war."[9] In addition, the right to wage war was contingent upon an offense having been committed. The need for public vengeance assumes that a fault exists. As Luther noted, war is "the punishment of wrong and evil."[10] Melanchthon agreed with this perspective and drew attention to the first king of Israel who started a war without a just cause. "People," he wrote, "start unjust wars and controversies which are dangerous to themselves and to their governments, as in the case of Saul. When he was moved by great jealousy and malice, he complained against David under the pretext that David was rebelling against him."[11] Finally, Melanchthon believed that a just war has the intention of keeping the peace, either confirming it or recovering it.[12] He maintained that David waged war so that "the church of God might be preserved" and that "the young people could gather in the schools and the people could come to hear sermons in safety." He added, "David considered these purposes every time he led forth his army, as often as he drew up his battle line, and as often as he attacked the army of the enemy."[13] Luther had

---

7. Melanchthon, *1543 Loci Communes*, 68.

8. Wengert, "Philip Melanchthon," 250, notes that Melanchthon had a deep appreciation for Augustine's theology.

9. Melancthon, *1543 Loci Communes*, 214.

10. Luther, "Whether Soldiers, Too," 95.

11. Melancthon, *1543 Loci Communes*, 219.

12. Melanchthon's perspective on the intention of war parallels his viewpoint on the intention of government: "Let us learn that in those who believe in Christ, the works of political and economic life are good works and acts of worship of God, and not merely secular works, because society must be preserved in order that God may become known in it" (Melanchthon, *Commentary on Romans*, 221).

13. Melancthon, *1543 Loci Communes*, 218.

taken the same view, making the comment, "Why does anyone go to war except he desires peace."[14]

It is possible in Melanchthon's view to have a just war, but his fundamental concern was to avoid unnecessary military engagements. He affirmed that "the devil" is the one who "often stirs up great wars on the most flimsy pretexts." He therefore insisted that wrongdoing did not necessarily mean that governments ought to rush into battle. Along with Luther, who urged political leaders to wait until they were compelled to fight, Melanchthon cautioned, "But let us employ equity which, even if offense has been given, is more concerned to bring peace than to destroy the innocent and bring immeasurable harm to the churches and the nation because of the errors of the few."[15]

## Philip Melanchthon, *1543 Loci Communes*. 215–17.

St. Louis: Concordia Publishing House, 1992. Used by permission.

In Luke 3 the Baptist preaches to the publicans and the soldiers; and he gives them very important counsel about their civic duty. Thus he gives his approval to this function when he teaches them about correct administration of their work: "Collect no more than is your right." Government cannot pay its expenses without collecting taxes. Thus he wants the taxes to be paid, but he does not want lawful taxes to become unbearable extortions. And "Do not intimidate or falsely accuse anyone." He wants justice to be practiced, but without contentions and lying. And finally he adds "Be content with your wages." The entire sermon is an approval of the civil status, the court system, and the military. And he makes a distinction between this order itself and the wickedness or confusion which human malice has mixed in.

The futile, insignificant, and stupid quibblings of the Anabaptists ought to be categorically rejected. They argue that the Baptist permitted these things out of his own imperfections, but that later on Christ taught differently. The sermons of the Baptist and of Christ are not opposed to one another. Nor should we get the idea that the authority of the Baptist is on a lower level. For his calling and office was so great that Christ Himself testifies to him, and God confirms his calling and teaching in a glorious

14. Luther, "Whether Soldiers, Too," 95.

15. Melancthon, *1543 Loci Communes*, 68. Luther's commitment to the idea that war ought to be a last resort is reflected in Luther, "Whether Soldiers, Too," 118.

testimony at the baptism of Christ. But the Anabaptists in their raving do not realize what they are saying when they speak contemptuously regarding the ministry of the Baptist.

"I said, 'You are gods'" (Ps 82:6) that is, they uphold the divinely established office as the defenders of justice and peace, which are divinely given blessings. God has imparted his own name to the rulers, because it is His will that they bestow with Him these blessings upon the people. Therefore He gives His approval to the office when He calls it a divine office. "When the peoples are gathered together and the kings that they may serve the Lord" (Ps 102:22); "Kings shall be your foster fathers, and queens your nursing mothers" (Isa 49:23). These statements and many more like them bear witness that kings and other rulers are members of the church of God and pleasing to God. Thus God gives his approval to governments and the civil order.

Confirmed by these testimonies, we must be constant in our condemnation of the Anabaptists, who contend that Christians do not have the right to serve as public officers. They disapprove of courts, laws, the military, and the rest of the civic order, as if these things are by their very nature sins and in conflict with the Gospel. In my opinion, many contentions have arisen over this dispute, with many people, including Carlstadt, Pelargus, Struthius and others; and many, after getting to know the fountains from which this dispute flows, have returned to the correct way by rejecting the ravings of the Anabaptists.

Further, to these points which I have adduced we need to add some examples—which are very numerous—of people who have truly invoked God, who have governed enormous realms down through the ages. It was the will of God that through some of these supportive people nations might be helped, both so that in their invocation their confession might shine brilliantly and the true doctrine be more widely spread, and so that the church might have a resting place. There is no doubt that our earliest fathers were in this group—men such as Adam, Enoch, and Noah, who were also civil rulers as we learn from the law of Noah regarding the punishment of murder. Then Melchizedek is expressly called a king. Abraham, although he was a guest in other lands, yet joined certain kings to the church, and ruled with political power over his family and waged war. Later on Joseph not only ruled but also established new laws for the nation of Egypt. Nor is there any doubt that the form of the Egyptian government which was established by Joseph, as long as it flourished, excelled the governmental systems of all other countries which later arose on earth, in Chaldaea, Ionia, Greece, and Rome.

Those people are in serious error who attribute greater political wisdom to Solon or Augustus than was found among the men who were ruling under the guidance of divine light and who were actually calling upon God, such as Joseph, Daniel, Ezra, and others like them. Not only did Joseph rightly call upon God while he was among the princes of Egypt, but as governor he drew to the knowledge of the true God the king who ruled in that era and many others who had positions of authority in the nation. In addition, there is no doubt that Moses and many other rulers among the people of Israel were also pleasing to God.

But when the raving Anabaptists say that this temple and political system was a concession made to the imperfection of the people of Israel, the answer is too easy. It was a singular blessing of God that He bestowed upon His church a certain temple and defended it for more than four hundred years. For it was the will of God that there would be a special place in which the testimonies of the divine promises might be made, and in which Christ might be born, as has been amply shown above in regard to the Old Testament. Among the people of Israel He approved a legal and political system, and often bore witness that He required these offices so that among the people invocation might be made and shine forth, and confession and love toward the church might be exercised. He was signifying that He also approved a legal and political order among the Gentiles, that they might set examples. For Joseph, Daniel, and many others had governed political systems among Gentiles. Therefore, we must consider the history of these matters in the case of other kingdoms outside the nation of Israel. Daniel ruled a province of Gentiles and under his administration he turned the leaders of the kingdom to the knowledge of the true God, including the conqueror of Jerusalem—Nebuchadnezzar—and his son Darius the Mede, Cyrus the Persian, and many princes. Therefore God dispersed the people of Israel into other kingdoms here and there in order that the true doctrine of God might be spread farther. In the Gospel accounts, mention is made of certain centurions who believed the Gospel. The Holy Spirit was even poured out with a marvelous miracle upon the whole household of Cornelius, a Roman soldier, just as he was upon the apostles.

We have such sure and clear testimonies and examples which show that civil and political order is pleasing to God, even that the offices in this civil order are filled with men who correctly call upon God that they may do their work in a godly way and carry out the prescribed worship of God. Therefore we must learn to respect civil offices, governments, rulers, laws, courts, the distinction of realms of service, and laws governing business affairs as gifts from God. We must confine all the works of civil life to these boundaries in order that we may be obedient to God in these ordinances and that our invocation and confession may shine like a bright light in this society and that we may practice our love for one another.

I have cited examples of rulers who were pleasing to God such as Joseph, Daniel, Naaman the Syrian, and others. Since it is obvious that they were helped by God, it is manifest that their governance was the work of God. Furthermore, I shall add to this list names of heroes from among the Gentiles who had no true knowledge of God, and yet, lest the human race come to complete destruction, these men were roused by God with sincere motives and were helped in their task of ruling, as was the case with Alexander, Scipio, and Augustus. The remarkable successes in the things such men have done have moved all prudent people to admit that they had better and happier intentions than the rest of mankind in general. Thus Cicero says that there is never a great man without a divine influence. God has grafted these outstanding ideas into such leaders and builders for the establishing of governments and the restoring of civil order and the maintenance of the arts. This clear testimony demonstrates this divine presence in our civil life, as Plato says, "Just as cattle are not governed by oxen, or goats by goats, but by a higher nature," namely, by men, "so human nature is too weak to rule over itself. Therefore, God has not placed men over citizens, but higher beings, a superior race of men who are closer to divinity, namely, the heroes, that is to say, people who since they have success for themselves are capable of governing us happily and easily. And they that take such care of us that they preserve peace, reverence, and freedom."

## CHAPTER 4

# Martin Bucer (1491–1551)

MARTIN BUCER, AN INFLUENTIAL Reformed theologian who served primarily in Strasbourg, was one of the most important, though often forgotten or neglected, of the Protestant reformers of the sixteenth century. The focus of much of his work was attempting to bring unity within the young Reformation church. He attempted to bring together Martin Luther and Huldrych Zwingli, especially with respect to their differing views on the meaning of the Lord's Supper. His desire for Protestant unity was enormous. He also attempted to unite Protestants and Catholics in Germany in an effort to create a national German church that would be separate from Rome. Bucer was a prolific writer of popular tracts and a voluminous letter-writer.

With respect to issues of war, peace, and justice, Bucer's primary contribution is in the larger realm of the development of Reformed political theory. His ideas are not so much about war as they are about the limits of political authority by the state or rulers and how those limits align with a Reformed understanding of biblical texts. His concern was articulating the purpose of political authority and government with respect to Christians individually and collectively.

Bucer was born in Sélestat (Schlettstadt), Alsace, a free imperial city of the Holy Roman Empire. The Holy Roman Empire of the sixteenth century was divided into many princely and city-states with enormous political rivalry among them. Free imperial cities were nominally under the control of the Emperor but were ruled by councils locally. The majority of Bucer's work until his exile to England in 1549 was in the free imperial city of Strasbourg.

Biographer Martin Greschat writes of Bucer:

In a rapidly and thoroughly changing world, Bucer was bent on understanding others and coming to agreement with them. This was hardly a craving for harmony and appeasement at any, or almost, any price. It is perhaps most fitting to describe Bucer as a theologian of dialogue. This does not mean he was not sure of what he believed. On the contrary, his own theological standpoint was quite clear and firm. But he did not use it primarily to contrast his own position over against that of his opponents, but rather as a point of departure for embarking in an exchange with them.[1]

Bucer's ideas about political authority and the Christian are illustrated in his 1531–1532 debate in Strasbourg regarding the limits of political authority with pacifist Pilgrim Marpeck (1495–1556), a municipal engineer and former town councilor from Rattenberg, who had recently arrived in Strasbourg espousing moderate Anabaptist theology.[2]

Both men grounded their argument in the biblical text and in their respective interpretation of biblical authority with respect to interactions between Christians and political authorities. "Each man developed a biblical justification of his political positions that was consistent with the justification of his respective theological position."[3] Both men argued on the basis of Scripture, but they approached it from different perspectives. Marpeck did so from an ideological vantage point and Bucer did so from the perspective of a leader and prominent figure in the Strasbourg community. Bucer was "defending the emerging theological and political status quo in Strasbourg."[4]

The two men debated before the town council in early December 1531. Marpeck wrote a twenty-nine-article Confession and Bucer responded point-by-point. Marpeck succinctly declared, "No external power may be present, used, or permitted to govern within the kingdom of Christ."[5] Although governments are "servants of God," those who wield authority, whether Christians or not, have no rule or government within the kingdom of Christ.[6] Bucer responded with a two-page refutation stating that political authority was ordained by God and when used appropriately by Christians

---

1. Greschat, *Martin Bucer*, 252–53.
2. Ziegler, "Marpeck versus Butzer," 95.
3. Ziegler, "Marpeck versus Butzer," 96.
4. Ziegler, "Marpeck versus Butzer," 100.
5. Marpeck, cited in Ziegler, "Marpeck versus Butzer," 96.
6. Ziegler, "Marpeck versus Butzer," 96.

political authority helped them glorify God. Further, he argued, political authority can aid in advancing the gospel by "putting a stop to wicked, erroneous corrupting teachings and actions."[7]

When Marpeck proclaimed that "earthly power in all its works has no place in the kingdom of Christ, whose kingdom is not of this world," Bucer rebutted "but it lives in this world!"[8] In these two statements can be seen the tensions of much of the political discourse among Reformation Christians—especially between those who followed the magisterial Reformers and the Anabaptists. It was the classic expression of contrasting political viewpoints and the realm in which Bucer's energies were focused. "By excluding any legitimate role whatsoever that government might play in the kingdom of God on earth, hence by asserting strict separation between church and state, Marpeck was affirming the tradition of limited government in an age of expanding governmental authority. . . . He was giving expression to an emerging tradition of individual liberty in Western Europe."[9] Countering this view, Bucer was a proponent of another evolving tradition, one that affirmed the primacy of government—not of the individual—in interpreting God's will on earth.

Not surprisingly, Marpeck's views failed to persuade the councilmen of Strasbourg, and he was expelled from the city. In spite of the debate with Marpeck, Bucer's reputation at the time and since has been one of an individual who sought peace and unity among Protestants. It was his hope that Protestants and Catholics would unite to create a German national church that would be separate from Rome, but the beginning years of the Council of Trent and the Schmalkaldic War dashed his hopes.

The military conflict of greatest concern for Bucer was the brief Schmalkaldic War of 1546–1547. The war pitted the military forces of Emperor Charles V of the Holy Roman Empire against those of the Lutheran princes within the Holy Roman Empire who had formed an alliance known as the Schmalkaldic League. The League was originally created in 1531 for religious purposes of mutual defense against military attack by Charles V. However, over time League members increasingly came to view it through a political lens wherein loyalty to the League displaced loyalty to the Empire. Membership in the league was contingent upon agreement with the Lutheran Augsburg or Tetrapolitan Confessions.

7. Bucer, cited in Ziegler, "Marpeck versus Butzer," 97.

8. Marpeck and Bucer, cited in Ziegler, "Marpeck versus Butzer," 100.

9. Ziegler, "Marpeck versus Butzer," 100–101.

Members of the League agreed to provide a military force of 10,000 infantry and 2,000 cavalry for mutual protection, and for 15 years there was no direct conflict between the League and the Empire. However, this lack of opposition from Charles V was due primarily to his preoccupation with fighting wars against France and the Ottoman Empire. Once conflicts between France and the Empire such as the Italian War of 1536–1538 and the Italian War of 1542–1546 ended, Charles V was able to concentrate his military forces on suppressing Protestant resistance within the Empire. This resulted in the 1546–1547 war against the Schmalkaldic League. The result was a disastrous military defeat for the League, though not for Protestantism, which was granted official status in the Empire three years later in the Peace of Augsburg. According to the established principle of *Cuius regio, eius religio* ("Whose realm, his religion"), princes were permitted to choose the official religion within the domains they controlled.

The victory eventually led to the exile of several princes and prominent reformers, Bucer among them. On May 15, 1548, before the Peace of Augsburg, an imperial decree known as the Augsburg Interim ordered Protestants to readopt Catholic beliefs and practices although there were some concessions to Protestant beliefs and practices.

When the city of Strasbourg accepted the Interim, Bucer was forced to leave and was exiled to England. In England, he influenced Thomas Cranmer in the second revision of the Book of Common Prayer. Bucer died in Cambridge in 1551.

Protestant defeat in the Schmalkaldic War caused Bucer to reflect theologically upon the events of the war. He interpreted the war theologically and understood the League's defeat as a punishment by God. His writings contain numerous instances of this interpretation.[10]

---

10. Greschat, *Martin Bucer*, 211n10 (provides 17 references).

# Part 2

# Swiss and French Reformers

CHAPTER 5

# Huldrych Zwingli (1484–1531)

HULDRYCH ZWINGLI WAS THE father of the Swiss Reformation, the first of the Reformed theologians. He was born in the village of Wildhaus in the Swiss canton of St. Gall on New Year's Day 1484, a little over seven weeks after the birth of Martin Luther. He studied at the University of Vienna before going to the University of Basel, where he earned a baccalaureate in 1504 and a master of liberal arts in 1506. Both universities introduced him to scholasticism and to humanism.[1]

Zwingli began his ministry as a priest in the small canton of Glarus in 1506. He then served at the Benedictine Abbey in Einsiedeln beginning in 1516 before he transferred and began his priestly work at the Zürich Great Church in 1518. He is remembered primarily for his reforming work as the leading pastor in the Swiss city of Zürich, officially launching his reform program on January 1, 1519, when he began to preach through the Gospel of Matthew.[2] It was his thirty-fifth birthday.

Zwingli developed major theological topics in *An Exposition of the Articles* (1523), a volume that developed the Sixty-Seven Articles that Zwingli had set forth at the first disputation, an event that the Zürich Council convened to discuss evangelical preaching and the dispute between the advocates and opponents of the reform program.[3] He presented his views

1. Stephens, "Huldrych Zwingli," 28, draws attention to the profound and permanent influence that the humanist movement had upon Zwingli. After Zwingli met Erasmus, "it was the fathers of the early church rather than the medieval schoolmen who engaged him" (29).

2. Snavely, "Huldrych Zwingli," 36, comments on Zwingli's powerful preaching, referring to one listener who said that he felt as if he had been "lifted by the hair and suspended in space."

3. Stephens, "Theology of Zwingli," 82, notes that the Bible was central in the Zwinglian reformation. "At the first disputation in January 1523 he pointed to the Bible, which

on government in ten of the Articles (Articles 34–43), already shaping the Reformed tradition in its earliest stage in the direction of a political orientation. He set forth his biblical doctrine of war in the context of a discussion on church and state relations.

Zwingli's teaching on war was certainly informed by his experience. He traveled as a chaplain with troops from Glarus to Italy and witnessed the devastation of war at the Battle of Marignano in 1515, which pitted the French Army led by King Francis I against the Old Swiss Confederacy. The French decisively prevailed on the battlefield over a Swiss force that was heavily outnumbered and outgunned. Six thousand Swiss soldiers lost their lives. The engagement was a turning point in Swiss history. It was the last battle fought by a Swiss army on foreign soil, the Swiss Confederacy never again mounting a military offensive against an external enemy. The bloodshed had a sobering effect on Zwingli. "In response to what he had experienced," Zwingli "came to believe that war was just only when hearth and home were attacked." He embraced the position that "unless attacked by a foreign power, the confederacy should remain neutral."[4]

Zwingli worked in a setting in which church and society were identical. The church was not a distinct entity in the larger society—an arrangement that did not please the Anabaptists who wanted a voluntary church of professing Christians who had been baptized as adults. The church and Zürich, however, were one and the same thing.[5] Zwingli did, though, distinguish between minister and magistrate. In Article 36 of *An Exposition of the Articles* he affirmed that the office of the minister is to teach the Word

---

had been brought into the assembly in Hebrew, Greek, and Latin, as the judge. He asserted that the sixty-seven articles that he was defending were based on the Bible. In this and in every subsequent debate he appealed to the authority of the Bible over against the authority of the church and its traditional authority." Gäbler, "Huldrych Zwingli," 149, points out that in the first disputation Zwingli was essentially providing a summary of his preaching in the Sixty-Seven Articles. "More than 600 persons met on January 29 for the disputation." The Zürich Council decided that the ministers of the city and countryside "had to preach in harmony with Zwingli's manner and spirit." "His conceptions" thereby "received a sort of normative status" (150).

4. Walton, "Zwingli," 77.

5. John Calvin also embraced the idea of a holy commonwealth. All the inhabitants of Geneva necessarily belonged to the church. The complete identification of church and society was the medieval ideal.

of God.[6] Rulers, on the other hand, "look after the office of the sword."[7] In this connection, Zwingli addressed the pope who wanted to take up arms against the Ottoman Turks who were threatening Europe. Zwingli exhorted, "Listen to Christ, oh pope, 'Put it away'"—referring here to the sword. "The secular princes," he said, "are undoubtedly quite capable of protecting their own land." He then added, "Take no other sword into your hand than the sword of the Spirit which is the word of God."[8]

Bishops, in addition, were not to rule temporal domains. "Priests should not govern at all, not even in the office which God has given them." He added, "They are to govern even less extensively in worldly matters."[9] In these statements Zwingli distanced himself from the medieval theory that regalian bishops (bishops who possessed the "regalia" of secular office) possessed both a religious and secular sword. It should be noted, however, that there is a disconnect between what Zwingli taught and what he did as a minister.[10] He actually did become involved in the political affairs of Zürich. When Zwingli died, the Zürich Council determined that his successors would not participate in civic affairs in the way that Zwingli had done—who probably inherited his political interest from his father, a rural chief magistrate in the Duchy of the Toggenburg.

Rule by kings and queens had been the government of choice through the Middle Ages. Zwingli, though, did not appreciate monarchies. He preferred an aristocracy, the kind of government reflected in the Zürich Council. Monarchies were particularly dangerous in his view because they tended to degenerate into tyranny.[11] Where monarchies existed there needed to be a constitutional provision for deposition. The tyrant "may be deposed in the name of God." "It is not to be done," however, "with killing, war and rioting." Zwingli reasoned that the individuals who installed the king had the right to remove him.[12] His advocacy of monarchical

6. All citations from Zwingli's *Exposition of the Articles* appear in Zwingli, *Defense of the Reformed Faith.*

7. Article 41 (Zwingli, *Defense of the Reformed Faith*, 247).

8. Article 36 (Zwingli, *Defense of the Reformed Faith*, 250).

9. Article 34 (Zwingli, *Defense of the Reformed Faith*, 245).

10. Gäbler, "Huldrych Zwingli," 153–55, provides a good discussion of Zwingli's political role in Zürich.

11. Calvin drew attention to the same danger in *Institutes* 4.20.8.

12. Zwingli stated that if the common people elected the monarch, "then the people are also to depose him." If the princes elevated him, they had the authority to "order him to be deposed" (Article 42 [Zwingli, *Defense of the Reformed Faith*, 279]).

deposition stood in the mainstream of the medieval tradition reflected in Thomas Aquinas and reiterated by Reformed theologians such as Peter Martyr Vermigli and John Calvin.[13]

The magistrates were to rule in accordance with God's law. They were to see to it that "all laws" were "brought into harmony with the law of God."[14] Some would contend that Zürich became theocratic under Zwingli's reform program. It was not, however, a theocracy in the strict definition of a state that is ruled by ministers or the church, in other words, "a political regime in which a priestly caste rules over human affairs."[15] This is reflected, for example, in the elimination of church courts. Zwingli insisted, "All judicial authority and the administration of justice which the so-called priestly estate appropriates to itself, really belongs to the temporal authority."[16]

This position corresponds with Zwingli's view that the sins of Christians should be punished by the state, not the church, a doctrine that was also followed in Lutheran countries where the right to discipline was likewise retained by the civil government.[17] Zwingli gave to the magistrate the authority to excommunicate, to remove members from the church for the good of the church. Calvin, who insisted that this power had to be exercised by a church consistory composed of pastors and elders, would later repudiate this policy. In Zürich itself, the Anabaptists who opposed any jurisdiction of the civil authorities in church life, placing ultimate authority in the local congregation, rejected Zwingli's acceptance of magisterial discipline in the church.[18]

13. It is interesting to note that Heinrich Bullinger, Zwingli's successor in Zürich, took the position of Martin Luther who opposed parliamentary resistance to tyrannical monarchs. Baker, "Covenant and Community," 23, draws attention to the fact that for Bullinger "there was no effective human check on magisterial power."

14. Article 39 (Zwingli, *Defense of the Reformed Faith*, 268).

15. Paquin, "Calvin and Theocracy in Geneva," 92. Walton, *Zwingli's Theocracy*, 1, affirms, "The word 'theocracy' assumes that a state which desires to realize the rule of God is governed by God's representative, the clergy. Zwingli certainly did wish to realize the rule of God at Zürich, but this did not mean that he endeavored to subordinate the city government to the power and influence of the clergy. If anything, Zwingli sought to deprive the clergy of the secular authority."

16. Article 36 (Zwingli, *Defense of the Reformed Faith*, 249).

17. This approach will later be designated Erastianism, named after Thomas Erastus who embraced the Zwinglian teaching on discipline in the church.

18. Zwinglian Christianity strongly opposed ecclesiastical discipline, favoring magisterial discipline instead. Kingdon, *Adultery and Divorce*, 20, cites the Republic of Bern that favored the Zwinglian variety of Protestantism as an example of a bastion of

The problem in the church, Zwingli noted, was that "there are still some rams among the flock of Christ who are so bold as to give no heed either to teaching or ban." Thus the "government has to see to it that the strong, well-fed rams do not destroy the poor, weak sheep." This means "they ought to see to it that they protect and punish."[19] The visible church, Zwingli noted, has members who are "insolent and hostile," people who "have no faith." In such cases, "there arises the need of government for the punishment of flagrant sinners, whether it be the government of princes or that of the nobility."[20]

The magistrate was to care for the church, but he also held the office of the sword. He alone in the domestic sphere had the authority to "impose the death penalty."[21] He was also to use the sword against foreign aggressors. On this specific issue, Zwingli alluded to the justice of war (*jus ad bellum*) and justice in war (*jus in bello*) categories of medieval moral theology. In addition, from the beginning of his ministry as a parish priest at Glarus, Zwingli attacked the mercenary trade as immoral and preached against it.[22] He later asserted that "professional warfare is inhuman, shameless and sinful."[23] It was his opposition to the Swiss mercenary system that forced him to leave Glarus for Einsiedeln.

When Zwingli formed an alliance of Evangelical cantons, the Roman Catholic cantons feeling threatened formed a rival alliance. All of this led to military conflict. Five Catholic cantons declared war on Zürich in 1531. A small Zürich army of two thousand men confronted a larger Catholic force of eight thousand near Kappel on October 11. Zwingli joined the Zürich forces as a chaplain. He had taught in continuity with Thomas Aquinas that ministers ought not to wield the sword, but he decided in the emergency of the moment to take up the sword and to fight alongside

---

Protestant religion that opposed significant disciplinary power being given to church officers.

19. Article 39 (Zwingli, *Defense of the Reformed Faith*, 269).

20. Zwingli, *Exposition of the Faith*, 266.

21. Article 40 (Zwingli, *Defense of the Reformed Faith*, 271).

22. The soldiers of the Swiss cantons had developed a reputation as skilled combatants and were in high demand as paid soldiers in foreign governments. They were renowned for attacks in huge columns with the long pike.

23. Article 40 (Zwingli, *Defense of the Reformed Faith*, 272). Zwingli argued that a major problem with the mercenary system was that Swiss soldiers ended up participating in campaigns that were initiated without a just cause.

his soldiers.[24] He died in the bloody engagement that lasted less than an hour. The Catholic soldiers desecrated his body, quartering and burning it, mixing it with cow dung, and cutting up his heart so that it might not become a relic for his followers.

Interpretations are varied on the tragedy at Kappel.[25] Luther believed that the judgment of God had come upon Zwingli. From another perspective, Zwingli can be seen as a brave patriot who gave his life in defense of the gospel and the church in Zürich.[26] His early death meant that he was not able to present a theological *magnum opus* for the Reformed world. Leadership in Zürich passed to his successor, Heinrich Bullinger.

## Huldrych Zwingli, Article 36 of "An Exposition of the Articles."

From *The Defense of the Reformed Faith*, by Huldrych Zwingli, 250–51. Translated by E. J. Furcha. Allison Park, PA: Pickwick, 1984. Used by permission.

The fact that it is not within the realm of so-called priests to guard the law does not mean that they should not by their teaching support the process of jurisprudence. Rather, it means that they should not at all undertake by force to protect courts and the seat of justice, as do the bishops in this our time who protect their rights with a mighty hand and their own bodies with so many soldiers and fighters that even a king or emperor would find them sufficient. Yet Christ bid Peter to put his sword into its sheath; for whoever fights with the sword, shall die by the sword. From this we clearly learn that the two swords with which Christ contends himself after the Supper do not indicate human power but rather the well-sharpened word of God, revealed in the Old and New Testament. Had Christ wanted his teaching and himself protected, he could easily have been able to gather troops other than the twelve poor fishermen. But he says, "Put it away." If then the pope

24. Peter Martyr Vermigli later taught theology in Zürich. He asserted that, generally speaking, "for the ministers of the church to bear arms" was "not lawful" (Vermigli, "Of Warre or Battell," 71). In an emergency situation though "the minister of the church may rightly take arms and repel violence, and do that which becomes a good citizen" (72).

25. Gäbler, "Huldrych Zwingli," 160.

26. Stephens, "Huldrych Zwingli," 27, draws attention to Zwingli's Swiss patriotism: "Zwingli himself saw this as stemming from his boyhood. In 1526 he recalled that as a boy he had resisted any one who slandered or abused the Swiss, risking danger on occasion."

is a successor to Peter why then does he not hear Christ saying to him, "Put it away?" For if he said it to Peter, he should also accept it without a doubt, since he wants to be successor and heir to Peter.

Now he wants to fight the Turks so that his household at Rome should not perish. Listen to Christ, oh pope, "Put it away." The secular princes are undoubtedly quite capable of protecting their own land. But you go and preach the kingdom of God. Are we to bemoan you more than Christ, should you be knifed to death? Or does one have to fight off the Turks, who rush toward you, more vehemently than one had to fend off the Jews who attacked Christ? You may well see then, unless you are blind, that such suffering of the faithful is inflicted on us by God on account of our sin; do you want to nullify the counsel of God? Go then and call sinful Sodom to repentance, not with guns and military marches, not with riding to and fro of dolled-up bishops but rather with the word of God; preach and shout— like Jonah, John and Christ—"Repent." And take no other sword into your hand than the sword of the Spirit which is the word of God and the other weapons which Paul forged in Eph 6:11–17, or else you shall perish. David cannot fight this in an iron breastplate. Or else, as long as you shout for weapons of iron, we will know that you are not a successor of Christ or Peter, but of the devil, indeed, that you are the true anti-Christ.

Do what God bids you do and rely on his word. He shall order everything well for one who depends on him. He shall find protection, though wicked Sodom shall be burned to ashes. Thanks be to God for visiting us. He reproves those whom he loves. He intends to pay us some day for the sake of our cunning and teach us that in future we ought not leave unpunished the great abomination which Rome dares commit before all the world without any shame. And since the entire Jewish nation was extinguished for the sake of evil priests and haters of Christ, it is undoubtedly God's intention to punish us all because we tolerated the dishonorable sins of the papists without any correction, and closed our eyes so as not to see them.

In sum: Every government will be the more peaceful when it does not permit any of the chapters or conventicles to judge in any way but, instead, takes under its own purview all court matters, not allowing any chapter or conventicle to do anything in isolation except they gather together in order to learn and listen; for, in short, as much as I have seen in my days, they are always against open authority and this is against God.

Finally, the maintaining of justice belongs to worldly authority though it may affect priests, monks and nuns. For Holy Scripture places these under worldly authority, inasmuch as it aims to be Christian, as shall become clear in the next Article. This I have included here so that the papists cannot object on the ground of Paul's opinion in 1 Cor 6:1–11, where he insists that Christians should settle their disputes among themselves and not drag them before unbelieving judges; now the papists turn this to mean that they themselves should judge among Christians and settle all disputes by their own justice. But Paul says nothing there which may be applied to the priesthood; for he says it with the following meaning in mind: Before you turn to judges who are unbelievers to settle the temporal affairs in which you are involved, you ought to seek out the poorest and most simple among you who may decide for you. But since all the princes among whom Christians live are Christians also, Christians should therefore accept judgment from them.

## The Kappel Wars (1529–1531)

The Kappel Wars were fought in Switzerland between the years 1529 and 1531. Although the two wars only witnessed one actual battle, the results of this climactic struggle would spell the end of the Reformation in Switzerland, as well as claim the life of one of Switzerland's foremost reformers—Huldrych Zwingli. The wars also furthered the process of fragmentation—not just of the Catholic Church, but of the Protestant denominations, which were forming their own sense of identity and competing amongst each other for adherents and legitimacy. The Protestant defeat in this war was not as much a result of the superiority of Catholic military prowess as it was a Protestant inability to unite forces in Switzerland with their brethren in the German states.

Zwingli published "Regarding Divine And Human Righteousness" in 1523, which was one of the first works of the Reformation to deal with social ethics "based on the divine and human righteousness."[27] This tract and others similar to it established Zwingli as one of the leading Church reformers in the Swiss Cantons. The differences between Luther and the Swiss reformers were important:

> Although Luther and the Swiss reformers, Zwingli and Bullinger, were largely in agreement on the nature and role of oath-taking by political office-bearers, the most important difference between these two reformational positions was the encapsulation of the oath within the covenant, as proposed by the Swiss reformers.

27. Raath and de Freitas, "Rebellion, Resistance," 2.

Zwingli, as early as 1523, in his debates with the Anabaptists, took the oath to be constitutive to the powers exercised by the political authorities.[28]

Zwingli began to consider that a military campaign might be necessary to secure the advances that the Swiss Reformation had so far made. His tract *Plan for a Military Campaign,* "which has no date, but is thought to have been written around 1527, was a shrewd assessment of the political situation in the Confederation."[29] Protestants feared a general prosecution in the wake of the martyrdom of one of their own—Jacob Kaiser (or Schlosser) in May, 1529.[30]

The high point of the Zwinglian Reformation occurred in the year 1530.[31] Philip Schaff observes, "Both parties organized for war, which broke out in 1529, and ended in a disastrous defeat for the Protestants in 1531."[32] War was declared on June 9, 1529. Zwingli "believed in the necessity of war; while Luther put his sole trust in the Word of God, although he stirred up the passions of war by his writings, and had himself the martyr's courage to go to the stake. Zwingli was a free republican, while Luther was a loyal monarchist."[33]

Only 16 days after the declaration of war, peace was declared. The first Kappel War ended without a general engagement of forces. Of tremendous consequence in the Eighteen Articles that formed the peace treaty was that for the first time in Europe

> the principle of parity or legal equality of the Roman Catholic and Protestant Churches—a principle which twenty-six years afterwards was recognized also in Germany (by the Augsburger Religionsfriede of 1555), but was not finally settled there until after the bloody baptism of the Thirty Years' War, in the Treaty of Westphalia in 1648.[34]

The outcome of the treaty was positive for the Reformation:

---

28. Raath and de Freitas, "Rebellion, Resistance," 12.
29. Gordon, *Swiss Reformation,* 123.
30. Schaff, *History of the Christian Church,* 8:166.
31. Schaff, *History of the Christian Church,* 8:166.
32. Schaff, *History of the Christian Church,* 8:166.
33. Schaff, *History of the Christian Church,* 8:167.
34. Schaff, *History of the Christian Church,* 8:171.

The effect of the first Peace of Kappel was favorable to the cause of the Reformation. It had now full legal recognition, and made progress in the Cantons and in the common territories. But the peace did not last long. The progress emboldened the Protestants, and embittered the Catholics.[35]

Yet, in spite of the positive results, there were also negative effects. "The collapse of the Swiss Reformation between 1529 and 1531 is a tale of fatal political compromises and bloodlust. It is a surprise that the Confederation survived at all."[36] Similarly, Baker observes: "The defeat at Kappel on 11 October 1531 ushered in a period of uncertainty and confusion in the Swiss Reformed cities; in Zürich, especially, it placed the entire structure in jeopardy."[37]

The Church suffered through a series of setbacks rather than experiencing the intended reform. The Kappel Wars furthered the fragmentation of the Church, and "from the 1530s onward, it was split into three: Orthodox, Catholic, and Protestant. And the Protestants themselves were split into ever more rival factions. The scandal was so great, and the fragmentation was so widespread, that people stopped talking about Christendom, and began to talk about 'Europe.'"[38]

---

35. Schaff, *History of the Christian Church*, 8:174.

36. Gordon, *Swiss Reformation*, 122.

37. Baker, "Church, State, and Dissent," 136.

38. Davies, *Europe*, 496.

## CHAPTER 6

# Heinrich Bullinger (1504–1575)

HEINRICH BULLINGER WAS A premier theologian among the Swiss Reformed in the sixteenth century. He was born near Zürich in the small town of Bremgarten in 1504. He studied at the University of Cologne, receiving a bachelor of arts and master of arts by the time he was eighteen years of age. While at Cologne, he attended lectures on Thomas Aquinas's *Summa Theologica*. In addition, the burning of Luther's books at the university piqued his interest in the church fathers. After he read them, he examined the writings of Luther and Melanchthon. His investigation of the New Testament led him to embrace the evangelical movement.[1]

In 1529, Bullinger became a pastor in his hometown of Bremgarten. The defeat of Zürich troops at Kappel in 1531 forced him to flee. Upon his arrival in Zürich, he succeeded Zwingli as the leading pastor in the city. Zürich was modeled after the Old Testament. This meant that the magistrates had the authority to discipline the Christian community.[2] Bullinger accepted the single sphere doctrine that prevailed in Zürich from the time of Zwingli in contrast to the two-sphere structure that Calvin would develop in Geneva in which the ecclesiastical sphere, not the civil, had authority over church discipline.[3]

---

1. Stephens, "Authority of the Bible," 27–28, provides a helpful discussion of Bullinger's embrace of the reform movement.

2. Baker, "Covenant and Community," 19–20, summarizes the Erastian outlook of Bullinger.

3. Baker, "Erastianism in England," 327–49. Raath, "Covenant and the Christian Community," 1003, makes the observation that in Bullinger's thinking, "the Christian magistrate was the head of the visible church." "The magistrate's laws were the only basis for community discipline—there was no separate church discipline" (Walton, "Institutionalization of the Reformation," 497–515).

Bullinger's workload as the lead pastor in Zürich and as professor of theology in the academy was enormous. He knew what it was to preach six to eight sermons a week. In addition, his theological production in writing was large and significant. He published more than one hundred titles—including sermons, biblical commentaries, and theological works. Unlike Calvin who never wrote a biblical exposition on the book of Revelation, Bullinger provided commentary in his one hundred sermons on the Apocalypse. His fifty sermons in the *Decades* provided a complete theology that was enormously influential, especially in Elizabethan England.[4]

The collected edition of the *Decades* was first published in 1552, while the English translation was published in 1587.[5] The sermons were preached in Latin, rather than in the German vernacular. They were probably delivered to the pastors and teachers of the city at the Zürich *Prophezei*, a learned circle of men who met weekly and who were committed to the study of the Bible along with mastering Hebrew, Greek, and Latin.

Bullinger's training in scholastic methodology is reflected in Sermons 6–9 of the *Second Decade*, where he presented his teaching on the civil magistrate and war. There is also evidence that he embraced the teaching of Aquinas on the matter of the justice of war (*jus ad bellum*). With respect to the category of justice in war (*jus in bello*), Bullinger opened the door to the holy war practice among the Reformed of fighting without restraint.[6] When it came to his discussion of the justice of war, however, he turned away from the holy war idea of fighting that is authorized by the church, embracing a classical just war perspective.

Bullinger treated the doctrine of war at length in Sermon 9, although he had briefly presented his understanding of the constituents of a just war already in Sermon 6. Bullinger insisted in continuity with Aquinas that a just war had to have a proper authority, the civil magistrate. He affirmed, secondly, that there had to be a just cause. He maintained, thirdly, that there had to be a right intention, the confirmation of peace.

---

4. Opitz, "Bullinger's *Decades*," 101, asserts concerning the influence of the *Decades*, "From the second half of the sixteenth century until well into the seventeenth century the *Decades* were one of the best-known theological works, performing a crucial role in the spread of the Reformed faith throughout Europe and beyond."

5. The 1587 English translation published in London by Ralph Newberie was entitled *Fifty Godlie and Learned Sermons, Divided into Five Decades Containing the Chiefe and Principall Points of Christian Religion*. All citations come from Bullinger, *Decades of Henry Bullinger*.

6. van Eijnatten, "Religionis Causa," 611.

Holy war advocates within the Christian political tradition believed that the church has the authority to declare war. Pope Urban II had proclaimed the First Crusade in 1095 to liberate Jerusalem from Muslim control and oppression. Bullinger rejected the crusade mentality at this point. Civil government alone has the authority to initiate war. He affirmed that it was "the civil magistrate" who "kills at God's commandment . . . when in defense of his people he does justly and necessarily arm himself to battle."[7] On the crucial point as to who may initiate war, Bullinger agreed with the position that had been spelled out by Aquinas. In order for a war to be just, there was a necessary preliminary constituent: "First, the authority of the sovereign by whose command the war is to be waged."[8]

In Sermon 9, Bullinger distinguished between the use of the sword in judicial punishment and its use in war. Like Aquinas, he reasoned from the lesser (defending the commonwealth against internal disturbances) to the greater (defending it against an even more serious threat, a large host of external enemies). "The use of the sword in the magistrate's hand is twofold," he said. "For either he punishes offenders therewith; or else he repels the enemy that . . . would spoil his people."[9]

With respect to the category of justice in war, Bullinger contemplated circumstances in which noncombatants, as well as armed soldiers, would be put to death in a time of war. This is the necessary implication from his statement that the laws of war in Deuteronomy 20 are still to be kept. He asserted, "The laws of war are recited in the twentieth chapter of Deuteronomy, both profitable and necessary, and therewithal so evident, that they need no words of mine to expound them. Moreover, in every place of scripture these laws of war are still bidden to be kept."[10]

The climactic statement of the Deuteronomy 20 passage is the divine mandate of holy war, the complete extermination of the pagan inhabitants of the Promised Land (Deut 20:16–18). There is also his statement regarding the civil magistrate that he has the duty to make war upon men who are incurable. Bullinger was here speaking about the prosecution of war without humanitarian restraint, that the Lord bids the civil magistrate at

---

7. Bullinger, "Sermon 6," 307.

8. Aquinas, *Summa Theologica* 2a2ae.40.1. This quotation of Aquinas's essay *Of War* is from the five-volume English translation of Aquinas, *Summa Theologica*.

9. Bullinger, "Sermon 9," 370.

10. Bullinger, "Sermon 9," 380.

times "to kill without pity or mercy." Such unrestrained war must be waged against the "incurable."[11]

The wars that Moses prosecuted against the Midianites (Num 31) provide one historical example of this kind of warfare. As Bullinger knew, the passage in Numbers supplies the account of noncombatants, captive Midianite women and male infants, being put to death. Killing without mercy was a violation of the limits of war traditionally developed in the doctrine of justice in war. By taking this position, Bullinger was drawing away from the medieval Peace of God trajectory, which culminated in the doctrine of noncombatant immunity in later just war teaching.[12]

In the ancient biblical world, killing without pity is seen in the wars of Moses against the Midianites. The same thing, Bullinger contended, applies to the present time: "Such are at this time those arrogant and seditious rebels as trouble commonwealths and kingdoms."[13] According to Bullinger, there must be no mercy to rebels, the people responsible for sedition.

Bullinger's teaching on war provided a remarkable synthesis of two opposing traditions within the church. Just war doctrine insisted that a war may only be authorized by the civil magistrate and that it must be prosecuted with restraint, offering protection to noncombatants. Holy war proponents believed that a religious figure, such as the pope, could legitimately authorize war and that such an engagement could be conducted without any concern for the protection of noncombatants. Bullinger combined features from each tradition, accepting the need for the civil authority to initiate the war, while at the same time allowing them in certain situations a free hand to prosecute the war without sparing.

By moving toward the possibility of holy war practice in a military campaign, Bullinger provided a foundation within the Reformed tradition for later holy war advocates among the English Reformed, such as William Gouge. His teaching at this point would have provided a justification for what happened at Drogheda under Cromwell's Puritan army in the 1649 massacre of Irish combatants and noncombatants alike.[14]

11. Bullinger, "Sermon 9," 376.

12. Johnson, *Just War*, 127. Johnson makes the point that eight kinds of people were to enjoy noncombatant immunity: "clerics, monks, friars, other religious, pilgrims, travelers, merchants, and peasants cultivating the soil."

13. Bullinger, "Sermon 9," 376.

14. McDonald, "Eighteenth-Century Warfare," 43, comments, "Cromwell's legions were capable of shuffling from this mortal coil thousands upon thousands of Irish or Scottish men, women, and children in a single outing."

# Heinrich Bullinger, "Sermon 9 of the Second Decade."

From *The Decades of Henry Bullinger*, 376–79. 1849. Reprint, New York: Johnson Reprint Company, 1968.

Princes therefore must precisely look into, and thoroughly examine, the cause of wars, before they begin or take them in hand. The causes are many, and of many sorts; but the chief are these that follow. For either the magistrate is compelled to send aid and raise the siege of his enemy, which doth environ the garrisons that he hath appointed for the defense of some of his cities; because it were an offence, and part of parricide, to forsake and give over, against oath and honesty, his cities and garrisons that are in extremity: or else the magistrate of duty is compelled to make war upon men which are incurable, whom the very judgment of the Lord condemneth and biddeth to kill without pity or mercy. Such were the war as Moses had with the Madianites, and Josue with the Amalechites. Of that sort are the wars wherein such men are oppressed, as of invincible malice will both perish themselves and draw other to destruction as well as themselves, with those also which, rejecting all justice and equity, do stubbornly go on to persist in their naughtiness. Such were the Benjamites, which were destroyed by sword and fire of the other eleven tribes. Such are at this day those arrogant and seditious rebels as trouble commonweals and kingdoms, as of old Absalom was in Israel, and Seba the sons of Bochri; of whom mention is made in the second books of Samuel.

Hereunto appertain the wars that are taken in hand for the defense of true religion against idolaters and enemies of the true and catholic faith. They err, that are of opinion that no wars may be made in defense of religion. The Lord, indeed, blamed Peter for striking with the sword, because he was an apostle; but thereby, notwithstanding, he bade not the magistrate to be negligent in looking to religion, neither forbad he him to defend and maintain the pureness of faith. For if it be lawful for the magistrate to defend with the sword the things of account, of which sort are liberty, wealth, chastity, and his subjects' bodies; why should he not defend and revenge the things of greater account, and those which are of greatest weight? But there is nothing of more and greater weight than sincere and true religion is. There is, moreover, a manifest and flat commandment of God touching this matter to be seen in Deuteronomium. For the Lord commandeth that every city, within the jurisdiction of every magistrate, which departeth from God and the worship of God, should be set on with warriors, and utterly rased, if it revolted not from idolatry betimes. The place is extant in the thirteenth of Deut. But if the magistrate be commanded to punish apostates by war, then it is lawful for him by war to defend the Church in danger to be drawn by any barbarous prince from true religion unto false idolatry. Josue would by war have suppressed the Reubenites with their confederates for building an altar against God's commandment. Judas Machabeus fought for the people of God against the people and soldiers of king Antiochus, who purposed to tread down the Jewish religion, which at that time was the true worship of God, and perforce to make all men receive and profess his heathenish superstition. Likewise also Paul commended greatly those Jewish captains or judges, which by faith withstood and turned away foreign enemies' invasions. And Paul himself did war in Cyprus against Elymas the false prophet, and struck him with blindness: he addeth the reason why he struck him blind, which he fetcheth from the keeping of religion, and saith: "Ceasest thou not to pervert the right ways of the Lord? &c." Act. xiii. For the same Paul again forty men do lie in wait, supposing, if he were once made away, that a good part of the preaching of the gospel would then come to an end, and that thereby the Jewish religion (which, notwithstanding, was utterly false) should have been set up and maintained for truth. But Paul was not negligent to remedy this case, neither turned he the other cheek to have that stricken too; but earnestly and humbly requireth delivery and defense, which he requested not of a christian magistrate (when as yet there was none), but of a Roman centurion: neither did he once gainsay him, when he saw that he chose out found hundred footmen and seventy horsemen, whom he placed in order of battle array, to conduct him safely from Hierusalem to Antipatridis: and by that means was Paul, the vessel of election, preserved by an armed band of Italian soldiers. Of the Armenians, whom Maximinus the emperor did tyrannously oppress, Eusebius in the ninth book and eighth chapter of his Ecclesiastical History saith: "The people of Armenia, having been long time both profitable and friends to the people of Rome, being at length compelled by Maximinus Caesar to change the use of Christian religion (whereunto the whole nation was most holily bent) into the worship of idols, and to honor devils instead of God, of friends became enemies and of fellows adversaries; and preparing by force of arms to defend themselves against his wicked edicts, do of their own accord make war upon him, and put him often too much trouble and business." Thus saith he. It is lawful, therefore, for the magistrate to defend his people and subjects against idolaters, and by war to maintain and uphold true religion.

Like to this there is another cause why the magistrate may take war in hand. For either some barbarous enemy invadeth the people committed to thy charge, tearing and spoiling them most cruelly, like a wolf in a flock of sheep; when as notwithstanding thou didst not first provoke him thereunto by injury, but also after his causeless beginning thou hast offered equal conditions of peace to be made. In such a case as this the magistrate is commanded to stand forth like a lion, and to defend his subjects against the open wrong of merciless cut-throats: (so did Moses, when he fought against Arad, Sehon, and Og, kings of the Amorites; so did Josaphat, when he fought against the Ammonites and inhabitants of mount Seir; so did David, when he understood the war made on him by the Syrians) or else the magistrate doth aid his confederates (for the magistrate may make league with the nations about him, so that thereby nothing be done against the word of God), when by tyrants they be wrongfully oppressed. For so did Josue deliver the Gabionites from the siege of their enemies, and Saul the men of Jabes Galaad, fighting for them against Nahas, a prince full of tyranny.

CHAPTER 7

# Peter Martyr Vermigli (1499–1562)

PETER MARTYR VERMIGLI WAS an Italian Reformed theologian who finished his career in Zürich laboring as a colleague of Heinrich Bullinger.[1] He was born in Florence in 1499 and from an early age desired to learn and teach the Bible. He entered the University of Padua at the age of nineteen, and he received his doctorate in theology, probably at the age of twenty-six. While at Padua, he mastered the theology of Thomas Aquinas.[2] Beginning in 1537, Vermigli became the abbot of San Pietro and Aram in Naples, where he became the friend of the Spanish reformer Juan de Valdés and first became acquainted with Protestant thought, reading Martin Bucer and Huldrych Zwingli. At this time, he embraced the doctrine of justification by faith alone. His last position in Italy was as prior of San Frediano at Lucca in which he established a Reformed school surrounding himself with scholars such as Girolamo Zanchi and Immanuel Tremellius. With the reinstitution of the Inquisition, Vermigli fled to Zürich in 1542.[3] He spent the final twenty years of his life teaching in Strasbourg, Oxford, and finally Zürich. He declined several invitations from Calvin to pastor the Italian congregation in Geneva.

Vermigli's most important contribution to Reformed theology may have been in his teaching on the Eucharist.[4] His political ideas, however, were "among the most developed" of those widely circulated in the Reformed community of the late sixteenth and early seventeenth centuries.[5]

1. Baschera, "Independent Yet Harmonious," 44.

2. Donnelly, "Italian Influences," 86.

3. Zuidema, "Peter Martyr," 377.

4. Kingdon, "Function of Law," 159–60.

5. Kingdon, "Function of Law," 161. See Kirby, "Political Theology," 401; cf. Kingdon, "Political Thought," 121–39.

One of the political topics that he examined in detail was the issue of war. He reflected the methodological style of medieval scholastic theology in his essay "Of War."[6] He also reproduced the substance of Aquinas's teaching on the just war, presenting instruction on the classical *justice of war* doctrine for the benefit of the Reformed churches of his time.[7] He deviated somewhat, though, from classical positions when it comes to the matter of *justice in war* doctrine.

In the thirteenth century, Thomas Aquinas, in continuity with the teaching of Augustine of Hippo, had affirmed that for a war to be just, there were three things that were necessary.[8] There must be the authority of the sovereign who gives the command that initiates the war. There must be a just cause that provides the reason for the war; and there has to be a rightful intention in going to war, namely, prosecuting the war in behalf of peace. It was this teaching that Vermigli set forth, reflecting the renewed interest in Thomist theology in the sixteenth century both among Catholic and Protestant theologians.

The treatment on war provided by Vermigli appeared originally at the end of his biblical commentary on 2 Samuel 2.[9] The structure of his commentaries included theological *loci* at strategic places in the midst of his running commentary on the biblical text. After Vermigli died, the essay on war was extracted from his commentary and placed in the fourth part of what became *The Common Places*.[10] His discussion on war appears in chapter 17, and it consists of 33 sections. The methodological approach of the medieval schools appears throughout his essay on war. There is the introduction of the *quaestio*, followed by the *disputatio*. The first of these questions that Vermigli addressed concerns whether or not it is lawful to wage war. The disputation begins with a presentation of the objections to war posed by the Anabaptists. Vermigli then moved from the *objectio* to his *responsio*. He began his response to Anabaptist objections by providing arguments in support of his case that just wars are lawful.

6. James, "Peter Martyr Vermigli," 67.

7. Donnelly, *Calvinism and Scholasticism*, 126.

8. Aquinas's famous treatment of just war doctrine is presented in *Summa Theologica* 2a2ae.40.1–4.

9. Donnelly, "Peter Martyr Vermigli's Political Ethics," 60–65, provides a brief survey of some of Vermigli's perspectives on war.

10. Kingdon, "Peter Martyr Vermigli," 203–4.

Vermigli provided a succinct definition of war: "It is an hostile dissension whereby through the prince's edict mischiefs are repressed by force and arms, to the intent that men may peaceably and quietly live by justice and godliness."[11] This one-sentence definition of a just war follows the order of Aquinas's delineation of the three things that are necessary for a just war—the authority of the sovereign, a just cause (there is a fault in those who are attacked), and a rightful intention (the advancement of the good).[12]

It is obvious that Vermigli did not embrace the holy war doctrine, reflected in the proclamation of the First Crusade by Pope Urban II in 1095, that the church has the authority to initiate armed conflict. He stood within the classic just war tradition, affirming that the civil magistrate alone has the right to declare and prosecute war when there is a just cause. Although the papacy in the sixteenth century continued to espouse the crusade ideology—asserting that it is legitimate for a bishop, including the pope, to wage war—such a holy war perspective found no advocate in Vermigli.

Key medieval thinkers affirmed that the right to make war was by no means restricted to the king or the prince. "That nobles might act to bridle the king was an old medieval idea."[13] Christine de Pisan, for example, had asserted that the right to do battle belonged not only to emperors and kings, but also to dukes and other secular lords. Aquinas agreed with this perspective, affirming that one government body could legitimately raise arms against the king. If a body had placed a man into kingship, it could depose him and move against him militarily, if he abused his power in a tyrannical way.

Aquinas's position at this point was revived in Vermigli's political theory when he justified a war against a tyrant on the same basis that Aquinas had. Vermigli drew attention to ancient political arrangements, mentioning both ephors and tribunes. The ephors and tribunes elected kings and consuls to office. Then in a move reminiscent of Aquinas, Vermigli drew the conclusion that the principle of installation brings with

11. Vermigli, "Of Warre or Battell," 61–62. Vermigli's definition with contemporary spelling has been updated.

12. Medieval theologians had developed complex discussions on what constituted a just war. To cite one example, Alexander of Hales had set forth six criteria for a war to be just. In his view, there had to be the proper authority, attitude, intention, condition, merit, and cause. It seems that Aquinas returned the just war formula back to the original definition proposed by Augustine.

13. Walzer, *Revolution of the Saints*, 60.

it the principle of deposition. He cited the Electors of the Holy Roman Empire as an example. The Electors not only selected the Emperor, but they also had the power of compulsion against him, including the right to make war against him who had become a tyrant.[14]

There was one point in which Vermigli dissented from Aquinas. This related to the issue of the defense of the commonwealth against foreign aggressors. Nature itself teaches that a citizen must rise to defend his country. Nevertheless, Aquinas had maintained that in such occasions it was not lawful for ministers to fight. It was not becoming for them to shed the blood of others. They should rather be ready to shed their own blood for Christ. Vermigli agreed that, generally speaking, ministers were not to bear arms. Perhaps with the example of Zwingli in mind, who armed himself and died at Kappel, Vermigli contemplated an exception to this general rule.[15] In an emergency situation, such as when the enemy had laid siege to the city and were storming the walls, ministers may lawfully take up arms in defense of the city, like any other good citizen."[16]

Vermigli moved in the direction of holy war practice in his teaching on justice in war. Holy war differs from just war on the issue of whether or not the war is prosecuted with humanity and restraint. According to just war doctrine, there ought to be respect toward prisoners, the sparing of noncombatants, and the restraint of violence within military necessity. Holy war, conversely, is prosecuted unsparingly against any number of possible victims including combatants and noncombatants—men, women, children, and prisoners as well. An example of this is to be found in the Middle Ages. It was a widespread practice for victorious knights to massacre defeated peasant infantry. Another instance comes from Vermigli's own lifetime at Mohacs in which the Turkish Sultan Suleyman massacred the prisoners whom he had taken in battle.

Vermigli did not espouse a full-fledged doctrine of holy war in which noncombatants would be annihilated. He did, however, move away from just war theory in his teaching on the treatment of prisoners of war. This is reflected in his essay "Whether Captives Ought to Be Kept or Put to Death," found in chapter 18 in *The Common Places*. With respect to the ethical question on hand, Vermigli stated that the issue is highly nuanced. He maintained that, if possible, it would be better to spare captives; but he did not

14. Vermigli, *Common Places*, 4.21.12.

15. Donnelly, "Peter Martyr Vermigli's Political Ethics," 62.

16. Vermigli, "Of Warre or Battell," 72.

believe that this ought always to be the case. Such a policy was not absolute, admitting of no exceptions. There were occasions when captives ought to be put to death. How should a government respond, for example, if the enemy slaughtered its prisoners of war? In such a case, it would be legitimate, Vermigli contended, for the vengeance of a government to be unleashed by way of reciprocal response. If the enemy massacred one's own soldiers, the same thing ought to be done to the enemy's soldiers.[17]

Vermigli positioned himself within the justice of war tradition articulated by Augustine in the ancient church and later reaffirmed by Aquinas. He was willing, though, to make revisions to the classical teaching on justice in war by maintaining that captives may at times be put to death.

## Peter Martyr Vermigli, "Of Warre or Battell."

From *The Political Thought of Peter Martyr Vermigli: Selected Texts and Commentary*, edited by Robert M. Kingdon, 71–73. Geneva: Droz, 1980. Used by permission.

11. But is it lawfull for the Ministers of the Church to beare armes? It is not lawfull. For they must avoide all things which may hinder their functions. And Aristotle in his Politicks saith, that two offices must not bee committed to any one man, because no man can be fit for both the functions, seeing either of both, requireth a perfect and whole man. Yea and scarcely can there be any one man founde that can well execute the one or the other. For first the office of a minister is to teach the people. Which function howe great it is by it selfe alone, everie one maie easily understand. Secondly to pray daie and night for the people: lastly also to exercise discipline. Who is able so to doe these three things, as he can have leasure besides to fight? Paul unto Timothie saieth: Suffer thou afflictions as a good souldier of Christ. Let no man going on warfare intangle himself with the affaires of this life, that he may please him which hath chosen him to warfare. There is no man crowned but he which hath lawfully contended. He warned Timothie, that he ought to be a good souldier, and therefore that he prepare himselfe to afflictions. For if thou wilt doe thine office rightly, thou must of necessitie suffer many things. And he addeth: No man going on warfare intangleth himself with the businesse of this life. For both in the Code and in the Digestes, Souldiers are commanded to leave both ye trade of Marchandize

17. Vermigli, *Common Places*, 4.18.1–4.

and also of husbandrie, to the intent that they may always doe that which they are commanded. But howe much rather must this be intended of the Ecclesiastical function? In holy services the Crier was woont to proclaime: Doe this: to the intent the Priest might understand, that he ought wholy to be occupied in holy things. The office of a good Pastor is no slight thing, which may be executed without singular diligence and attention. None shall be Crowned (saieth Paul) but he that hath striven lawfully: that is, he that hath done even so much as the lawe commaundeth. And Paul in another place: Our weapons (saith he) be not carnall but the power of God, to cast downe everie high thing that advaunceth it selfe against God. This is the armour that must be committed unto Ministers. Howbeit if an enemie upon the sudden besiege the Citie, and hath even now laide siege to the walles, the Minister of the Church may rightly take Armes and repell violence, and doe that which becommeth a good Citizen. Notwithstanding when other souldiers shall come, he must retire himself to his office. But this will the Bishops never graunt. For if any man perhaps shall kill an enemie, him they account for irregular. And for the proofe hereof they alleage (forsooth) the fact and example of David. God saieth unto him: Thou canst not build a Temple unto mee because thou hast shead bloud. Beholde (say they) he is forbidden to build the temple because of bloud justly shead. Howbeit these things are mere trifles: for that temple was a shadow of the Church. And because Christ builded his Church not be violence or by bloud, therefore God woulde have his temple to be builded not by David but by Salomon the peaceable king. Moreover Salomon in himself did shadowe Christ. But Christ gathered himself unto himself men that came not against their willes, but a willing people. For that cause God made this aunswere unto David. And whereas they say that this must be understood of bloud justly shead by David, it is false. Nay it ought rather to be understood of the betraying of Urias, and of those souldiers which were slain together with him. This fact although God had forgiven David before, yet would he appoint some discipline for it. But let these men which be so sharpe and wittie tell me, whether Peter, when he slue Ananias and Saphira, or Paul, when he had blinded Elimas, were irregular. Or else if they were not from that time forwarde exercised in the office of Apostles.

12. But in a Campe there be, and ought to be Ministers, howbeit, not to fight, but to instruct the souldiers, and to minister the Sacramentes if neede require. In Deuteronomium God commanded the Priestes to be in the Campe, who should sound with the Trumpets. And when as Ministers

doe teach vertues and the worshipping of God, they may often put men in remembrance of those thinges which pertaine unto the ende. And if the Prince be overslacke, they may stirre him up unto virtue, and utter this saying unto him: The Lord commaundeth that evill should be taken away from among the people. Ioiada, a good high priest preserved Ioas the king, and when he was now growen to be a young man, he created him king, and by just battell chased away Athalia, although that he fought not with his own hand. Yet notwithstanding Moses together with his Levites slue a great number of idolaters. And Samuel slue Agag. But these thinges because they were particular must not be drawn in example. Howbeit, whether Byshops have the right of both swordes, I will speake nothing in this place. Onelie this one thing I will say, that it is not convenient, seeing they cannot be fit for both functions. But the Assamonites thou wilt say, held both the head byshoprick and the kingdome. I aunswere, in that they delivered their Countrie and preserved Religion, they are to be praysed: But in that they would retaine unto themselves the kingdome, I allow it not: seeing they usurpe an other mans right. For the promise of the kingdome was made to the Tribe of Iuda, and to the house of David. Hostientis in this matter is altogether of my minde, and addeth at the last: Let the laws say, let the Canons decree, let men cry out as much as they will, yet will our Cleargie men be warriors. And assuredlie, ever since the times of Adrian the Pope, which called Charles the Great into Italie, the Byshops and Cardinals have never ceased from warres.

## CHAPTER 8

# John Calvin (1509–1564)

JOHN CALVIN, THE FRENCH reformer in Geneva, was born in Noyon in northern France in 1509. He was a student at the University of Paris before he studied law at the universities in Orléans and Bourges. When his friend Nicholas Cop delivered a Lutheran-influenced address at the University of Paris, the Sorbonne was so infuriated that Cop and Calvin had to flee for their lives. Basel became Calvin's first place of refuge and the location where he published the 1536 edition of the *Institutes of the Christian Religion*. He then labored with William Farel in the reform effort in Geneva. He was expelled from the city in 1538 due to the fact that he could not tolerate the government's control of the church.[1] This led to three years of ministry with Martin Bucer in Strasbourg, pastoring a French-speaking congregation. He agreed to return to Geneva in 1541 upon the condition that he be allowed to draft a church constitution in which he could incorporate ecclesiastical rather than magisterial discipline.[2] Geneva then became the place of his life's work, where Calvin served as the church's organizer and the lead pastor in the city. In addition to preaching two times each Sunday and daily every other week, Calvin wrote biblical commentaries on much of the Old Testament and New Testament and refined his theological text, the *Institutes*, with the final edition appearing in 1559. He also laid the

---

1. Olson, "Calvin and Social-Ethical Issues," 155, nicely covers the dispute between Calvin and the early Geneva city council; cf. Mühling, "Calvin and the Swiss Confederation," 66. Cheneviére, "Did Calvin Advocate Theocracy?" 168, states, "From 1536 to 1541 Geneva was governed by a regime in which the State claimed to direct both the religious and the civil life of the citizens. This system of caesaropapism prevailed at the period in most of the Swiss towns."

2. Naphy, "Church and State," 14; cf. Olson, "Church and Society," 202–6.

foundation for what was to become the University of Geneva, an institution that attracted students from all over Europe.[3]

There is no question that Calvin was the most influential of the Reformed theologians of the sixteenth century. At the same time he is probably the most distorted in contemporary portraits of his political teaching. He is often presented as a theocratic tyrant ruling Geneva with an iron fist and believing in holy war against the infidels. The stereotypical presentation is that Calvin implemented a theocratic structure in which he ruled the Republic of Geneva, even while he believed in the prosecution of war without humanitarian restraint.[4] The reality is that Calvin rejected theocracy, granting the Geneva consistory a limited spiritual jurisdiction, focusing upon the moral conduct and doctrinal beliefs of the church members in Geneva. In addition, he deliberately positioned himself in the medieval just war tradition as it had been developed by Augustine of Hippo.

Calvin repudiated a theocratic arrangement in which the clergy would have direct civil authority, the kind of arrangement that was found in the Jewish ghettos of Europe in which the head of the community was the rabbi and the constitution was the Torah, the Talmud, and rabbinic commentaries.[5] He taught a doctrine of two spheres, separating church and state with respect to their distinct jurisdictions and giving different roles to ministers and magistrates. Pastors were called to wield the sword of the Spirit in the preaching of the Word of God.[6] Princes were appointed to unleash the sword of justice in the punishment of domestic evil and in battle against

3. Note the excellent discussion in Olson, "Calvin and Social-Ethical Issues," 158–59.

4. Paquin, "Calvin and Theocracy in Geneva," 92, properly observes that Geneva "was never submitted to the ruling power of any clergy after the Genevans solemnly adopted the Reformation in May 1536." Brauer, "Rule of the Saints," is an example of a scholar who provides an overly broad definition of what a theocracy actually is. He states, "The New England Puritans set up a theocracy, if by theocracy one means the church and saints exercising definitive power in the political order." He adds, "Such a 'theocracy' did not necessarily demand the rule of the clergy. It only demanded the rule of the saints." McNeill, "Democratic Element in Calvin's Thought," 162, properly states regarding Calvin, "At heart he is a political republican."

5 Pfeffer, *Church, State, and Freedom*, 8. Mundry, "John Calvin and Anabaptists," 240; Jeong Koo Jeon, "Calvin and the Two Kingdoms," 305, 314.

6. Calvin forcefully asserted this position in the constitution that he wrote for the church in Geneva, the *Ecclesiastical Ordinances*. Near the end of the document, Calvin wrote, "All this is to be done in such a way that the ministers have no civil jurisdiction and wield only the spiritual sword of the Word of God." Furthermore, he added, "There is no derogation by this consistory from the authority of the Seigneury or the magistracy; but the civil power shall continue in its entirety" (Calvin, *Register*, 49).

hostile foreign powers.[7] Calvin insisted that the best condition for citizens was to live in a republic, for the people to be under the civil authority of the men whom they had chosen to political office. "A system compounded of aristocracy and democracy, far excels all others," he said.[8] "In this especially consists the best condition of the people," he contended, "when they can choose by common consent, their own shepherds."[9]

There is no question that some of the Reformed leaders and thinkers moved in the direction of holy war. The Puritan armies in the English Civil War, for example, put holy war doctrine into practice. The Roundheads prosecuted the war effort against the Cavaliers and their supporters with ruthless abandon, eliminating combatants and noncombatants in their engagements. After the September 1649 massacre of Irish men, women, and children at Drogheda, Peter Sterry (1613–1672) responded with a sermon dedicated to giving thanks to God for the glorious Parliamentary victory.[10]

Calvin understood that holy war deviated from the restraints advocated by the proponents of justice in war. Holy war entailed, as he put it, "the indiscriminate and promiscuous slaughter, making no distinction of age or sex, but including alike women and children, the aged and the decrepit."[11] He denied that it was right "in the present day" to "slay all the ungodly" in a holy war campaign.[12] He also spoke against the slaughter of prisoners of war, affirming that it entailed the defiance of God.[13] He was probably opposing at this point the widespread practice in the Middle Ages of defeated infantry being massacred by victorious knights.

Calvin repudiated holy war doctrine, positioning himself in the mainstream of the just war tradition of the church. In his discussion of just war doctrine in the *Institutes*, he connected his teaching with Augustine of

---

7. Britz, "Politics and Social Life," 440–41, draws attention to Calvin's acceptance of a two-kingdom doctrine.

8. Calvin, *Institutes* 4.20.8.

9. Calvin, *Commentaries*, 14:309–10. Kingdon, "Church and State," 356, notes that Calvin "came to prefer" government run by collectives. Indeed, "the Genevan state was run during Calvin's ministry by a hierarchy of councils, headed by a Small Council of twenty-five native-born citizens, re-elected every year, supervised by four executives called syndics, elected every year for a term of only one year."

10. Sterry, *Coming Forth of Christ*.

11. Calvin, *Commentaries*, 4:97.

12. Calvin, *Commentaries*, 4:268.

13. Calvin, *Sermons on Deuteronomy*, 734.

Hippo, referring to him two times by name.[14] He also included the same three justice of war constituents that Augustine had developed—proper authority, just cause, and right intention. He asserted that the civil magistrate alone is authorized to declare and prosecute war: "Princes must be armed to defend by war the dominions entrusted to their safekeeping."[15] The prince may initiate war, but it must be on the basis of a just cause. Something must have already happened that justifies going to war. A fault exists. Wrongdoing has been committed. In such a case, the prince is armed in order that he may "execute public vengeance." Examples would include disturbing "the common tranquility of all," the raising of "seditious tumults," and "vile misdeeds."[16] A just cause might well lead a prince to make war, but he had to do so with the right intention of seeking the peace of the community. In his biblical commentary on Deuteronomy, Calvin maintained that "wars must not be undertaken except that we may live in unmolested peace."[17]

Calvin went beyond Augustine in his justice of war discussion. He added a fourth constituent, stressing that war must be an option of last resort. Governments, he affirmed, ought not to go to war "unless they are driven to it by extreme necessity." "Everything else ought to be tried before recourse is had to arms."[18] Calvin was probably referring here to a diplomatic solution to problems. That is what he preferred. "An ambassador," he asserted, "ought to be favored because he tends to maintain peace among men, or to remove troubles which have already started."[19]

One of the most influential aspects of Calvin's doctrine of war relates to his teaching on parliamentary resistance, i.e., warring by the popular magistrates as a response to a tyrannical monarch.[20] Calvin appealed here to the existence of the *populares magistratus*, calling them "magistrates of

---

14. Calvin, *Institutes* 4.20.12.

15. Calvin, *Institutes* 4.20.11.

16. Calvin, *Institutes* 4.20.11.

17. Calvin, *Commentaries*, 2:52.

18. Calvin, *Institutes* 4.20.12.

19. Calvin, Sermons on 2 Samuel, 451.

20. Calvin's discussion at this point occurs in the context of his reflections on the tyrant, the "savage prince" (Calvin, *Institutes* 4.20.29). In his *Commentaries on the Prophet Amos* (Calvin, *Commentaries*, 14:269–70), Calvin notes that the despot sees to it that "no freedom of speech" is "allowed." More than that, tyrants were known for "plundering houses, raping virgins and matrons, and slaughtering the innocent" (Calvin, *Institutes* 4.20.24).

the people, appointed to restrain the willfulness of kings."[21] The idea in the expression *populares magistratus* was that these individuals constituted a representative body that was appointed in an elective manner. Calvin left his readers with no ambiguity as to the kind of representative assembly that he had in mind. He alluded to the various European parliamentary bodies, referring to the "three estates," which no doubt included the French Estates-General. Such parliamentary bodies had the duty to "withstand . . . the fierce licentiousness of kings . . . who violently fall upon and assault the lowly common people." They had the responsibility to take up arms, if necessary, in behalf of the people for whom they had been "appointed protectors by God's ordinance."[22]

Calvin's teaching at this point had an influence at the time of the American Revolution. The magistrates of the people who had been sent to Philadelphia by the colonial governments formed a representative body in the Second Continental Congress for the express purpose of confronting the problem of British tyranny, namely, the trampling down of legal rights. It was Calvin's doctrine of resistance by a parliamentary body that provided theological and moral legitimacy among Reformed Christians for armed resistance to tyranny in the American Revolution.

## John Calvin, *Institutes of the Christian Religion.*

1517–20. Translated by Ford Lewis Battles. Philadelphia: Westminster, 1960. Used by permission.

4.20.30. Here are revealed his goodness, his power, and his providence. For sometimes he raises up open avengers from among his servants, and arms them with his command to punish the wicked government and deliver his people, oppressed in unjust ways, from miserable calamity. Sometimes he directs to this end the rage of men with other intentions and other endeavors. Thus he delivered the people of Israel from the tyranny of Pharaoh through Moses; from the violence of Chusen, king of Syria, through Othniel; and from other servitudes through other kings or judges. Thus he tamed the pride of Tyre by the Egyptians, the insolence of the Egyptians

---

21. Calvin, *Institutes* 4.20.31; cf. Kingdon, "Church and State," 360.

22. Calvin, *Institutes* 4.20.31. Calvin's position regarding armed parliamentary resistance to tyranny was nothing new. It was an old medieval idea that was implemented, for example, in the uprising led by Simon de Montfort in 1258 when he led the barons to victory over the royal army. See Stevenson, "Calvin and Political Issues," 184–85.

by the Assyrians, the fierceness of the Assyrians by the Chaldeans; the arrogance of Babylon by the Medes and Persians, after Cyrus had already subjugated the Medes. The ungratefulness of the kings of Judah and Israel and their impious obstinacy toward his many benefits, he sometimes by the Assyrians, sometimes by the Babylonians, crushed and afflicted—although not all in the same way.

For the first kind of men, when they had been sent by God's lawful calling to carry out such acts, in taking up arms against kings, did not at all violate that majesty which is implanted in kings by God's ordination; but, armed from heaven, they subdued the lesser power with the greater, just as it is lawful for kings to punish their subordinates. But the latter kind of men, although they were directed by God's hand whither he pleased, and executed his work unwittingly, yet planned in their minds to do nothing but an evil act.

4.20.31. But however these deeds of men are judged in themselves, still the Lord accomplished his work through them alike when he broke the bloody scepters of arrogant kings and when he overturned intolerable governments. Let the princes hear and be afraid.

But we must, in the meantime, be very careful not to despise or violate that authority of magistrates, full of venerable majesty, which God has established by the weightiest decrees, even though it may reside with the most unworthy men, who defile it as much as they can with their own wickedness. For, if the correction of unbridled despotism is the Lord's to avenge, let us not at once think that it is entrusted to us, to whom no command has been given except to obey and suffer.

I am speaking all the while of private individuals. For if there are now any magistrates of the people, appointed to restrain the willfulness of kings (as in ancient times the ephors were set against the Spartan kings, or the tribunes of the people against the Roman consuls, or the demarchs against the senate of the Athenians; and perhaps, as things now are, such power as the three estates exercise in every realm when they hold their chief assemblies), I am so far from forbidding them to withstand, in accordance with their duty, the fierce licentiousness of kings, that, if they wink at kings who violently fall upon and assault the lowly common folk, I declare that their dissimulation involves nefarious perfidy, because they dishonestly betray the freedom of the people, of which they know that they have been appointed protectors by God's ordinance.

4.20.32. But in that obedience which we have shown to be due the authority of rulers, we are always to make this exception, indeed, to observe it as primary, that such obedience is never to lead us away from obedience to him, to whose will the desires of all kings ought to be subject, to whose decrees all their commands ought to yield, to whose majesty their scepters ought to be submitted. And how absurd would it be that in satisfying men you should incur the displeasure of him for whose sake you obey men themselves! The Lord, therefore, is the King of Kings, who, when he has opened his sacred mouth, must alone be heard, before all and above all men; next to him we are subject to those men who are in authority over us, but only in him. If they command anything against him, let it go unesteemed. And here let us not be concerned about all that dignity which the magistrates possess; for no harm is done to it when it is humbled before that singular and truly supreme power of God. On this consideration, Daniel denies that he has committed any offense against the king when he has not obeyed his impious edict. For the king had exceeded his limits, and had not only been a wrongdoer against men, but, in lifting up his horns against God, had himself abrogated his power.

# CHAPTER 9

# Theodore Beza (1519–1605)

UPON THE DEATH OF Swiss reformer John Calvin in May 1564, leadership of the Genevan church was designated by Calvin to go to his friend and fellow French exile Theodore Beza.

Born at Vézelay, in Burgandy, France, Beza descended from a family of distinction; his father was lesser nobility, king's baliff, and royal governor of Vézelay. Beza's family lineage proved advantageous and instrumental on numerous occasions during his lifetime, providing entrée into royal, political, and religious circles from which others were excluded.

When he was nine years old, his father sent him to Orléans to study with the humanist Melchior Wolmar (1497–1560) under whom Beza was introduced to ideas of the Reformation and subsequently followed to the University of Bourges. In 1535, Beza's father ordered him to return to Orléans to complete legal studies. In 1539, with a degree in law, Beza moved to Paris to practice law. He also continued his pursuit of humanist interests and reading of Reformed literature. Gradually he changed his spiritual and theological ideas and in 1548 fled to Geneva, which had become a city of refuge for adherents of the Reformation.

In 1549, through the assistance of Pierre Viret (1511–1571), Beza secured an appointment as professor of Greek at the Lausanne academy. Upon the death of Calvin in 1564, Beza joined the Genevan clergy and was elected moderator of the Compagnie des Pasteurs ("company of pastors"), a post he held until 1580. He became leader of the Genevan Protestants and chief counselor to French Reformed churches and other European Protestants. He travelled to France and elsewhere on behalf of Protestants, and he took special interest in the Waldensians of the Piedmont region of Italy who were being harassed by French authorities. Throughout the 1580s he attempted theological reconciliation between Lutheran and Reformed proponents on matters of the Lord's Supper and other theological differences. Beyond the importance of theological distinctions, there were political ramifications because some German Lutheran princes were deciding where or if they would support the different factions of the French Wars of Religion. Some German princes supported Henry III (the Roman Catholic Guise faction) and others supported Henry of Navarre (leader of the Huguenot faction).

Beza remained in Geneva throughout his ministerial and educational life. He also was actively teaching until 1597. The conversion of Henry IV (previously Henry III, King of Navarre) to Roman Catholicism greatly saddened Beza. Henry had been baptized as a Catholic but raised as a Protestant by his mother Jeanne d'Albret, Queen of Navarre. Upon her death in 1572, Henry inherited that throne. He barely escaped death in the St. Bartholomew's Day massacre of August 24, 1572, and during the Wars of Religion led Huguenot forces against the royal (and Catholic) army. In 1589, upon the death of his brother-in-law and distant cousin Henry III of France, he was called by French succession to the throne by Salic law (the ancient Salian Frankish civil law code compiled by the first Frankish King, Clovis, in the sixth century). On July 25, 1593, and against the earnest pleadings of Beza, Henry renounced Protestantism and converted to Roman Catholicism in order to gain the crown and throne, reportedly declaring "Paris is well worth a mass." For Beza, it was the saddest day of his latter life. He died in Geneva a dozen years later on October 13, 1519.

Often obscured by the shadow of his predecessor, Beza was instrumental in directing what he understood to be a program of Protestant evangelization across Europe and especially in his native country, France. Through his prolific correspondence, he maintained contact with Reformed churches throughout Europe and England. Beza scholar Scott Manetsch observes:

> Like Calvin, Theodore Beza viewed himself as a spokesman for Protestants in the diaspora, a reformer of the refugee church. . . . Calvin perceived himself not solely as a minister of a city or territory, but a pastor of refugees. Stationed in Geneva, Calvin's vision extended to his native France and beyond to the four corners of Europe. . . . While the Peace of Augsburg (1555) largely froze Lutheranism within the territorial boundaries of Germany, Calvin's program of reform, with Geneva as its command-center, achieved dramatic successes in France and through much of Europe during the middle decades of the sixteenth century.[1]

1. Manetsch, *Theodore Beza*, 2–3.

Although Beza spent most of his life in Geneva, he always monitored political and religious activities in his native country of France, especially during the era of the French Wars of Religion between 1562 and 1598. When
called upon, he engaged in political and diplomatic negotiations on behalf
of Protestants, and he also became embroiled in the political intrigue of his
day. As a teacher at the academy in Geneva that trained many of the Protestant pastors of Reformed Europe (e.g., England, Scotland, the Netherlands,
Poland, Hungary, and the Palatinate) his influence was enormous. Indeed,
he would boast that the school in Geneva was the "nursery-garden of the
ministers of France . . . of England . . . [and] of Flanders."[2] Additionally, in
France the church organizations and structures created by leaders in Geneva as part of the larger Calvinist movement became useful after 1560 and
1561; local synods in southwestern France began mustering and recruiting
soldiers using the local churches as military units thus enabling rapid re-
cruitment and large numbers once revolt became public at the onset of the
Wars of Religion in 1562.[3]

Theology and ecclesiastical organization produced faithful soldiers
committed to combat. Further, it was necessary to have leadership from the
nobility, the only ones to have such experience, training, and resources to
offer any chance of success on the battlefield. French Calvinists found such
a leader in Louis de Bourbon, Prince of Condé (1530–1569), who was later
killed in the 1569 Battle of Jarnac.

It was against the backdrop of the French Wars of Religion that Beza
ministered, seeking support for Protestant refugees fleeing to Geneva and
elsewhere, even appealing to England's Queen Elizabeth for relief and sanctuary for them. Another result of the conflict that touched Beza and biblical
scholarship was the taking by Huguenots (French Calvinist Protestants) of
the fifth-century codex of the New Testament in 1562 from the monastic
library of St. Irenaeus at Lyon during the wars in which Huguenots captured the city. They gave the codex to Beza who in 1581, for comparative
safety and security, gave it to the University of Cambridge, thus accounting
for its historic designation *Codex Bezae Cantabrigensis*. Interestingly, even
after Henry of Navarre converted to Catholicism in order to accede to the
French throne as Henry IV, there was correspondence between him and
Beza, with Beza meeting with him as late as 1600.

2. Beza, cited in Kingdon, "Political Resistance of the Calvinists," 222.

3. Kingdon, "Political Resistance of the Calvinists," 222.

Both Calvin and Beza had an international perspective and vision for their theology and their ministries. Through his publications and letters, Beza counseled princes and encouraged persecuted Protestants far beyond Geneva's borders. In his lectures and teaching as a theology professor at the Genevan Academy during the years 1555–1599, he trained many of the religious and political leaders of Reformed Protestantism and his influence and thought had wide geographic dispersion. Beza's thought influenced many people, among them, thinkers as diverse as French jurist and Calvinist theologian Lambert Daneau (c. 1535-c. 1590), Dutch theologian Jacob Arminius (Jakob Hermanszoon, 1560–1609), and English cleric and theologian William Perkins (1558–1602).

Although Beza is remembered primarily for his work in Geneva, his biblical scholarship on the text of New Testament, and his theological writings, he also authored an important political treatise that set forth his ideas on political resistance theory and just war. News of the St. Bartholomew's Day massacre of French Calvinists in August 1572 jolted Reformation leaders and adherents. The massacre that began on August 24th in Paris and continued for weeks soon spread to other cities. "This royally sanctioned pogrom unleashed, in turn, an unexpected orgy of popular violence within the city, as frenzied Catholic crowds looted Huguenot homes and murdered neighbors suspected of heresy . . . mob violence spread like a deadly pestilence to major provincial cities, including Tours, Lyon, Rouen, and Orléans."[4] As a result, thousands of French Protestants were killed and thousands of others fled, seeking refuge in Huguenot strongholds such as La Rochelle, Sancerre, and Montauban. Still others left France entirely for sanctuary in Protestant cities such as London, Strasbourg, Basel, and Geneva. "Three months of savagery had effectively eviscerated the military and religious leadership of the Huguenot movement. At the same time, the massacres decisively altered the Protestant expectations for the future: the very survival of the Reformed religion in France now seemed in jeopardy."[5]

The St. Bartholomew's Day massacre was "a defining moment in the Calvinist tradition.[6]" The pogrom sent shock waves through Protestant Europe. Protestant leaders feared that it would ignite a greater persecution and movement rolling back decades of Protestant gain. News of the slaughter reached Geneva in less than a week, and by Sunday, August 31,

4. Manetsch, *Theodore Beza*, 31.
5. Manetsch, *Theodore Beza*, 31.
6. Witte, *Reformation of Rights*, 83.

1572, Beza and other ministers announced it in their Sunday sermons.[7] Manetsch observes:

> In addition to responding to the humanitarian disaster, the Genevan clergy worked frantically to shape international opinion about the massacres as well as to offset the damage incurred by wide-spread "apostasy" in the French churches. . . . The anger, suspicion, and fear fostered by the Huguenot diaspora in Geneva created a volatile social climate particularly conducive to the growth of radical ideas and explosive actions. Protestant Geneva had never faced a crisis of such magnitude as the one it confronted in the fall of 1572.[8]

Further information regarding the massacre and Beza's response will be seen below, but as one steps back from the incident and views Beza's work in a larger context of war, peace, and justice, Beza emerges as a key figure in the development of broader Protestant political theory in the sixteenth century. His writings and thought had an enormous effect on shaping the future of Protestant, and especially, English Protestant ideas of rights, civil disobedience, rebellion, and revolution.

Beza first wrote of political theory in a 1554 treatise (almost twenty years before the St. Bartholomew's Day massacre) titled *The Punishment of Heretics* (*De haereticis a civili magistratu puniendis*), which was a vigorous defense of the execution of Michael Servetus. Beza argued that the execution was just and necessary and an exemplary case of ecclesiastical and civil leaders working together to maintain order and discipline in a Christian community.[9] At that time this could be accomplished only in the local or territorial level, but he hoped that in time the Reformed faith would spread throughout the world and there would be a unitary Christian society in what he variously termed the "City of God on earth," "the republic of the Christian Church," and a "visible form of the invisible body of Christ" (*corpus Christianum*).[10] In this early writing Beza drew upon the experience of Lutheran pastors in Magdeburg in 1550 in the document known as the Magdeburg Confession. This document arose in response to the imposition of Roman Catholicism in Magdeburg and argued that leaders of the city had the right to resist imperial law when faced with a situation where the

---

7. Manetsch, *Theodore Beza*, 32.
8. Manetsch, *Theodore Beza*, 32.
9. Witte, *Reformation of Rights*, 92.
10. Witte, *Reformation of Rights*, 92. See also Kingdon, "First Expression," 88–100.

"supreme authority" was working to destroy true religion. This confession was "the first Protestant religious justification of the right of defense against unjust higher authorities."[11]

In Beza's *The Punishment of Heretics* he stated:

> When then several Princes abuse their office, whoever still feels it necessary to refuse to use the Christian Magistrates offered by God against external violence whether of the unfaithful or of heretics, I charge deprives the Church of God of a most useful, and (as often as it pleses the Lord) necessary defense.[12]

Kingdon writes of Beza's words:

> In this statement I see an embryonic justification of democratic revolution. . . . This is one of the first justifications of popular right to overthrow tyrannical government every expressed by a Calvinist. And in historical fact this right of inferior magistrates to revolt was expanded to permit whole populations, even without the benevolent supervision of the Church, to revolt against royal government.[13]

As with all ideas, there is an intellectual genealogy. No idea arises in a vacuum. Within Protestantism, Beza's thought was one of the progenitors that would eventually lead to broader ideas regarding tyranny, freedom, and revolution in the English Civil War of the seventeenth century and in America and Europe in the eighteenth century.

Beza's major political writing was the 1574 *Concerning the Rights of Rulers over Their Subjects and the Duty of Subjects towards Their Rulers*. Written first in Latin and subsequently translated and published in French, the work in part addressed emerging theories of natural rights and political covenant. In this writing Beza returned again to the historical example of Magdeburg and well as other illustrations from history and the biblical text.

For Beza, the constitutional monarchy had boundaries and was also subject to abuse by the monarch. He believed that there was a long history dating to biblical times of monarchs overstepping the legitimate boundaries of their reigns.

---

11. Lindberg, *European Reformations,* 196. See also, Olson, "Theology of Revolution," 56–79.

12. Beza, cited in Kingdon, "First Expression," 92.

13. Kingdon, "First Expression," 92–93.

Beza's writing became an extremely influential work in the shaping of Calvinist resistance theory.[14] As legal historian John Witte, Jr., notes: "Beza, of course, did not operate alone. He called on five decades of Protestant and five centuries of Catholic teachings on law, politics, and society as well as a whole arsenal of classical and Patristic sources."[15] He also drew on the inspiration and instruction of many English, Scottish, French, and Swiss contemporaries and other reformers. Among them were the Marian exiles from England and Scotland, including John Ponet, John Knox, Christopher Goodman, Antoine de Chandieu, Lambert Daneau, Simon Gouart, Francois Hotman, Hubert Languet, Philippe DuPlessis Mornay, Peter Martyr Vermigli, Heinrich Bullinger, Pierre Viret, and several Dutch pamphleteers.[16]

*Concerning the Rights of Rulers* was very methodical and reasoned, unlike many of the Huguenot pamphlets that responded to the massacre with exuberant and passionate oratory. Each of the work's ten sections, written in the form of a question, focused on a particular aspect of the political relationship between political rulers ("Magistrates") and subjects. Within the political structure that Beza addressed there was the monarch, the lesser or "inferior" magistrates, and the Estates-General. Beza believed that those who had the lawful power to create a monarch also had the right to depose the monarch if the monarch acted tyrannically and refused to change. For Beza, the lawful (and biblical) way to depose a tyrant rested not with individuals but with the people led by proper magistrates.[17] Because the lesser magistrates had taken an oath to defend the kingdom, there was a moral obligation and duty to take up arms against a tyrant if necessary. In so doing, they and those who followed them would be defending the kingdom. Beza argued that just as David had "taken to defend himself by means of arms"[18] against King Saul, so too could the inferior magistrates do the same when necessary. Such action was not to be impulsive. The "recourse to arms" was to come "after all those [previously discussed by Beza] remedies have been put to the test."[19] In Question 8 he

---

14. Kingdon, "First Expression," 88–89.

15. Kingdon, "First Expression," 89.

16. Kingdon, "First Expression," 89.

17. Gosselin, "David in *Tempore Belli*," 35.

18. Beza, *Right of Magistrates,* 13.

19. Beza, *Right of Magistrates,* 14.

reiterated the same idea, stating that it "befits a wise man to make trial of all things by deliberation before armed force."[20]

However, it must also be noted as Robert M. Kingdon states: "The subordination of Calvinist political thought to theology means that it takes many forms. Different writers, and often the same writer in different circumstances, advocated very different forms of government, and presented very different doctrines of the duty of political obedience."[21] With respect to the importance and influence of the ideas of Beza, Witte writes:

> Beza's core theory of a political covenant with fundamental rights that could not be breached with impunity became a standard argument for Western revolutionaries thereafter. In France, the most famous expansion of this argument came in the 1579 tract, *Vindiciae, Contra Tyrannos: Or Concerning the Legitimate Power of the Prince Over the People, and of the People Over the Prince,* which even the eighteenth-century Jacobins would later cite with reverence. In Scotland, the most powerful exposition of Beza's ideas was George Buchanan's *Dialogue Concerning the Rights of the Crown and the People of Scotland* (1579/61), which would become an anchor text for later Scottish Enlightenment theories of "common sense." In the Netherlands, Beza's ideas were axiomatic for the powerful Calvinist logic of revolution against Spanish tyranny, that was set out in more than 10,000 pamphlets and sermons published from 1570–1610, and all manner of learned tracts that poured forth from major Dutch universities over the next two centuries. The Dutch revolutionary writers were soon outdone by the 22,000 plus Calvinist tracts published in England from 1640–1660 in defense of the Puritan revolution against the tyrannical King Charles and the ultimate execution of this tyrant by public beheading in 1649. And, eventually, this Christian covenantal theory of society and the state would be transmitted into increasingly secularized forms of the English, French, and American Enlightenments, most notably by such cradle Calvinists who later went their own way–John Locke, Jean Jacques Rousseau, and John Adams.[22]

Beza's influence on political thought should not be under-estimated.

For many, if not most, Calvinists the culmination of political resistance theory rested in the concept of the role of the lesser or "inferior magistrate" in government. Such leaders shared with the monarchs the

20. Beza, *Right of Magistrates,* 38.

21. Kingdon, "Political Resistance of the Calvinists," 226.

22. Witte, "Rights, Resistance, and Revolution," 569–70.

duty of maintaining "true" religion. When they failed to do so, or worse, tried to suppress "true religion," it was the right (but not duty) of the lesser magistrates to resist their superiors, with force if necessary.[23] This concept formed the core of Calvinist resistance theory.

It is also important to note that Protestant resistance theory was not solely Calvinist in origin. Calvinists such as Beza and Philippe Marnix van Sint Aldegonde (1540–1598) were master political polemicists who were able to draw on the Lutheran experience of armed defiance and resistance in the document of 1550, the *Confession, Instruction and Warning* in the city of Magdeburg, Germany at the end of the Smalkaldic War (1546–1547).[24]

The combination of Calvinist synodical organization, noble leadership, and a theory of resistance created a potent theological and political vitality that spread geographically far beyond Geneva.[25] Witte writes:

> Napoleon Bonaparte once quipped: "I would rather face ten thousand Italians coming from mass, than one thousand Presbyterians rising from their knees." There's more to this than Napoleon's notorious anti-papalism and French snobbery against Italians. He was signaling the real danger of the fierce righteous warrior who was a Calvinist. Calvinists did not start out as fierce warriors, and their founder John Calvin was notoriously averse to sponsoring offensive or defensive wars or bloodshed, save in narrow circumstances. Calvin's successors were not nearly so reticent, especially as they faced pogroms, inquisitions, and genocides that were killing their coreligionists by the tens of thousands. Within a decade of Calvin's death in 1564, his followers had gone from turning checks to swinging swords in support of their righteous cases. Calvin's followers continued his trademark penchant for due process, orderly decisionmaking, and constitutional structures in deciding on the justice of their military cause and on the methods for executing it. But once Calvinists decided on war, and rose from their knees after seeking God's blessing, woe to their enemies![26]

Beza's influence on ideas of revolt and war were enormous and were ideological and theological. They arose largely in the context of the Huguenot experience in France, especially in the aftermath of the St. Bartholomew's

23. Kingdon, "Political Resistance of the Calvinists," 226.

24. Kingdon, "Political Resistance of the Calvinists," 227–30; Olson, "Theology of Revolution," 56–79.

25. Kingdon, "Political Resistance of the Calvinists," 230.

26. Witte, "Rights, Resistance, and Revolution," 550.

Day massacre. His ideas would be evaluated, expanded, and reshaped in the decades and centuries that followed, and one can see a direct linkage between his thought and that of the revolutionary ideas of the eighteenth century. Though he likely would not have agreed with all that came after his work, he had given much to Protestant political theorists who followed in his wake.

## Theodore Beza, *Question 10. Whether those who suffer persecution for the sake of their religion can defend themselves against tyrants without hurt to their consciences.*

From *Concerning the Rights of Rulers over Their Subjects and the Duty of Subjects towards Their Rulers.* Translated by Henri-Louis Gonin. Capetown and Pretoria: HAUM, 1956.

It finally remains for me to solve a question of the greatest moment, namely, whether it is allowable, in accordance with the condition and distinctions laid down above, to offer resistance by armed force to tyranny assailing the true religion and even stamping it out as far as may be, and to contend against persecution. The following may be the principal reasons for entertaining doubts (*on this score*): firstly, since religion touches the consciences (*of people*) which can in no way be subjected to violence, it would appear that it should not be rendered secure or be defended by means of any armed force; for that reason we perceive that it has thus far been propagated by the preaching of the Word of God, by prayers and by patience. There are besides many passages to be found in the Scriptures from which the difference between the kingdoms of this world and the spiritual kingdom of Christ appears. To these may finally be added the example of the holy Prophets and in the last instance that of Christ Himself, our Lord, for although all authority, power and virtue dwelt in Him, yet He Himself never adopted this method of defense, just as the Apostles themselves and all the martyrs after them refrained from doing so; so much so that not even entire legions of the faithful of Christ, abundantly furnished with arms, declined to meet death rather than defend themselves by drawing the sword and assailing the very enemies of truth.

I answer first that it is an absurd, nay even a false opinion that the means by which the objects and affairs of this world are defended, such as both courts of law and armed force, not merely differ from the means by which things spiritual can be defended, but are as it were diametrically opposed to them and are so incompatible with them that they neither can nor ought to find any application in a matter of religion. But on the contrary I declare that it is the principal duty of a most excellent and pious ruler that there should apply whatever means, authority and power has been granted him by God to this end entirely that God may truly be recognized among his subjects and may, being recognized, be worshipped and adored as the supreme king of all kings. Therefore the man of that description will not merely put forth all the power of his jurisdiction and the authority of the laws against the despisers or disturbers of the true religion who have shown themselves not the least amenable to ecclesiastical words of rebuke and admonition, but will even punish with armed force those who cannot otherwise be restrained from impiety. In support of this view the Scriptures themselves furnish us with innumerable reasons and examples. The reasons are of the following kind:

a. Since the purpose of all well-ordered polities is not simply peace and quiet in this life, as some heathen philosophers have imagined, but the glory of God, towards which the whole present life of men should be directed, it therefore follows that those who are set over nations, ought to bring to bear all their zeal and all the faculties they have received from God to this end that the pure worship of God upon which His glory depends should in the highest degree be maintained and increased among the people over whom they hold sway.

b. Finally, even if we were to concede that the ultimate purpose of polities was the undisturbed preservation of this life, yet we should have to admit that this was the sole reason for obtaining and preserving it, (namely) if God, both the author and the director of our life, be piously and rightly worshipped.

Proofs or example (*of this*) are quite innumerable in the Scriptures:

a. For it is particularly clear that those patriarchs of old were simultaneously the highest priests and the supreme rulers among their people; this is expressly recorded concerning Melchizedek and Eli and although these two offices were afterward separated by the Lord, this did not happen because they were incompatible with each other but because one man could scarcely be equal to the performance of both.

b. Furthermore, when the king is bidden to have with him a book of law that he may practice himself in the reading of it day and night, that is demanded of him not as of a private citizen but as of a king and a public magistrate.

c. And among the laws of which the execution is entrusted to the rulers, those are deemed the principal which condemn to death the despisers of the true religion. The application of these laws we remark in the case of David who by means of fixed laws rendered inviolable the entire worship of God, and in the case of Solomon who supplemented the decree of his father against transgressors; likewise in the edicts of the Kings Asa, Jehoshaphat, Hezekiah, and Josiah, nay even of Nebuchadnezzar and Darius when they were persuaded by the prophet Daniel to worship God.

d. Lastly, when the Apostle declares that kings and princes have been appointed by God to this end not merely that we may pass life honorably, but also piously, that is, not merely that we may live as it befits honest and respectable men, and in accordance with piety towards God, it admits of no doubt but that he has stated this whole question most succinctly. Hence we observe that the earliest Councils against heretics were summoned not upon the authority of the Roman Pontiffs who had not yet appeared in the character in which they came to light much later but by the decree of the emperors, (*in order that*) by means of this remedy they might hear the case in accordance with the persuasive arguments of the pious bishops. There are also extant innumerable constitutions (i.e., laws) and canons of the Church enacted by the Emperor Justinian as well as by his successors and even by Charlemagne and others approving of the same course.

But to what end are monarchs even today being so furiously incited by that whore of Rome to persecute with fire and sword and to banish those whom they themselves style heretics, unless it holds that this duty falls within their province? And in this matter it does indeed rest upon the best and surest foundation, but abuses it no less than innumerable other testimonies of truth to support forsooth and to defend its own impieties and blasphemies. But, you will say, why such a longwinded digression? For the question is not whether kings or rulers ought to defend and promote piety, but whether subjects can defend themselves by force or arms against persecutors. I therefore reply to the earlier of the two questions proposed above: It is one thing now for the first time to introduce religion into some part and another to preserve it when it has already been received somewhere or to wish to restore it when it has gone to ruin and has been buried as a result of the connivance or ignorance or malice of men. For I grant that initially it should be introduced and spread by the influence of the Spirit of God alone, and that by the Word of God (which is) suited to teaching, conviction and exhortation. For this is the particular task of the Holy Spirit which employs spiritual instruments.

It will therefore be the part of a pious ruler who wishes to entice his people away from idolatry and false superstitions to the true religion, to see to it in the first instance that they are instructed in piety by means of true and reliable argument, just as on the other hand it is in the part of the subjects to give their assent to truth and reason and readily to submit. Finally the ruler will be fully occupied in rendering the true religion secure by means of good and noble decrees against those who assail and resist it out of pure obstinacy, as we have seen done in our times in England, Denmark, Sweden, Scotland, and the greater part of Germany and Switzerland against the Papists, the Anabaptists and other heretics. If the other nations preferred following their example rather than trusting and obeying that bloodstained whore of Rome, could greater tranquillity indeed by seen in the whole world in the sphere of religion as well as of politics? What therefore will subjects have to do if on the other hand they are compelled by their ruler to worship idols? Assuredly reason does not permit them to force their ruler to a complete change in their condition; nay rather, they will consider it needful patiently to bear with him even to persecution, while they worship God purely in the meantime, or altogether to go into exile and seek new abodes. But if the free exercise of the true religion has once been granted by means of decrees lawfully passed and settled and confirmed by public authority, then I declare that the ruler is so much the more bound to have them observed as a matter of religion is of greater moment compared with all others, so much so that he has no right to repeal them upon his own arbitrary decision, and without having heard the case, but only with the intervention of that same authority by which they were in the first instance enacted. If he acts otherwise I declare that he is practicing manifest tyranny; and with due allowance for the observations made above, (his subjects) will be all the more free to oppose him as we are bound to set greater store and value by the salvation of our souls and the freedom of our conscience than by any other matters however desirable. It should therefore now be no cause of surprise to anyone that our Lord Jesus Christ, the Prophets and the

Apostles, too, or the other martyrs, since they were men in private station, confined themselves within the limits of their calling.

And as regards those who held public office or those legions which in the midst of battle suffered martyrdom with their commanders without offering any resistance even though their attackers were acting in violation of the decrees previously passed in favor of Christians, as happened especially under the Emperors Diocletian and Julian, there is, I say, a twofold answer. First, although certain emperors before Diocletian had made the persecution somewhat less severe, as it is certain that Hadrian, Antonius and Alexander did, yet none of them had ever permitted the public exercise of the Christian religion. Next, I also repeat the well-known saying that whatever is lawful, is not always expedient as well. For I should not be inclined to assert that a religion made lawful by public decrees must needs always be defended and held fast by means of arms against manifest tyranny, but that even so that is the right and lawful course especially for those upon whom this burden rests and to whom God has granted the opportunity, as the example of the people of Libnah against Jehoram and of the people of Jerusalem against Amaziah and the war of Constantine against Maxentius undertaken at the request of the citizens of Rome as described above abundantly prove. Hence I conclude that among the martyrs should be counted not only those who have defeated the tyranny of the enemies of the truth by no other defense than patience, but those also who, duly supported by the authority of laws or of those whose right it is to defend the laws, devoted their strength to God in defense of the true religion.

And these arguments so far I decided to urge in reply to the last objection that I might satisfy those who raise it so as not to violate their consciences because they are genuinely afraid of sinning against God if they attempt anything of that kind. But as regards that class of men who confer no other benefit upon the world but that they fill it with innocent blood while they abuse the authority of rulers that from their ruin they may pursue and advance their own interests and who meantime are characterized by such shamelessness that they dare to attack and assail with these objections those who do not spontaneously present themselves to them for slaughter, thus of course cloaking their cruelty and unbridled license under the false pretext of religion and zeal—this class of men, I say, would merit no other reply than that which would deservedly be given to robbers who summoned merchants and other travelers before the court for not undertaking a journey without girding on the sword for their defense, declaring that they had no right to do so, though they themselves adopted every kind of weapon to murder them.

Nay, they put me in mind of that abominable Roman Fimbria, whose like of hired assassins may be seen in large numbers at the present time; for so insolent was his daring, or rather so shameless his effrontery that when at the time of the Sullan proscription he had had a wound dealt to Scaevola, a man famous among the citizens of Rome for his extraordinary virtue and honesty, and the latter did not succumb to it as he was wishing, he was bold enough to complain and to threaten Scaevola that he would have him before court as if he had been most outrageously wronged because the other had not unresistingly admitted the dagger to enter his very heart. But because all discussion with men of that kind would be otiose and to no purpose, they should all of them be referred by me not so much to their own personal conscience (in which the majority are entire lacking) as to the tribunal of Him whose supreme authority and judgment—as by unmistakable evidence time and reality at length have proved—they themselves have not been able to escape.

## St. Bartholomew's Day Massacre

The massacre that occurred on St. Bartholomew's Day on August 24, 1572, was the worst religious massacre of the sixteenth century. The slaughter took place within the context of the French Wars of Religion and was directed against the French Calvinist Protestants, known as Huguenots.[27]

The bloodshed began after the wedding of Margaret, the daughter of Catherine de Medici, on August 18, 1572, to the Protestant prince Henry of Navarre. An assassin attempted to take the life of the French Calvinist Admiral Gaspard de Coligny on August 22. He was shot from an upstairs window and seriously wounded. King Charles IX visited Coligny at his bedside that afternoon, promising justice for what had happened. On the next day, August 23, the king and Catherine his mother decided to eliminate Coligny and some two or three dozen members of the Huguenot nobility who were still in Paris following the wedding.

In the early morning hours of August 24, assassins acting on the orders of the king broke into the bedroom of Coligny. After stabbing him to death, they threw his body out the window where it fell into the hands of a mob gathered in the courtyard below. They proceeded to drag the corpse through

27. Kingdon, *Myths about St. Bartholomew's Day Massacres, 1572–76.*

the streets of Paris, now missing head, hands, and genitals. A pogrom was then initiated by ringing bells for matins before dawn at the monastery of St. Germain l'Auxerrois. This was the signal for the soldiers and the Catholic mob to break into the homes of Calvinists, slaughtering men, women, and children at will. The butchery in Paris lasted for almost a week. The bodies of the dead were thrown into the Seine. In the coming weeks, the savagery spread to many other cities. In two months, perhaps 100,000 Huguenots lost their lives. Before the end of the year, another civil war erupted in France between the Protestants and the Catholics. When the king appeared before the Parlement of Paris, he announced that he had ordered the massacre in order to thwart a Huguenot plot against the royal family.

How did Catholics and Calvinists respond to these events? Reactions among Catholics were mixed. Pope Gregory XIII congratulated the king by sending him a golden rose and by striking a medal commemorating the slaughter showing an angel bearing a cross and sword next to Protestant corpses. Moderate French Catholics, conversely, began to doubt whether religious uniformity was worth the shedding of so much blood. Beza responded to the massacre by writing one of the most significant Protestant works on political theory in the sixteenth century, *Concerning the Rights of Rulers over Their Subjects and the Duty of Subjects towards Their Rulers*.[28]

As noted earlier, Beza was the Rector of the Geneva Academy and following the death of John Calvin became the moderator of the Company of Pastors. Although he gave his life to serving the Geneva Church, his thoughts were directed to the well-being of France, the country of his childhood and youth.[29] He even served as the chaplain to Louis of Bourbon in the first war of religion.[30] At times, such as at the Battle of Dreux in 1562, Beza could "smell the smoke of battle."

Beza's immediate concern in writing *Du droit des magistrats* was focused on the Valois monarchy in the person of Charles IX.[31] The king of France was a tyrant. His political rule was nothing but tyranny. As Beza explained it, tyranny relates to the issue of opposition to law. He asked, "What

---

28. Kingdon, "Reactions to St. Bartholomew Massacres," 30; Gosselin, "David in *Tempore Belli*," 33, 36; Witte, "Rights, Resistance, and Revolution," 545–70.

29. Baumgartner, *Henry II*, 1.

30. Holt, *French Wars of Religion*, 48–49.

31. Beza wrote the original text in Latin (*De Iure Magistratum*), but his treatise was first published in French in the city of Lyon in 1574. The French text is found in Beza, *Du droit des magistrat*.

else is tyranny but authority setting itself against the laws?"[32] He declared, "The mark of tyranny and as it were its peculiar concomitant is a persistent malice which strives with might and main to subvert the constitution and the laws upon which the kingdom rests as upon foundations."[33]

Although Beza did not mention Charles IX by name, his description of how a tyrant acts corresponds to the historical record of the king's deeds in connection with the St. Bartholomew massacres. Beza asserted that the tyrant destroys his subjects: "[Tyrants] do not strive to have subjects in their power for any other reason but to persecute and crush them to their destruction."[34] He added a statement referring to "tyranny assailing the true religion and even stamping it out as far as may be."[35] He alluded to the king, describing him as a ruler who "wantonly proceeds to such a pitch of license that he savagely slays the parents of his subjects, ravishes their wives and daughters, pillages their houses and possessions and finally murders them individually as the fancy takes him."[36]

The immediate problem in France, Beza contended, was a royal government that had descended into tyranny. Beza therefore wrote his treatise in order to instruct the Estates-General, the inferior magistrates, and the private citizens as to their biblical and constitutional duties.[37] There was, however, an even more fundamental concern that Beza had in writing *Concerning the Rights of Rulers*. Beza's treatise is significant not only for its theory of resistance to tyrannical government, but also for its warning against royal absolutism, the doctrine that there ought not to be any restrictions to the authority of the monarch.

Beza recognized that there were those who maintained that "the king is not bound by the laws."[38] There were theorists "who so far exalt the authority of kings and supreme rulers as to dare maintain that they have no other Judge but God alone to whom they are bound to render account of

---

32. Beza, *Concerning the Rights of Rulers*, 48.

33. Beza, *Concerning the Rights of Rulers*, 80.

34. Beza, *Concerning the Rights of Rulers*, 70.

35. Beza, *Concerning the Rights of Rulers*, 82.

36. Beza, *Concerning the Rights of Rulers*, 66. Smither, "St. Bartholomew's Day Massacre," 41, observes that "this last point was aimed directly at Charles IX and his supporters, who had massacred the king's faithful subjects for no reason."

37. Manetsch, *Theodore Beza*, 1572–98.

38. Beza, *Concerning the Rights of Rulers*, 68.

their deeds."[39] There were people who viewed the transformation of "the French monarchy into a tyranny" as "the emancipation of the sovereign of his release from slavery."[40]

The problem with the theory of absolutism, as Beza understood it, was that boundless and unlimited power eventually leads to the abuse of that power. "Since the origin of the world," Beza wrote, "there has never been a king" who "did not in some measure abuse his authority."[41] Beza therefore countered the absolutist position with his arguments. He pointed out that "boundless and unlimited power" did not "commend itself to the Roman people."[42] He noted that the people in Poland "limited the authority of their king by the wisest laws and for having as it were confined it within bounds."[43]

Calvin, it has been noted, was "a farsighted political scientist."[44] The same thing may be said regarding his successor, Theodore Beza.[45] That which has been affirmed concerning Calvin's political perceptiveness may likewise be applied to Beza: "He knew that the future of his Europe depended on taming absolutism." Moreover, "it was clear to him that no European order would emerge unless royal absolutism were to be contained and harnessed by the rule of law."[46]

## Theodore Beza, *Question 6. What is the duty of subjects towards their superiors who have fallen into tyranny?*

From *Concerning the Rights of Rulers over Their Subjects and the Duty of Subjects towards Their Rulers*, 49–52. Translated by Henri-Louis Gonin. Capetown and Pretoria: HAUM, 1956.

Let us now proceed to the polity of Israel, the most perfect of all that ever were, if only the Israelites had been satisfied with it. The fact that the eternal God was from the beginning its sole monarch exalted that polity as it were

39. Beza, *Concerning the Rights of Rulers*, 64.
40. Beza, *Concerning the Rights of Rulers*, 61.
41. Beza, *Concerning the Rights of Rulers*, 49.
42. Beza, *Concerning the Rights of Rulers*, 46.
43. Beza, *Concerning the Rights of Rulers*, 54.
44. Oberman, "*Europa afflicta*," 107.
45. Baumgartner, *France in the Sixteenth Century*, 301–2.
46. Oberman, "*Europa afflicta*," 107.

beyond the stars, not merely because He himself held supreme authority over all things, but (*also*) because He did so in a unique way; for through Moses He visibly drew up their laws for the Israelites; through Joshua as it were with arms thrust out He brought his people into the promised land; and finally He commanded and governed them, that it is in the person of those men whom He himself had directly appointed to the government of that (*polity and*) who were called Judges.

At that time therefore the Jewish polity was truly monarchical (although God employed the service of certain men in accordance with His will), and if all kingdoms had this Monarch, or at least if all monarchs always allowed themselves to be directed by this supreme Lord of the universe, this present enquiry would be no less redundant than it is now (*universally*) recognized to be indispensable. For that blessed state of this commonwealth (which never befell any other people but this) was changed in an amazing and unusual way. For the monarchical constitutions of other nations have degenerated into tyrannies by the fault of the monarchs themselves; but the Israelites, not recognizing such a great boon, as it were against His will compelled that true Monarch of theirs, who could never have become a tyrant, to appoint for them a human king as for other people also. The Lord therefore at length granted their wishes but in anger and indignation, not that He desired by that act to disapprove of a monarchical constitution as such, but because this change had proceeded from a hot-headed and stubborn people.

Meanwhile the fact neither can nor should be disguised that since the origin of the world there has never been a king—even if you were to select the very best—who did not in some measure abuse his authority so that it must be indeed conceded, as the philosophers enlightened by natural reason alone have recognized also, that monarchical rule brings ruin and destruction upon the people rather than protection and welfare unless it is curbed by certain reins, so that by them it may come about that the greatest boon which can derive from it may be secured, and that the great evil which otherwise must of necessity result from it may be avoided and impeded.

I am giving this introduction while entering upon my discussion of the origins of the Israelite kingship since clear examples of all these things are to be found there; it would be worth the effort if both kings and nations paid careful attention to these that the one class might not so often come to be oppressed by the other but that rather the glory of God, from whom alone all tranquility comes, might be such an object of care to both, that rulers and subjects alike might be content to maintain themselves peacefully. But to return to the point from where I digressed, the Lord being rightly incensed against His people, that he might clearly make known to them what they were to expect from that reckless disposition by which they were being disturbed, prophesied to them through Samuel in wondrous words indeed what that right would be which history calls the royal prerogative, namely, in short, that the king would arbitrarily seize the persons and possessions of his subjects and convert them to his own uses, (*conduct*) which is doubtless tyrannical rather than royal. For who would dare to doubt seriously that God alone is competent to thrust His arbitrary will in the place of reason since nothing can be called just but what God has first willed? For the will of God alone is the true and certain rule of all justice, as was maintained from the beginning. But the contrary happens in the case of men whose reason too should be subject to and guided by just and inviolable laws, particularly in the case of those who are placed in authority of others; so that they are entirely mistaken who interpret Samuel's words as if he desired to be the authority of kings for the commission of any daring deed, or approved of whatever they did in blind willfulness; equally accursed is the saying of the notorious incestuous woman "Si libet, licet" a standpoint which, alas, is excessively bandied about and acted upon in this present century. Nay rather the works of Samuel must be interpreted as if he spoke them to rebuke Israel: "It suffices not for you to have God Himself as your monarch as it has thus far been by some extraordinary favor; but you are demanding another and such as the other nations have; therefore shall such an one fall to your lot. But again listen to what right he shall claim over you and with what fairness and justice he shall hold sway over you." That this was the purpose of Samuel's words the subsequent course of history itself has shown.

I therefore maintain that though God had expressly elected David, yet he had to be elected by the people also and that they in electing him rightly, as they should, followed the will of God. The same thing occurred in the case of Solomon also who after being first elected by God, was in the second instance made king by the people. And in general: although the royal crown in accordance with the command of God by hereditary right belonged to the House of David, yet as we have shown above the people ever elected from among the children of the late king that one whom it preferred to hold sway. And with this (*election*) went a twofold obligation, as appears from the history of Joash. For both the king and the people first promised God under solemn oath to observe His laws both ecclesiastical and political. Afterwards another mutual oath too was taken between the king himself and the people. "But," someone will say, "did the people, that is the Estates of the people, for that reason have the right to punish their elected candidate when he failed to perform his duty?" They certainly had that right as can be particularly proved by four examples.

For if David might defend himself against the tyranny of Saul, as appeared a while ago, and if the people of Libnah, who however were but subordinate magistrates, might revolt from their allegiance to Jehoram, shall I not rightly thence infer that the royal Estates per se (ipso iure) had many more rights? Relevant to this point is also the deed that was done by those very Estates upon the wise counsel of Jehoida the priest against Athaliah, who had been appointed queen and had reigned over the kingdom for six whole years. Lastly the example of Amaziah is much clearer still; him the people of Jerusalem pursued even till they slew him. But if anyone were to think that this was done seditiously and not lawfully, I would have him attend carefully to the following arguments. It is nowhere declared that Amaziah was slain by the slaves of his household, as we read happened to his father Joash and to Amon the son of Manasseh, but rather by some common agreement of the people of Jerusalem; and this happened not secretly and as it were by way of ambush, as the end of tyrants has mostly been, but by undisguised violence and as it were upon the authority of the people; nor yet as the result of some sudden uprising but after he had betaken himself in flight to the city of Lachish where it is recorded that his body was returned and buried in the sepulcher of his fathers. In short, neither before nor after the death of Amaziah is anything to be found here offering any indication of revolt, but all the circumstances rather prove clearly that everything was attempted and carried into effect in accordance with the resolution and studied deliberation of the people of Jerusalem, and also by the tacit treaty of those joined (*in the undertaking*), presumably a majority of the tribes although this befell in an exceptional and as it were perfunctory way; (*it was*) certainly (*done*) not from any private feeling of animosity, but as a result of his wickedness by which he had in great part violated his oath. For that reason we nowhere read that after his death any complaint or inquiry (*occurred*) or that in short any punishment was secured or meted out against the perpetrators of the murder either by the people or by his children as happened after the deaths of Amon and Joash, for the conspirators who slew them though they were from their household, were visited with just punishments albeit that they had both been wicked. But on the other hand we read that the corpse of the latter was from reverence for both the royal dignity and his family carried back to Jerusalem on horseback, and that his son Azariah was by the entire people of Judah set as king in his stead. And this again clearly shows that what had been done by the stronger part of the Estates, that is by the people of Jerusalem, was subsequently confirmed by general consent as concerning a just cause and as having been carried into effect by those who were competent to do so. Hence I conclude that the Orders or Estates of the people of Israel had authority to choose for themselves from the family of David whom they wished, and afterwards, when he had been elected, either to drive him out or even to execute sentence of death upon him as the occasion demanded.

## CHAPTER 10

# Pierre Viret (1511–1571)

THROUGHOUT THE MID-SIXTEENTH CENTURY, religious and political dissent in Scotland, England, and Europe was fueled by the religious writings and sermons of leaders such as John Knox, John Ponet, and Christopher Goodman. These reformers drew from each other as well as from earlier Christian writers and other contemporaries such as Pierre Viret (1511–1571). During the tumultuous era of the Reformation, Viret, termed by some scholars as "the forgotten Reformer," articulated what was the earliest known presentation of resistance theory from a Calvinist perspective. This little-known individual was one of the most influential and popular of the Reformers.[1]

Swiss-born theologian Pierre Viret was a close friend and associate of John Calvin (1509–1564). Viret's influence among Protestants in French-speaking Switzerland and France during the Reformation was enormous. He was born in Orbe, Switzerland, not far from Lausanne, into a staunch Roman Catholic family. During the years 1527–1530 he attended the Collège de Montaigu, one of the colleges of the University of Paris, where he was preceded by Desiderius Erasmus (1466–1536) and Calvin who studied at Collège de la Marche at the university. It was here that Viret converted to the theology of the Reformation in 1528–1529. In 1530, he returned to Orbe and met Guillaume Farel (1489–1565), who encouraged Viret to become a minister. He subsequently worked closely with Farel and spent much of his time in Lausanne and Geneva, Switzerland, but also preached throughout France with great reception.

Viret is best known as a popularizer of the views of Calvin and for his own views advocating the right of resistance by religious and political

---

1. See Linder, "Forgotten Reformer," 35–37. We are indebted to Linder's decades of research and publishing on this often overlooked Reformer's writings that provide the fullest analysis available of Viret with respect to political theory.

dissenters as well as a philosophy of political toleration for religious dissenters. He also was a supporter of the just war tradition. However, not everyone liked his message, and Viret survived an assassination attempt by stabbing and a second attempt to take his life as well. He died in Orthez, France in 1571.

While in Geneva in 1534, Viret assisted Farel in public disputations with Dominican friar Guy Furbity, the leading Roman Catholic apologist in the city. The debate created public enthusiasm, brought many citizens to the side of the Reformation, but ended in a riot. The civil response to this was that the city came under siege from the duke of Savoy in alliance with an exiled bishop of Geneva. This allowed Viret and Farel to link Protestantism with the city's struggle for political independence, and in 1536, based upon the unique political process in Switzerland at the time, the city became a Protestant city. Viret then moved to Lausanne where public disputations were repeated with the result that Lausanne also aligned with Protestantism.

## Viret and Resistance Theory

In 1547 Viret wrote a work titled *Remonstrances aux fideles qui conversent entre les Papistes*. This was the earliest known exposition of a Calvinist resistance theory. In the work Viret argued that Christians had the political and religious right *and* obligation to take up arms and oppose the state for reasons of both religious and political tyranny. However, this was permissible only in a circumstance where the legitimately constituted magistrates were leading in the resistance. It was not to be done by individual Christians acting on their own initiative.

Much of the religious thought during the era with respect to war and political resistance was the result of the breakup of the monolithic political structure of Christianity from medieval Europe. With the rise of the Reformation, two or more expressions of Christianity were present in the West where there had previously only been one—Roman Catholicism. Now, Protestants and Roman Catholics had to address the question of what would happen when the civil government and the church (whichever variety) opposed each other. The answers to this question varied considerably depending upon where one lived geographically.

Christian ideas of resistance during the Reformation were closely tied to the varied political circumstances in which the Reformers and Protestant leaders found themselves. Thus, while all looked to the Bible and their theology for guidance, the immediate political environment, often hostile, in which they lived and wrote, also affected their views. Although there are similarities in core ideas, there are also differences. German Lutherans, Swiss Calvinists, French Huguenots, and Marian exiles all built their political ideas by drawing from common theology and the diverse political realities of the geographic regions in which they lived. Additionally, there was a maturing of political ideas among individuals and groups as writings were shared, letters exchanged, and political events unfolded. The result was the growth and development of the idea of resistance.

However, the idea of resistance was not new in the Reformation era. Reflection on and discussion of the idea had a long medieval heritage wherein resistance was understood to be a rare exception to the political order and did not extend to the right to reorganize a political and social structure.[2]

As a result of the political ramifications of the Protestant Reformation in Europe and what is now the United Kingdom, resistance as a theo-political idea arose in such a way that there is linkage between the political ideas of some of the Protestant reformers and later political thought (secular and religious) that ultimately affected those involved in the struggle of the American colonists for independence. Among those whose influence can be directly traced are John Knox, John Ponet, and Christopher Goodman. For these men, civil disobedience and the responsibility to resist arose in part because of the reign of a Roman Catholic and female monarch on the throne of England—Mary Tudor (r. 1553–1558). During her reign and under her re-Catholicizing measures many Protestants left England and Scotland for Protestant Reformed centers in Europe such as Geneva and Strasbourg. Once there, they interacted with Continental Calvinist Protestants, published and preached anti-Marian works and sermons, and articulated theo-political ideas in response to what they considered to be the lawless and blasphemous rule and actions of Mary Tudor, "Bloody Mary"—the English "Jezebel."[3] Part of the theological and political heritage that theologians, political philosophers, and political activists would draw upon in the seventeenth and eighteenth centuries was that of Pierre Viret, a minor Reformer with a major influence.

---

2. Shoenberger, "Development of the Lutheran Theory," 62–63.

3. For an overview, see Danner, "Resistance and the Ungodly Magistrate," 471–81.

## Just War

Viret requested and was granted leave from his pastoral responsibilities in Geneva to visit Huguenots in France in 1561. He eventually settled in Montpellier, but his brief and successful ministry there was interrupted by the first French War of Religion. He returned to Lyon where he had first gone after arriving in France and provided pastoral counsel to Protestant soldiers and ministered amidst civil war and a plague outbreak. It was in Lyon that Viret wrote and published his enormous two-volume theology entitled *Instruction chrestienne* (1564). The work has a discussion of just war and other aspects of Viret's political theory.[4] He also discusses just war in his 1565 work *L'Interim, fait par dialogues*. Both of these works were read and distributed widely during the first years of the French Wars of Religion.[5]

In 1563 royal authority was re-established in Lyon, and in 1565 Viret was forced by royal order to leave the kingdom of France. However, instead of entirely leaving, he went to Bearn in Navarre in southwestern France and what was then a semi-autonomous kingdom. During France's Third Religious War (1568–1570), Viret was captured by Roman Catholic forces along with eleven other Reformed ministers. The military commander ordered his execution, but Viret was spared because of his reputation. Several weeks later he was rescued and freed by Protestant forces and returned to his ministry. He died in 1571, the year following the conclusion of the third religious war. War was not an abstract idea and debate for Viert—he was intimately acquainted with it.

As with the other Reformers, Viret broke with the medieval legacy of the crusade philosophy of war, favoring instead, as did many Roman Catholics and Protestants, the just-war tradition that followed the heritage of Augustine and Aquinas. Nor did Viret believe, as did crusaders, that the spreading of the gospel should be accomplished through force.[6]

Leading Viret scholar Robert D. Linder notes of Viret's theology as a whole and of just-war thought:

> Both Calvin and Viret discussed the Christian's role in organized combat in terms of a just war. Viret, as much or perhaps even more than Calvin, demonstrates that first-generation Calvinism was much less aggressive than many in the past have supposed. In

4. Linder, "Pierre Viret's Concept," 214–15.
5. Linder, "Pierre Viret's Concept," 215.
6. Linder, "Pierre Viret's Concept," 217.

fact, if anything, Viret might be said to have advocated a position which, relatively speaking, could be called liberal Calvinism.[7]

## The Similarity of Viret's and Calvin's Ideas

Viret's thought on just war followed the ideas articulated by Augustine more than a thousand years earlier. While Viret does not cite Augustine directly in the just war section in *Instruction chrestienne* (1:482–509), he does follow Augustine's views. He knew them well from his studies in Paris, especially through Noël Béda (1470–1537) whose Augustinian theology dominated Collège Montaigu during Viret's studies.[8] Viret frequently cites Augustine elsewhere in his writings.[9] Like Augustine, he believed that all wars were evil, though some were necessary.

Viret's clearest expressions of his own views on war are found in his discussion of the Sixth Commandment: "You shall not murder" (Exod 20:13). He believes that the magistrate (government) is ordained by God "for the defense of the good and the punishment of evil" and is "given the right to wage a just war" when necessary.[10]

Viret believed that it was the responsibility of the soldier, and especially the Christian soldier, to obey the orders of the magistrate. It was not the soldier's responsibility to determine the justice of the cause.[11] However, using the biblical account of the unjust death of Naboth (1 Kgs 21:1–16), Viret argues that the obedience to the magistrate is not an absolute requirement. If the order is so egregious that it blatantly violates biblical teaching, then the soldier is not obligated to obey. Indeed, the obligation is to disobey even though it may mean "great jeopardy."[12]

His support for this position is to be found in the words of Jesus, "And do not fear those who kill the body, but are unable to kill the soul; but rather fear Him who is able to destroy both soul and body in hell" (Matt 10:28). The

7. Linder, "Pierre Viret's Concept," 217.

8. Linder, "Pierre Viret's Concept," 220, 220n18.

9. Linder, "Pierre Viret's Concept," 218, 218n12.

10. Viret, cited in Linder, "Pierre Viret's Concept," 219.

11. Viret, cited in Linder, "Pierre Viret's Concept," 221.

12. Viret, cited in Linder, "Pierre Viret's Concept," 221.

teaching of the apostles also stood behind his thinking, "We must obey God rather than men" (Acts 5:29).[13]

For Viret, killing is an act that must be done only in self-defense or in the context of a war that is truly a just war. Because the magistrates and princes are "ordained by God to preserve the peace,"[14] Christians are to obey them, but it is not an unqualified obedience.

## War against Other Christians

Unlike some of the other Reformers, Viret did not think force should be used against Anabaptists and other Christian groups who dissented from Reformed theology. He believed that their doctrinal positions should be answered, but he opposed persecution of other Christians. Such persecution, he argued, weakened Christianity from within and was not reflective of the message of true faith. Additionally, it could cause dissension, trouble, and even rebellion against the magistrates and princes.[15] Persecution of "true Christians" was not to occur, although determining who was and was not a true Christian was part of the larger theological and ideological conflict of the Reformation. Viret believed that there were true Christians across the spectrum of those proclaiming the Christian faith, but it was a matter that was between the individual and God.[16]

Viret also articulated his understanding of non-persecution of Christians against the backdrop of Roman Catholic persecution of Reformed Christians. He was an early advocate for "liberty of conscience" (*liberté de sa conscience*). Linder notes that this was "based upon an argument that . . . the hearts and consciences of men cannot be forced but instead God must be operative to change the heart and bring men to faith in Christ."[17] Linder summarizes: "Viret did not mean full religious liberty but freedom from being forced to worship contrary to one's convictions. He was willing to go so far as to grant this liberty to other groups if it could be obtained

---

13. Viret, cited in Linder, "Pierre Viret's Concept," 221–22.
14. Viret, cited in Linder, "Pierre Viret's Concept," 222.
15. Linder, *Political Ideas of Pierre Viret*, 152.
16. Linder, "Pierre Viret's Concept," 224.
17. Linder, *Political Ideas of Pierre Viret*, 152.

for his own movement as well."[18] Persecution and forced conversion were contrary to human, divine, and natural law.[19]

Viret was the first to articulate the idea that it was inconsistent for papal policy to advance persecution of Protestants in France while at the same time protecting Jews in southeastern France. This argument would later become common among French Huguenots.[20]

Viret also opposed the execution of those deemed to be heretics. He wrote:

> Taking away the lives of men is no small matter in the sight of God. But the crime is a great deal more serious when men take away life in the name of God when instead it ought to be preserved, which course of action is to be recommended to all, principally to lords and magistrates.[21]

He believed that just as with the Anabaptists, heretics needed to be answered and vehemently opposed, but not with the sword. In this view he was more moderate than his contemporaries Calvin and Beza.

## War against the Ottoman Turks

Viret opposed contemporary calls for war against the Muslim Ottoman Turks, but he did so on the basis that he believed such efforts, including the medieval crusades, diminished Christianity. For Viret, conversion was not something that should be forced. Rather, it was to come through the preaching of the gospel of Jesus Christ. Whereas Luther had argued against such military endeavors because of the financial cost and the belief that without general repentance the efforts would be futile, Viret opposed them as corrosive to the Christian faith.[22]

## Views of Peace

Viret did not offer a systematic approach or a fully developed theory of peace, but he did present scattered ideas about peace throughout his writings.

18. Linder, *Political Ideas of Pierre Viret*, 152.
19. Linder, *Political Ideas of Pierre Viret*, 153.
20. Linder, "Pierre Viret's Concept," 224n28.
21. Viret, cited in Linder, *Political Ideas of Pierre Viret*, 153.
22. Linder, "Pierre Viret's Concept," 223.

Agreeing with his contemporaries, Viret argued that the major cause of war was sin: "The main cause of wars in our time is our own sins."[23] For this, repentance was necessary. Although war was first and foremost a theological matter, Viret believed that some peace could be obtained through social and economic systems that fostered justice rather than exploitation. He linked peace with labor and meaningful employment, stating, for example: "For what better way is there to bring peace to the land and to show the true love of God than to provide the poor and oppressed with an opportunity to engage in the dignity of labor."[24] A third stepping stone beyond repentance and social justice was religious toleration. In Linder's words, "He not only advocated religious toleration as a cornerstone to true peace in the world (especially among Christian nations), but he was also, in fact, among the most tolerant of the first-generation Calvinist reformers."[25]

## Conclusion

In France, political and religious circumstances were entirely different than in England, Germany, and Switzerland such that the course of political ideas (including religious freedom, rights, and the nature of government) followed a separate history. The course of the Protestant Reformation in France included the rise of the French Calvinists known as Huguenots, religious and political tensions of eight civil wars known as the French Wars of Religion (1562–1598), the famous St. Bartholomew's Day Massacre (August 23, 1572), and the Edict of Nantes (1598), wherein Henry IV of France granted substantial civil rights to Protestants. Also included in the edict was the famous phrase pertaining to *cuius regio, eius religio* ("Whose realm, his religion"). Although the edict was a step toward religious toleration of some Protestants, it was only a beginning that would not be finalized for French Calvinists until the 1648 Treaty of Westphalia. Although many scholars previously believed that the St. Bartholomew's Day Massacre was a beginning point for Protestant resistance thought in France, Viret's writings show that such is not the case and that religious views on political resistance were influencing individuals and events for almost thirty years before the tragic massacre.

23. Viret, cited in Linder, "Pierre Viret's Concept," 226.
24. Viret, cited in Linder, "Pierre Viret's Concept," 227.
25. Linder, "Pierre Viret's Concept," 227–28.

# Part 3

# Anabaptist Reformers

## CHAPTER II

# Conrad Grebel (1498–1526)

## Establishing a "Radical Reformational" Context

IT HAS BECOME CUSTOMARY for historians of the sixteenth century to speak not of "the Reformation" but of "reformations." Four of these reform movements—each with its own character—are usually noted: Lutheranism, Calvinism, Anglicanism, and the Radical Reformation. Although some such as Roland Bainton and John T. McNeill have used the language of "the left wing of the Reformation" to depict the latter movement,[1] others prefer a different mode of characterization insofar as "left-wing" is a more modern description.[2] Moreover, not all radical reformers of the early sixteenth century would hold to a strict separation of the church from the temporal realities. For example, the Swiss Brethren would be strict separationists, in strong contrast to the revolutionary theocracy of Thomas Müntzer and Münster Anabaptists, while Balthasar Hubmaier would welcome protection from the princes of Moravia. And a generation removed, Menno Simons would affirm an enduring "Anabaptist" tradition in which relative versus absolute separation would be normative.

George H. Williams has helpfully distinguished between three groups constituting the radical reformation: Anabaptists, spiritualists, and

---

1. McNeill, "Left-Wing Religious Movements," 127; Bainton, "Leftut Wing of the Reformation," 127.

2. Zuck, *Christianity and Revolution*, 3–10, prefers to speak of the radical reformation as the "second Reformation." The weakness of this designation, however, is that the "first" and "second" movements were simply different expressions of the same chronological revolt. We freely grant that no historian is immune from imposing modern values and categories on the sixteenth century, since the interpretation of history is ideological, theological, political and sociological in nature.

evangelical rationalists.[3] While these divisions—and the nomenclature attached thereto—are neither exact nor always holding to be true, they are for the most part accurate and permit us to make certain necessary distinctions among the reform movements of the early sixteenth century. Characteristic of Anabaptism, whose beginnings in the third decade of the sixteenth century this chapter attempts to elucidate, are several identifying markers—among these: the priority of individual confessed faith, brotherhood, communitarianism and the need for collective discipline, free will and voluntarism, personal piety, adult baptism, restoration of the New Testament as model and pattern, and pacifism. And even Anabaptism, which has generally been viewed as the most unified strand of Reformation radicalism, is itself best understood as emerging from differing origins.

Social and cultural conditions of the late fifteenth and early sixteenth century leave little doubt that reform of any type was in the air—be it ecclesial, political, or socio-economic in nature. While the precise connection between the "Peasants' War" of 1524–25 in Germany and the emergence of Anabaptism is controversial among sixteenth-century historians, it is nevertheless the case that Reformation radicalism must necessarily be considered in the context of this powerful social development. Radical reformers represented an emergent popular "evangelical" movement during the 1520s that was sweeping significant parts of Germany and Switzerland. These reformers were insistent that reform be thoroughgoing as it affected not only devotional practice or sacramental life but the entire church as a corrupt institution; hence, a fervency and impatience characterize their efforts—efforts that often are couched in apocalypticism and anti-clericalism.[4]

Radicals would differ with other, more "moderate" or "magisterial" reformers not only over matters of Christian doctrine—for example, the mass, the sacraments, the place of Scripture and the nature of the true church—but also over scope and strategy in terms of popularizing and spreading the message of reform. This would be particularly true in the case of Conrad Grebel, who as a disciple of Ulrich Zwingli would come to view his mentor as a traitor to the reformation cause. While the magisterial reformers were in rebellion against ecclesial authority's perceived corruptions of the church based on their reading of Scripture, they nevertheless affirmed the

3. Williams, *Spiritual and Anabaptist Writers*, 20; *Radical Reformation*, xxiii-xxxi. Fast, *Der linke Flügel der Reformation*, assumes a three-fold classification in his treatment of the radicals but speaks of "Enthusiasts" and "Anti-trinitarians" to describe the latter two groups identified by Williams.

4. Baylor, *Radical Reformation*, xii.

authority of existing secular political authorities. These individuals hoped for reform, but a reform that had the backing and blessing of the princes. In the spirit of Luther, they wished for a "princely authorization," and as Zwingli in Zürich, they hoped to win the backing of city councils, which over time would initiate change.[5]

Michael Baylor, who has done us the great service of collecting key sixteenth-century texts, describes the vision of the magisterial reformers, against whom radical and Anabaptist reformers would react, in the following way:

> Rejecting traditional ecclesiastical authority, they [magisterial reformers] clung more firmly to existing secular authority, which they held to be ordained by God. They also deeply distrusted the common man and feared that his participation in politics would lead to anarchy. They were willing to proceed only as far as authorization would allow. The ecclesiastical counterpart to this view of secular authority was the magisterial reformers' view that the power to proclaim the meaning of the gospel—and to advise secular authorities about the interpretation of Scripture—should remain in the hands of a university-trained, properly ordained clergy. Reformation radicalism was, in the first instance, "internal dissent'" within the Reformation—opposition to the paradigm for change set forth by such magisterial reformers as Luther and Zwingli.[6]

As one quickly learns, to sift through the literature that chronicles sixteenth-century ferment is to discover a lively debate among historians that has characterized recent decades. Thus, for example, Claus-Peter Clasen's magisterial *Anabaptism: A Social History, 1525–1618* argues with considerable force that there is no real relationship between social conditions and ecclesiastical dissent. Hans-Jürgen Goertz's *Pfaffenhaus und gross Geschrei: Die reformatorischen Bewegungen in Deutschland 1517–1529* and James M. Stayer's *The German Peasants' War and Anabaptist Community of Goods* dispute that point of view, arguing that both theological connections and the emphasis on community—particularly parts of Germany, Switzerland and Austria—were formative and hence important for our understanding.[7]

---

5. Baylor, *Radical Reformation*, xiii.

6. Baylor, *Radical Reformation*, xiii.

7. So, for example, Clasen, *Anabaptism*; Goertz, *Pfaffenhaus*; Stayer, *German Peasants' War*. Franz, *Der deutsche Bauerkrieg*, takes an intermediary position, arguing that the peasants' war was chiefly a socio-economic phenomenon, and any relationship to Anabaptism was random.

Stayer's historiographical conclusion is thusly qualified: "Although Anabaptism is not important for the understanding of the Peasant War, the Peasant War is very important for understanding Anabaptism."[8]

Some consequences of the Lutheran reformation, of course, were inevitable. Thus, once people began reading the Bible for themselves, they would begin interpreting it for themselves, with no particular interpretation guaranteed. In relative terms, it is a very small step from the "priesthood of every believer" to "prophetic" and strongly dissenting views. In the words of one historian, liberation can easily lead to disorientation.[9]

## Early "Anabaptism" and the Role of Conrad Grebel

In many respects, the matter of Anabaptist origins remains a lively one, both among Anabaptist and non-Anabaptist historians.[10] What remains uncontroversial, however, is the fact that its beginnings were neither in Wittenberg nor in Münster but in Zürich, the womb of Zwinglian reformation.[11] The situation in Zürich matured at several levels. The city, along with other "reformed" cities and cantons, aspired toward unity against a potentially aggressive or intolerant Catholicism. But what now in the early-to-mid 1520s threatened that hopeful unity were "radical reformers" who were perceived as abetting—or even indirectly contributing toward—any sort of "counter-Reformation."[12] Surely the irony here was not lost on Roman Catholic opponents of the Protestant reform. The Catholic polemicist Johann Eck, to cite but one example, derided Zwingli for "tormenting" and "torturing" the Anabaptists.[13] And to extend the irony, here were former disciples of Zwingli turning the very weapon he had been using—namely, Scripture—against him.

---

8. Stayer, *German Peasants' War*, 4.

9. Cohn, *Pursuit of the Millennium*, 252.

10. Not only the matter of origins but classification, as well, has been the focus of lively debate in recent decades. Illustrative of this debate, for example, are Eire, *Reformations*, 254; Lindberg, *European Reformations*, 201–4; Kaufman, "Social History," 527–55; Stayer et al., "From Monogenesis to Polygenesis," 83–121.

11. Anabaptist historian Harold Bender identifies three principal enduring groups of Anabaptism: the Swiss Brethren, the Hutterites of Moravia and Slovakia, and the Mennonites of Holland. See Bender, "Swiss Brethren," 670.

12. Lindberg, *European Reformations*, 202.

13. Gerrish, cited in Lindberg, *European Reformations*, 203.

The first "Anabaptists" (German: *Wiedertäufer*; literally, the "re-baptized"),[14] two of whose leaders—Conrad Grebel and Felix Mantz—initially had been disciples of Ulrich Zwingli in the early 1520s but who subsequently broke with the reformer, would advocate a "believer's baptism," and in January of 1525 Grebel would baptize the first Anabaptist "convert." Shortly thereafter, in a letter dated November of 1526, Zwingli will describe Grebel as the Anabaptist "ringleader" (*coryphaeus*),[15] while Mantz would be the first Anabaptist martyr.[16] Without Grebel, according to the chief biographer of Grebel in the English-speaking world, Anabaptism in its historic form would probably not have come into existence.[17]

Any attempt to trace Grebel's history, theology, or impact encounters severe obstacles, given his very brief life; he will die of the plague at the age of 28.[18] In bald contrast to other reformers—indeed, other Anabaptist reformers—the only writing he prepared for publication, a brief pamphlet of under 5,000 words, has been lost, though parts thereof have been somewhat reconstructed through Zwingli's counter-attack that appeared in 1527.[19] At the same time, an important source of information comes through letters—some 69 in number—that Grebel penned between September of 1517 and July of 1525, the year he baptized his first convert, one Georg Blaurock.[20]

It is generally thought that the phenomenon of Anabaptism arose from socially and economically oppressed lower classes.[21] But this was not the case with Grebel, whose family pedigree and education proved to be

---

14. The early dissenters did not call themselves "Anabaptists" (*Wiedertäufer*); this was the name given to them by their opponents.

15. Zwingli, *Huldreich Zwinglis Sämtliche Werke*, 8:780. A second source refers to Grebel as the "arch-anabaptist" (Erzwidertouffer). See Kessler, *Johannes Kesslers Sabbata*, 142–43, 314.

16. Mantz was publicly executed by drowning in January of 1527.

17. Bender, "Conrad Grebel," 566.

18. The only account of Grebel's origin is found in the chronicles of the Hutterian Brethren, under the title *Geschicht-Buch der Hutterischen Brüder*. The Brethren, whose recorded history begins in 1524, settled in Austria but claim as their origin Zürich.

19. Zwingli, *Huldreich Zwinglis Sämtliche Werke*, 6:1–196.

20. Two of these letters were written to Zwingli, one to Thomas Müntzer, one to a co-worker in Zürich (Andreas Castelberger), nine to an Oswald Myconius of Lucerne, and fifty-six to a close friend, Joachim von Watt, a fellow reformer in the Swiss city of St. Gall. Unfortunately, most of these letters were written when Grebel was a student in Paris and Vienna and not as an "Anabaptist" leader.

21. For example, see Niebuhr, *Social Sources of Denominationalism*, 38–39.

quite the opposite. Grebel was the "promising son of a Zürich patrician,"[22] the second of six children of Junker Jacob Grebel and Dorothea Fries. The Grebels had been a leading family in Zürich for generations in terms of political and economic affairs.[23] Thus it was that young Conrad was sent to the best universities—Basel,[24] Vienna[25] and Paris[26]—to study. While a student in Paris in the years 1518–1520 and without moorings, Grebel was part of a group of students who were responsible for killing two Frenchmen as the result of nationalistic fervor. His conversion several years later was thoroughgoing, probably deepened by what had become an unhappy relationship to his father.[27]

The year 1522 would mark significant change for Grebel, whose education up to that point had not answered his questions regarding images, sacrifice in the mass, clerical benefits, and tithing, among other issues. At this time he was being increasingly drawn to the preaching of Zwingli and the idea of reform in Zürich; in short order the two would become close. This friendship would also be short-lived, until the second Zürich disputation of October 1523, due to a growing schism. By the Fall of 1524 the break between the two was complete, leading to denunciation and counter-denunciation.[28]

As was particularly the case in the Swiss confederacy, public disputations were typically held to adjudicate over important issues bearing on the civic polity. As a rule, these usually lasted a day or two and were presided over by town or city councils. In the Swiss context, the public was generally

22. Fast, "Conrad Grebel," 118.

23. Bender, an Anabaptist authority on Conrad Grebel, writes that for two generations prior to the Protestant Reformation, "no important political event took place in Zürich in which a Grebel did not have part" (Bender, "Conrad Grebel," 160).

24. Upon arriving at the University of Basel in October of 1514, where Erasmus had taken up a teaching position, Grebel would have been exposed to humanist scholarship.

25. Grebel's father transferred him to the University of Vienna where he was to receive a four-year stipend from the emperor Maximillian (Bender, "Conrad Grebel," 162).

26. After three years at Vienna, Grebel would transfer to Paris for another two years of study; however, he would return to Zürich due to personal issues without finishing his education formally.

27. This is suggested by Fast, "Conrad Grebel," 129. Most sources are generally agreed that Conrad's marriage to a girl of lesser status alienated him from his family, resulting in a break in or about the year 1522.

28. Grebel's final break with Zwingli and the Zürich church would be over infant baptism. The issue, for Grebel, reduced to what constitutes the real church and true Christian discipleship.

allowed to attend.[29] In late 1523, Grebel and company began organizing, following the realization of a growing split with Zwingli. This breach would result in several disputations before the city council. Grebel's position was uncompromising: Zwingli, who had wished for a growing reformed consensus to emerge, with Zürich helping to lead the way, was too accommodating to the authorities, and this compromised the church in its essence and its witness to the world.

The October 1523 disputation, from the dissenters' vantage-point, was intended to pressure the city council to institute reforms in the city's church life through abolishing the mass and removing images. At bottom, Zwingli was willing to be more patient with the council; Grebel was not. For Grebel, the issue reduced to this: should civil authorities dictate the faith and worship of the church, or should pastors and laity change things based on the requirements of the Word of God? That is, should the church be state-controlled or voluntary? Grebel felt betrayed by Zwingli, while Zwingli viewed Grebel as a young radical. In the end, Zwingli was willing to accommodate the authorities, but Grebel was not. Meanwhile, Grebel would decide to write Karlstadt in the summer of 1524, who had broken with Luther along similar lines, and then he will hear of another former Lutheran who had broken with the Wittenberg reformer—a radical by the name of Thomas Müntzer. Here Grebel assumed that he would find support, since Müntzer had rejected Luther's sympathies toward the magistrate.

Grebel writes his letter and sends it on behalf of "seven new young Müntzers" in the faith. His letter makes clear the common ground that they share with Müntzer: they are "brothers" in Jesus Christ—brothers who lament the state of a corrupt church, fallen into error and in neglect of the holy Scriptures. Grebel writes that one of Müntzer's writings has come into their possession, which simultaneously encourages them—given its condemnation of the church's errant ways—and at the same time raises concerns, based on news that Müntzer advocates use of the sword by the saints with inspiration drawn from Old Testament law. The rationale undergirding Grebel's concern is as follows:

> One should not protect the gospel and those who accept it with the sword, nor should they protect themselves, as we have learned . . . that you believe and that you subscribe to. Truly believing Christians are sheep in the midst of wolves, sheep for slaughtering. They must be baptized in fear, need, grief, persecution, suffering,

---

29. Here on see Clasen, *Anabaptism*, 395–97.

and dying. They must be tested in the fire, and they must not find the haven of eternal rest by killing their bodily enemies; rather they must attain it by killing their spiritual enemies. Also, true Christians use neither the worldly sword nor war, for among them killing has been totally abolished. Indeed, believers practiced these things at the time of the old law [Old Testament], during which time (so far as we know) after they had conquered the promised land, war became a plague.[30]

Following a public debate on January 17, 1525, strict mandates by the Zürich city council were put in place, whereby (a) a cessation of activity by Grebel and his fellow dissenters was ordered and (b) the group was forbidden from meeting, and (c) a baptizing of all unbaptized infants was mandated.[31] Both sides were hardened. On January 21, the dissenters met, and Grebel baptized Georg Blaurock, with some 80 more baptisms occurring before the month's end.[32] The new mandates made it impossible for Grebel to remain in the city area; thus, he would begin to itinerate, then return to Zürich twice in between. In October of 1525 he was arrested and imprisoned, but escaped in March of 1526 and continued to preach, until several months later, when his health would give out.

## Grebel and Early-Anabaptist Theological Commitments

In terms of the major Christian doctrines, Grebel was in basic agreement with Zwingli. Their chief differences, according to Zwingli himself, were baptism and the role of secular authority—and specifically, whether a Christian can serve as a magistrate.[33] Grebel's biographer, Harold Bender (see above), has attempted to identify the theological underpinnings of Grebel's understanding of the Christian's relationship to the world; following are basic presuppositions that are thought to govern the true disciple:

- The Christian community must be separate from the world.

- Secular authorities cannot shape the church.

- The church must overcome the world by winning individuals over voluntarily.

30. "Letter to Thomas Muntzer," reproduced in Baylor, *Radical Reformation*, 42–43.

31. At this time, Grebel happened to have a two-week-old daughter.

32. Lindberg, *European Reformations*, 214.

33. Zwingli, *Huldreich Zwinglis Sämtliche Werke*, 3:872.

- Because the church and the governing authorities are separate, the Christian can expect to suffer.

- The church is bound by the New Testament but not the Old Testament.

- The Christian cannot participate with the state because of its use of coercive force and the sword.[34]

Anabaptist beliefs would be crystallized among the Swiss Brethren in the seven articles of the *Schleitheim Confession* (on which, see below) in 1527. The moniker "Swiss Brethren" was not foremost a geographical designation; rather, it referred more broadly to "Anabaptists" who were followers of Conrad Grebel. The fundamental differences between Swiss Anabaptists and Protestant reformed leaders in the 1520s and 1530s suggest that Anabaptists were first and foremost reacting against—and rejecting—an institutionalization of the Reformation cause. It is generally accurate to say that radical reformers—and the Anabaptists as the chief expression of the radical reformation—were equally distant from magisterial Protestantism and Roman Catholicism. And while fellow (magisterial) reformers worked toward reformation, the goal of Anabaptist reform was restitution, i.e., a return to the apostolic church and the perceived New Testament model.[35]

Although Anabaptism was neither homogenous nor centrally organized, its varied communities sought to model themselves on what they viewed as the pattern of the early church. Not theology per se but brotherhood and solidarity based on social practices and exclusivity/separation were their defining marks. A central reason for this was their deep-seated suspicion of the state and secular authority. This distrust and commitment to separation, of course, is lodged in their genesis. Political authority, as embodied in the magistrate and represented by the sword, inevitably was used against them. Both ecclesiastical and political authority viewed radical reformers as heretical, seditious, treasonous, and a genuine threat to the common good, given their refusal to bear arms and take oaths (a common late-medieval expression of citizenship and loyalty to the city/political community),[36] their refusal to pay the tithe, and their rejection of the need for political authority or participation in military service.[37] As the

34. Bender, "Conrad Grebel," 571–73.

35. Williams, "Radical Elements in the Reformation," 33.

36. Refusing to take oaths was important because citizens were sworn to maintain the common good, take up defense, avoid perjury, and uphold public service.

37. Citizen-soldiers guaranteed the public order, insofar as there was no standing

*Schleitheim Confession* concisely states, the sword, taking oaths, and political coercion are necessary for unbelievers but not the community of Christ. Furthermore, they rejected the magisterial reformers' position due to its "uncritical" and "undiscerning" attitude toward secular authority. Anabaptist reformers viewed themselves as "small islands of righteousness amidst an ocean of iniquity."[38] Thus, it is not surprising that Anabaptists were perceived as a threat, as social-political revolutionaries. Most—though not all—were pacifistic and neither revolutionary nor militant.[39] Nevertheless, after the Peasants' War both the authorities and fellow magisterial reformers grew increasingly hostile, given the common fear among authorities of disloyalty, anarchy, and lack of solidarity among the citizenry. In this respect, Anabaptists were aware that they were violating laws by refusing to bear arms and take oaths. Grebel had admonished his followers that God, not government, must have precedence.

Earlier we noted that at about the time of the final Zürich disputation and Grebel's final break with Zwingli, Grebel set about to consult other "radicals" in south and central Germany—among them Müntzer. In contrast to Müntzer, who had been influenced by the early stages of the Lutheran reformation but who had broken with Luther and advocated the use of violence to accomplish reform, Grebel insisted that no force must be used.[40] Contents of his letter, noted above, are instructive and constitute a primary source of Grebel's theological commitments.

army per se in sixteenth-century Switzerland.

38. Cohn, *Pursuit of the Millennium,* 254.

39. In south Germany, revolutionary Anabaptism remained negligible and disappeared entirely by 1530. This, however, was not the case in the north and in the Netherlands.

40. Although Heinrich Bullinger, by 1560, had inherited the view that Thomas Müntzer was the father of the Anabaptist movement, Anabaptist—and especially Mennonite—historians have denied this linkage, for obvious reasons, seeking to distance themselves from Müntzer. An important piece of evidence is the letter (noted above) from Grebel and his colleagues to Müntzer that simultaneously applauded him for his commitment to radical change yet decried his tendency to resort to violence. In the end, the degree to which Zürich dissenters were influenced at all by Müntzer remains speculative. There is no evidence that Grebel ever met Müntzer before the former died in 1526.

# Grebel and Early-Anabaptist Views of Political Authority

The matter of how to understand the relationship between the church and the state, between the Christian community and the secular authorities, was without question one of the most controversial subjects that confronted leaders of Protestant reform—from Luther and Calvin to various kinds of Anabaptists—in the sixteenth century. In Luther's understanding, it will be remembered, the church was entrusted with the gospel, whereas the state existed to administer justice and maintain an ordered society. Insofar as Lutheran theology neither equated not conflated the spheres—or "estates"—of church and state, the sword properly belonged to only one domain, the magistrate, as distinct from medieval conceptions of authority that allowed for the "two swords" of papal theocracy and the political magistrate. Because, in Luther's theology, (a) Christians cannot dismiss their citizenship in either the earthly or heavenly kingdom and given (b) the reality of human depravity and thus (c) the need for maintaining an ordered community, coercive force remains a necessary part of the state's function.

With other magisterial reformers, Luther distinguished his understanding of Christian discipleship from "radical reformers" with his ability to reconcile New Testament apostolic teaching—e.g., the Pauline teaching in Romans 13 and the Petrine teaching in 1 Peter 2—with Jesus' teaching in the so-called "Sermon on the Mount." To the extent that he did this he remained in continuity with classic Christian teaching and mainstream Christian thinkers to come. Based on natural law reasoning and scriptural exhortation, "the sword" is wielded by the secular authority for the benefit of society, and where and when rulers violate the natural moral law by not applying it, their authority is undermined. What is required, then, of the Christian is to realize that neither a "Christianization" of the world nor a separation from it are legitimate. Public spheres such as governing, soldiering, and judging are, like the work of farmers, cobblers, and fathers raising families, noble duties and, in fact, every bit as high a calling as church work, the priesthood or monastic life.

This vision of social reform, it needs emphasizing, spread in rather remarkable ways—both demographically and geographically. Nowhere was this rate of change more pronounced than in the Swiss territories to the south, where reformers such as Huldrych Zwingli, Conrad Grebel, Felix Mantz, Balthasar Hubmaier, and Hans Hut pressed for reform of both faith and practice. Whereas Anabaptists today are fairly uniform in their practice, their diversity in the early-sixteenth century is striking. So-called "spiritualists" such as Johann Denck are known for their emphasis on an inner light that was viewed as superior to Scripture. Others, such as Thomas Müntzer, were relatively self-educated but attentive to the Lutheran and reformed accent on the authority of scripture and the priesthood of the believer, in the end fashioning themselves as apocalyptic visionaries. Their convictions, often informed by Old Testament narratives in which Yahweh had commanded the faithful to slay the wicked, led them to affirm that the sword existed for the purpose of slaying the godless. Yet others, though a distinct minority, with Hubmaier believed, as Luther, that a Christian could serve as a soldier, a ruler, even a henchman—the implication being that war may or may not be justified. Still other radical reformers—indeed, we would argue most early Anabaptists—embraced varying degrees of "apolitical" pacifism. This belief very often led to severe persecution or martyrdom.

Despite the radical nature of early-sixteenth-century Anabaptism—in which one can observe an oscillation between the polar antitheses of revolution and pacifism—most of these dissenters arrived at what historian James Stayer calls a "radical apoliticism," i.e., a denial that political and coercive force might achieve ethical goals, given the explicit commitment to be separate from the world.[41] Unlike moderate apoliticism, radical apoliticism denies that force is necessary on occasion to preserve the common good.

## From Grebel to the Swiss Brethren: The Schleitheim Confession of Faith and Practice

Among the earliest—and best known—of radically apolitical groups were the Swiss Brethren and the Hutterites, who were soon joined in their extreme pacifistic stance by the Mennonites a generation later. In order to better understand their beliefs and self-identity, let us examine what is considered to be the earliest of Anabaptist documents, published under the title "*Brüderliche Vereinigung etlicher Kinder Gottes/sieben Artickel betreffend*" ("Brotherly Agreement of a Number of Children of God concerning Seven Articles"), otherwise known as the Schleitheim Confession of Faith, so named for the location of a synod that took place near the north Swiss-German border on February 24, 1527.[42] The Schleitheim Confession is significant not for its theological detail but rather because in time it would be

41. Stayer, *Anabaptists and the Sword*, 3–4.

42. For a representative English translation, see Wenger, "Schleitheim Confession of Faith," 243–53.

considered a normative Anabaptist confession and because it enumerates those practices that were thought to distinguish true Christians, as embodied in their fellowship, from "the world."

The Brethren, under the leadership of Michael Sattler, a former Benedictine monk, had been influenced by reform efforts in and round Zürich under the leadership of Conrad Grebel and Felix Mantz. The particular aim of this synod was to discuss seven specific matters of the free-church movement that were thought to be of critical importance to their faith and practice. The seven matters, each being addressed in the form of an article of faith, were as follows: baptism, the ban (excommunication), the breaking of bread, separation from the world, pastoral duties, the sword, and the oath (vows). These matters of faith and practice stressed the separation of true believers from "the world." The confession was an attempt, if not to codify and consolidate creedal convictions, at least to formulate belief and practice in such a way as to (a) address those supposed "fringe" elements that deviated from Anabaptist belief and/or (b) emphasize what was shared by all Anabaptist groups. The degree to which the confession is representative of Anabaptism continues to be debated today among scholars of its own tradition.[43] Nevertheless, for our own purposes we shall assume the significance of the confession as a charter document and the crystallization point of early Anabaptism.[44]

What is noteworthy about the Confession is its oppositional tone and emphasis. Pronounced antagonism rather than differentiation undergirds the articles of faith. Correlatively, the chief argument being set forth appears to be that of separation from the world. In the introduction, the document reads, "We who have been and shall be separated from the world in everything . . . [are] completely at peace." And in the fourth article, we read:

> We are agreed on separation: A separation shall be made from the
> evil and from the wickedness which the devil planted in the world;
> in this manner, simply that we shall not have fellowship with them

43. Some contemporary Anabaptist scholars bristle at the suggestion that their tradition, as mirrored in the Schleitheim Confession, is "separatist" and that the document was influential, prototypical, or separatist in reality; rather, they would argue that documents such as the confession are a product of *cultural engagement* and *not* withdrawal. The nuances of this debate are helpfully illustrated in Biesecker-Mast, "Anabaptist Separation," 381–402.

44. This is the view of least several contemporary Anabaptist writers—among these, for example, are Hostetler, *American Mennonites*; Snyder "Influence of the Schleitheim Articles," 323–44.

[the wicked]] and not run with them in the multitude of their abominations. . . . Since all who do not walk in the obedience of faith, and [who] have not united themselves with God so that they wish to do His will, are a great abomination before God, it is not possible for anything to grow or issue from them except abominable things. For truly all creatures are in but two classes, good and bad, believing and unbelieving, darkness and light, the world and those who have come out of the world, God's temple and idols, Christ and Belial; and none can have part with the other.[45]

Alas, the clear thrust of the Confession is that the Brethren are to be unified in their separation.

The sixth and longest of the seven articles of the Confession concerns "the sword." Here one finds a dualism in the Confession's formulation of what is required by Christian faith. On the one hand, the "sword" is "ordained by God," "guards and protects the good," and is "ordained to be used by the worldly magistrates." On the other hand, it is "outside the perfection of Christ" and for this reason is not to be employed by Christians. In anticipation of an objection, article six reasons: "Now it will be asked by many who do not recognize [this stance regarding the sword as] the will of Christ for us, whether a Christian may or should employ the sword against the wicked for the defense and protection of the good, or for the sake of love." The Brethren's reply to this question is "unanimous" and consists of a fourfold rationale:

- Christ's teaching and example point in the direction of mercy and forgiveness.

- Christ's example was not to pass judgment.

- Christ's example was not to rule as a king or prince, and in fact, Christ explicitly "forbids the [use of] the force of the sword saying 'The worldly princes lord it over them, etc. but not so shall it be with you'"[46]—an example that is supported by Paul's statement that God predestined his own to be conformed to the image of his Son (Rom 8:29) and Peter's reminder that because Christ suffered, we are left with an example (1 Pet 2:21).

45. Here, the translation found in Biesecker-Mast, "Anabaptist Separation," is being used.

46. This statement, found in all three synoptic gospels, is taken out of context by the Brethren. The purpose of Jesus' teaching here is to emphasize the attitude of *being a servant of all* rather than wanting to be served and "lord it over" others.

- Christian citizenship is spiritual and heavenly; therefore, the work of ruling and magistracy, because it is "worldly," is out of line with the Christian's true nature.

The final point is the most substantial of the Brethren's answers to why a Christian may not employ the sword:

> Finally it will be observed that it is not appropriate for a Christian to serve as a magistrate because of these points: The government magistracy is according to the flesh, but the Christians' is according to the Spirit; their houses and dwellings remain in this world, but the Christians' are in heaven; their citizenship is in this world, but the Christians' citizenship is in heaven; the weapons of their conflict and war are carnal and against the flesh only, but the Christians' weapons are spiritual, against the fortification of the devil. The worldlings are armed with steel and iron, but the Christians are armed with the armor of God, with truth, righteousness, peace, faith, salvation and the Word of God.[47]

The absolutist approach to the Confession's dualism inevitably and inexorably breeds withdrawal from the world. On the one hand, the Swiss Brethren, as reflective of most sixteenth-century Anabaptists, were true children of the Reformation, and they agreed with Luther on one temporal sword. At the same time, their separation was far more radical than that of Luther or any of the magisterial reformers, none of whom was apolitical. The Brethren, and the Anabaptists as a whole, derived their separation— and hence their radical apoliticism—from a particular view of Christian discipleship that issued out of their view of the world.

As we attempt five centuries removed to interpret accurately the radical reformers, an interpretation that begins with Grebel and other devotees of Ulrich Zwingli in Zürich, it needs pointing out that their view of "the world" arose from their experience with "the world"—an experience of intense persecution that emanated from both Catholic and fellow-Protestant sides. As James Turner Johnson reminds us, neither the separatism of the early Anabaptists nor their pacifism and absolute dualism between the affairs of this world and the kingdom of God were developed in a social or political vacuum. They became separatists and pacifists as a result of their attempt to distance themselves from a world in which magisterial and princely power had been used not infrequently for unjust purposes. Not having the power themselves to resist the misuse of the sword, they separated themselves for

---

47. Reliance on the Biesecker-Master translation is being made here.

spiritual purposes, therewith renouncing for themselves any recourse to the use of the sword.[48] In point of fact, it was only a matter of months after the Schleitheim synod that Michael Sattler, generally considered the author of the Schleitheim Confession, was executed in Catholic Austria. Hence, we do well to resist attempting to understand proto-Anabaptist views apart from their own documentary evidence and the specific religious, social, and political contexts in which they arise.[49]

In sum, the early sixteenth century constitutes something of a new and remarkable chapter in Christian thinking about not only the church as an ecclesial structure but social life, political authority, and the uneasy relationship between church and state. While magisterial reformers generally maintained a dependence on Augustinian theory which seeks to mediate the tension between our two citizenships, the city of God and the city of man, new developments begin to dramatically alter the landscape. A rethinking of the church's relationship to the sword, as mirrored in the earliest form of "Anabaptism," indicates an emergent break with medieval life and tradition. This break and resultant stark polarity between "the kingdom of Christ" and "the kingdom of this world" will be maintained by the end of the sixteenth century—a break that more or less remains yet today.

48. Johnson, *Quest for Peace*, 164–65.

49. Surely, it can be argued that with the proliferation of sects and churches that issued out of early sixteenth-century reformation movements, arguments for religious toleration and religious freedom were severely lacking; each group, after all, professed to have a corner on revealed truth. Thus, as one reformer observed, "the papists anathematize the Lutherans, the Lutherans anathematize the Zwinglians, the Zwinglians persecute the Anabaptists, [and] the Anabaptists anathematize all the others" (*Corpus Schwenkfeldianorum* cited in Baker, "Church, State, and Dissent," 146).

CHAPTER 12

# Thomas Müntzer (1488–1525)

## Politics and Religious Faith among
## the Radical Reformers

IN THE EARLY 1520S, following the Church's condemnation of Luther, the student of history notes the emergence of a powerful current of unrest at the popular level in Germany and Switzerland that convulsed society. Dissenting preachers of "evangelicalism" surfaced both in urban and rural areas, notwithstanding the role of the university in propagating the Lutheran evangelical message. In the words of one historian: "As the Reformation spread—through a flood of printed literature, but, more importantly for lay commoners, through sermons, public debates, and less formal oral channels—it also absorbed preexisting socio-economic grievances and political aspirations, and [it] gained a revolutionary momentum."[1] These popular convulsions, alas, would culminate in the Peasants' War of 1524–25.

The radicalism of the Reformation is best understood in the light of these socio-economic and political "grievances." But it cannot be understood apart from those religious forces that loosed it, first in Swiss and German society and then, a generation later, in the Netherlands. Religious discourse of the early-sixteenth century possessed an "unavoidable dimension of political reference," and to attempt, from a modern or ultra-modern perspective, to distinguish between "religious" and "political" life is anachronistic.[2] Correlatively, radical reformers would not have been interested

1. Baylor, *Radical Reformation*, xi.

2. Baylor, *Radical Reformation*, xvii. Baylor helpfully uses infant baptism to illustrate this unity by pointing out that baptism at the time was a rite with decisively *socio-political* implications—an agreement, as it were, in the mold of a social contract. Refusing to baptize one's infant, for the radicals, would not generally have been viewed as rebellious or seditious per se; it simply represented for them an encroachment on the Christian

in political theory as some abstract set of doctrines or propositions about government. Rather, as one sixteenth-century authority observes,

> their writings contained a set of norms for living, [i.e.,] practical values and principles about how socio-political life should be conducted among people who call themselves Christians. In this sense, their political theory was implicit, a sense of social morality embedded in everyday life . . . [while their] standard of justice derived from Scripture. What gave the ideas of the radicals political force was that many commoners shared their view that the moral economy of society was dislocated, and that the behavior of the clergy and secular rulers contradicted the values they professed.[3]

In fact, it would appear that many citizens shared, at least to some extent, the radicals' belief in an egalitarian and autonomous local community, without the need for the blessing of the secular authorities.

It is, of course, inevitable that both local and princely authorities would come to view these radical attitudes as a genuine threat to the social-political order and hence opposed—even suppressed—them actively, although this was not the case everywhere. Where suppression did exist, the political issue was forced upon them as to whether and how to mount active resistance. That any sort of violent expression would have been considered revolutionary or illegal goes without saying. And where forceful or violent protest and resistance did manifest itself, the very credibility of the Reformation was called into question. It is in this light that Luther, Zwingli, and the magisterial reformers interpreted radical reform. In short order, they found it necessary to denounce the radicals, insofar as the willingness of some radicals to resort to violence threatened to undo the very cause of Reformation protest that was formally lodged in 1517.

While on matters of Scriptural authority and evangelical reform over against a corrupt church all of the reformers—magisterial as well as radical— were united, what is significant about the radical reformers is the manner in which they diverged from their magisterial counterparts. The clear fault line expresses their underlying disagreement over authority, and specifically political authority. While the magisterial reformers—in some cases to a fault—were careful to seek the blessing and support of secular authorities,

---

community by the authorities, who were perceived as corrupt. The authorities themselves, however, would have viewed the radicals' refusal to baptize their infants as *inherently* subversive, threatening the very foundations of community life, citizenship, and obedience.

3. Baylor, *Radical Reformation*, xviii.

the radical reformers were impelled by a fervency and an impatience to witness radical and widespread reform, based on their reading of the New Testament (and sometimes the Old). For radical reformers such as Conrad Grebel and Michael Sattler, that impatience was nevertheless yoked to a reading of Scripture that required not only separation from the very world that was persecuting them, but an ideological pacifism that understood itself as following the example of Jesus. For a select few such as Balthasar Hubmaier—and this category of radical reformer was indeed a distinct minority—the secular authorities were perceived in generally Lutheran terms; that is, they were divinely ordained for the protection of civil society. For others, however, a commitment to a biblical literalism—a literalism that depended on a particular reading of the Old Testament and which failed to make hermeneutical distinctions—and a marked apocalypticism fed this "impatience" both with the Church as an ecclesiastical institution and with the magisterial reformers' vision. No figure of the early sixteenth century can be cast as more "impatient" than Thomas Müntzer.

Those who desired change more radical than Luther had envisioned it were not a few. They would emerge in Zürich, Strasbourg, Nürnberg, and a multitude of other places. All radicals agreed with the Reformation in principle, but they disagreed over how to restore what they understood to be genuine Christianity. While the radicals owed their message and vision in some respects to Luther and fellow magisterial reformers, they generally came to differ with their more "moderate" counterparts over matters of scope and strategy in spreading reform. It was in their fundamental rejection of the structure of politics and secular authority that they distinguished themselves perhaps most radically. Luther, Zwingli, and others had rebelled against the traditional structures of ecclesiastical authority, but they moved forward in the hopes of winning the approval of princes and magistrates,[4] whose authority for them was ordained by God.

The early stages of radicalism in the Reformation were first and foremost a matter of "internal dissent" among those who espoused reform. That is, their dissent was not only against the corruptions of the traditional Church; it was marked by a radical rejection of the magisterial reformers' view of secular authority. And nowhere was this "internal dissent" stronger

---

4. In Switzerland, which was divided into various confederacies, local authority often rested in the hands of city councils, as was the case in Zürich. Hence, the early disciples of Huldrych Zwingli, moved by his evangelical vision and preaching, in little time grew impatient with his commitment to work through the existing authority that was vested in the city council.

and more vehement than in the life of Müntzer, a former Luther devotee.[5] Müntzer is the earliest—and, in some respects, the most tragic—radical among those who were affected by the Reformation message. Among both Catholics and fellow Protestants he would be labelled the "arch-devil of Allstedt," a heretic, and a disturber of civil law and disorder.[6] Müntzer utilizes in the years of 1523 and 1524 the political and geographical foundations that were created by Luther for the very purpose of countering Luther. He would become convinced that Luther had not gone far enough; in fact, following his rejection of Luther's agenda he attacked Luther in no uncertain terms, viewing him as a puppet of secular rulers and a pampered theologian within the walls of the academy whose faith was meager and wholly inadequate to the task of real social change. Notably in his *Sermon to the Princes* (see below) and his *Highly Provoked Defense*, the latter of which represents the culmination of his dissent, Müntzer is unsparing of Luther (whom he believes has "befouled" and "perverted" the faith by his "theft of Holy Scripture"), as he is of all secular authority. Not for nothing does one historian call Müntzer Luther's "tormented ally."[7] But we get ahead of ourselves.

## Thomas Müntzer in the Making

Born in 1488, Müntzer entered the University of Leipzig, founded in 1409 by dissidents who left the University of Prague, then studied at the University of Frankfurt, founded in 1506, where the adjective "seditious" was affixed to his name by the university as part of his application and acceptance. We have little information about the earliest years of Müntzer's life, although we do know that he grew up in Stolberg, a small town near the Harz mountains, near the western border of the former GDR. One historian seems justified in calling him "restless and erratic."[8] In time, Müntzer entered the priesthood. Following his exposure to Luther's preaching in the early 1520s and conversion to evangelical ideas, Luther recommended Müntzer as an interim pastor to the Marienkirche in Zwickau, in eastern

---

5. Müntzer will break, in short order, with Luther—a break that was initially predicated on the rejection of infant baptism, although Müntzer would never become an "Anabaptist" in the formal sense.

6. Hillerbrand, *Reformation,* 215. Understandably, Marxists have tended to view Müntzer quite favorably.

7. Ozment, *Mysticism and Dissent,* 61.

8. Ozment, *Mysticism and Dissent,* 216.

Saxony, a city considered to be a business center, given the presence of important commercial and trade routes therein.[9] Müntzer arrived in Zwickau in May of 1520. There, however, he would not remain for long, and in April of 1521 he leaves Zwickau due to civil unrest as a result of his contact with certain Zwickau "prophets," who encourage in him an even greater prophetic radicalism.[10]

It is likely that Müntzer, at some point, involved himself in controversies over indulgences, given existing letters associating him with the city of Braunschweig.[11] This would correlate with Luther's posting of the 95 theses in 1517, which addressed this very issue. We know that Müntzer spent about two years, between 1517 and 1519, in Wittenberg and attended Luther's lectures.[12] Exactly how Luther and Müntzer met we do not know, even when Luther writes that Müntzer got into a fight in his (i.e., Luther's) cloister.[13] We know that in 1519 Luther supported Müntzer as a reformer, following local complaints by the local Catholic bishop about Müntzer's "heretical" preaching as well as those by Luther's nemesis Johann Eck.

Müntzer would migrate to the city of Prague (the first of several brief visits there), where he would spend a period of eight months and attempt in vain to incite Hussite Brethren to an uprising. Apparently, Hussite territory seemed the best place for radical reform. There he penned the *Prague Protest* on All Saints Day (Nov. 1) of 1521, mimicking Luther's action in 1517 by posting a manifesto which begins:

> I, Thomas Müntzer of Stolberg and residing in Prague, the city of the precious and holy fighter Jan Hus, think that the loud and moving trumpets [that once sounded in this city] were filled with the praise of the holy spirit. With my whole heart I will testify about my faith and lamentingly complain about present conditions to the whole church and to the whole world, wherever this document may be received. Christ and all the elect who have known me from my youth on confirm such a project. . . . I pledge

9. Wappler, *Thomas Müntzer*, 7–20.

10. For several decades Zwickau had developed the reputation as a "boom town" due to the advent of silver-mining. Its population increased to three times the size of Dresden, drawing workers from central and even south Germany. See Cohn, *Pursuit of the Millennium*, 237. When Müntzer lands in Allstedt in 1523, his preaching will have the effect of drawing many miners.

11. Gritsch, *Thomas Müntzer*, 5–6.

12. Bubenheimer, "Thomas Müntzer's Wittenberger Studienzeit," 168–211.

13. Luther notes this in Luther, "Letter to the Princes of Saxony," 52.

on my highest honor that I have applied my most concentrated and highest diligence in order that I might have or obtain a higher knowledge than other people of the foundations on which the holy and invincible Christian faith is based.[14]

Based on the introduction to *Protest*, in order to gain a reception Müntzer finds it necessary to identify with—and further—the reform movement begun by Jan Hus, who was martyred a century earlier. But unlike Hus, Müntzer "damns" everything conceivable—notably, the clergy ("hell-based parsons," "villainous and treacherous parsons"), theologians ("donkey-fart doctors of theology"), and the church ("a whore at the hands of seducing parsons"). "In the spirit of Elijah," Müntzer claims to have come to Prague to "demonstrate . . . a skillful mastery of the truth." The manifesto closes with an exhortation to the people to embrace him as a prophet of God who was being sent to initiate the final stage of world history. To not accept him and receive his message, he warns, is to await divine judgment "in the hands of the Turks."[15] As the *Protest* illustrates, the conspicuously apocalyptic dimension of Müntzer's preaching and writing is one of the first features that strikes the eye.

Müntzer would return to Saxony in April of 1523 and settle in the city of Allstedt as pastor of the Johanniskirche, with a view to set up the "new Jerusalem," even if that meant by force. Müntzer desired to see Allstedt, a small city in Saxony, become a religious-political center based on his version of the gospel—a sort of "counter-Wittenberg,"[16] from which, then, he hoped that a religious and social revolution might spread to all of Germany.

In response to Müntzer's growing radicalism, Luther decides to write to the princes of Saxony, calling on them to counter "the spirit of Allstedt."[17] The authorities, according to Müntzer's increasingly apocalyptic outlook, had come to represent the devil.

A closer look at Müntzer's theological convictions and modus operandi is illuminating. Simply put, Müntzer believed that the Holy Spirit and inner light (*das innere Licht*), and not merely Scripture in the Lutheran sense, was to be the Christian's guide. The Spirit, as he understood it, called for something *new*, breaking with *all* tradition. Müntzer held to a

14. Reliance is being made on the translation of the *Prague Protest* found in Baylor, *Radical Reformation*, 1–2.

15. Baylor, *Radical Reformation*, 10.

16. Hinrichs, *Luther und Müntzer*, 1.

17. Luther, *WA* 18:85.

seven-fold gifting of the Holy Spirit—the apex of authentic faith—which was closely correlated with his belief that dreams, visions, and ecstatic utterances were normative among the "elect" of God. Suffering as modeled on Christ's example was to be normative as well, given the world's resistance to God's purposes on earth. Ultimately, an apocalyptic eschatology was understood to usher in the "new Jerusalem." Relatedly, the Old Testament was thought to be read and contemporized—noted examples being Joshua's taking of the promised land by the sword and Daniel's vision of the collapsing kingdoms in Daniel 2—in order for the saints to prepare for the consummation of God's kingdom. In Müntzer's escalating criticism, whether of the Catholic Church or of Luther and Wittenberg, Müntzer was led to a conspicuously Old Testament and "theocratic" conclusion: "cleansing" would need to come by means of "slaughter."

In the meantime, the Zürich reformer Conrad Grebel and fellow radicals had recently broken with Ulrich Zwingli over the nature and pace of the Swiss Reformation. Hence they write to Müntzer, who appears to be a kindred spirit, based on what they have heard. They express solidarity with Müntzer in terms that are quite glowing. In the letter Müntzer is addressed as a "truthful and faithful proclaimer of the gospel," as one who has read the Scripture properly, in order to ascertain "the true faith and practices of God" over against the corruptions of the institutional church, and as one who rightly understands baptism. Grebel and the Swiss brethren, however, express grave concern over what they have heard: i.e., that Müntzer affirms the use of the sword in the propagation of the gospel.

In the summer of 1524 Luther will write a letter to the princes of Saxony which is dismissive of Müntzer—a conclusion that is based on the fruit of his work.[18] The princes, however, decide to grant Müntzer a hearing, on which occasion Müntzer delivers his famous *Fürstenpredigt* ("Sermon to the Princes") with its exposition of Daniel 2 and in which he denounces Luther as "Brother Fattened Swine."[19]

## Müntzer's Sermon to the Princes

It has been estimated by one German historian that, by the spring of 1524, Müntzer had influenced approximately 2000 people in Allstedt with

18. Luther, *WA* 15:217.10ff.
19. Williams, *Spiritual and Anabaptist Writers*, 54, 61.

his vision.[20] On July 13 of 1524 Müntzer is invited before several Saxon princes to present his radicalized understanding of Protestant reform. In this presentation of his interpretation of Daniel 2, the radical Reformation reaches a "high-water mark" in terms of its "revolutionary spiritualism" and counter-Lutheran emphasis.[21] The sermon is delivered in the presence of Duke John, brother of Frederick the Wise, protector of Luther, as well as multiple town officials. Herein Müntzer insists that divine revelation has not stopped; rather, it is a sign of the last days, he is a prophet, and the Spirit of God is speaking through him.

Godly princes, he argues, help end the abominable mixture of clerical and secular power which is rampant in his day and which was foreseen by Daniel the prophet. Christ requires nothing less than the stone of Daniel 2: namely, complete destruction of the earthly kingdoms. And because Nebuchadnezzar perceived in Daniel the wisdom of God speaking (Dan 2:46), so should the rulers of Allstedt and Duke John. The "stone" without hands, in Daniel's vision, strips the rulers of their power, and in this case, the rulers in question are the princes of Saxony. Müntzer is convinced that if the German princes properly understood God's wrath, they would purge the surrounding idolatry in the spirit of Jehu or Elisha, or in the spirit of Joshua who did not spare the sword. Luther's teaching concerning the state and the secular authorities has wrongly protected them, he warns.[22] The "day of the Lord" is upon Allstedt. The political authorities of Saxony, in the end, are responsible for ushering in the "New Jerusalem," given Müntzer's conviction that the will of God is directly mediated by rulers, based on Old Testament texts (e.g., 1 Sam 8:5ff; Hos 13:11). In his program, Müntzer assumes that the end is near. The end of the age equates to harvest, which means gathering and burning what is chaff (Matt 13:38–40).

In the words of historian Steven Ozment, Müntzer is quickly becoming a "bitter and disillusioned" man, inasmuch as both the ecclesiastical and political orders are corrupt beyond hope. For this reason the radical reformer can insist, "I tell you truly that the time has come for bloodshed to fall upon this impenitent world for its unbelief."[23] Accordingly, "lords and princes as they now present themselves are not Christians. Your priests

---

20. Hinrichs, *Luther und Müntzer*, 11.

21. Hinrichs, *Luther und Müntzer*, 47.

22. Surely, Müntzer has in mind Frederick the Wise, who had given Luther refuge.

23. Ozment, *Mysticism and Dissent*, 78.

and monks pray to the Devil, and there are ever fewer Christians."[24] For Müntzer, authority per se has become the equivalent of the devil himself. The great irony here, particularly in Müntzer's *Sermon*, is that Duke John and Prince Frederick were among the more tolerant rulers; hence, one can only imagine their sense of disorientation upon hearing Müntzer's message. Probably realizing that his days were numbered, Müntzer considers at this point taking his Daniel sermon to the peasants of Thuringia (present-day Thüringen), a neighbor state in eastern Germany.

Müntzer would be executed on May 27, 1525 only days after 5,000 of his followers were massacred in Frankenhausen. The words of one sixteenth-century historian are worth savoring: "Though few would praise—much less repeat—his revolutionary tactics, he, more than any other, is the magister of sixteenth-century dissent."[25]

## Luther against Müntzer: Conflicting Visions

In the eyes of Luther, Müntzer is the extension—the tragic though very logical development—of Karlstadt, a fellow Wittenberger who had turned on Luther as well. Fanatics (*Schwärmer*) like Karlstadt and the well-known Zwickau "prophets" would create unrest in Wittenberg in 1520–1521 during Luther's absence and unplanned "stay" in Wartburg.[26] Luther worried much, as would his younger university colleague Philip Melanchthon, about the wider direction of this sort of radicalized thinking as it came to bear on political authority and social cohesion. Originally, Luther did not foresee the possibility of uprising, nor did he wish to witness it. Luther, it is true, shared Müntzer's basic assumptions about the corruption of the church and the ecclesiastical structures. But for Müntzer, it was *both* the church *and* the secular authorities, embodied in the princes that constituted the problem. From Luther's perspective, the need for reform was chiefly ecclesiastical.

---

24. Ozment, *Mysticism and Dissent*, 78.

25. Ozment, *Mysticism and Dissent*, 97.

26. Similarly, in Zürich, Zwingli would reject not only the supposed "New Testament pattern" of the church being advanced by Conrad Grebel and fellow reformers but also their total rejection of the magistrate's role in terms of protecting the faith. For this reason the Swiss reformers would look to people such as Karlstadt and Müntzer for inspiration and advice. In fact, Grebel et al. will write two letters to Müntzer in September of 1524, signing them as "your brethren" and "seven new Müntzers against Luther" (Williams, *Spiritual and Anabaptist Writers*, 85).

The political implications of the Lutheran view become readily apparent. The gospel of peace requires an external, political protection by the authorities because of the sin problem in the world; hence, God has ordained the magistrate, in accordance with St. Paul's teaching in Romans 13. What occurs through the use of an ordered force is not the same as uprising (*Aufruhr*) and tumult. Luther rejects the badly misguided notion, which has germinated in Müntzer's thinking, that we now kill the wicked. Tumult has no place and, what's more, not infrequently affects the innocent as much as the guilty. Uprisings, therefore, cannot be justified. It is for this very reason that the magistrate is divinely ordained to bear the sword; he alone is justified in this capacity. From the standpoint of Christian faith, the magistrate is the sole arbiter of justice, and this for the purpose of preserving the social order. In the "two-kingdom" framework of Luther, both realms—church and secular power—have their own boundaries which should not be over-stepped.[27]

It is true, Luther concedes, that we can implore and admonish political authority. But we do not force its hand; uprisings are per se unjust. In fact, uprisings have the effect of discrediting the Reformation cause. We preach the word of God, we admonish the Pope, we condemn corrupt practices, but in all this we aim for the heart, which for Luther accomplishes more than innumerable uprisings. These convictions, in fact, were expressed by Luther even before the tensions that shook Wittenberg in late 1521 and in 1522, and they are on display in Luther's *Letter to Princes of Saxony*. Luther rejects the radicals' use of the Old Testament: if we interpret it literally, he insists, then it follows necessarily that we must be circumcised and do the works of the law, in addition to exterminating all unbelievers like the Canaanites and the Amorites. And according to "the spirit of Allstedt," those who are not killed must be strangled, so that the righteous, ultimately, are not judged by God.

In the end, the chief—though by no means sole—difference between Luther and Müntzer reduces to two diametrically opposed understandings of political authority in the Pauline teaching of Romans 13.[28] For Luther, uprising and tumult are devilish, inspired by false prophets and unclean spirits; they represent anarchy, against which both the kingdom of God and divinely-ordained political authority stand in opposition. For Müntzer, revolution is viewed as a right—a right to resist godless authority—and hence it is spiritually justified. The magistrate's sword is to punish the wicked and protect

27. Luther, *WA* 60:24, 239.

28. Hinrichs, *Luther and Müntzer*, 162.

the godly, according to Romans 13; however, when the social situation is reversed and the magistrate ends up protecting the wicked, then the sword is to be taken up by the people in order to bring down the wicked.

What particular writings of Müntzer did Luther have in view as he denounced Müntzer as a source of anarchy? It would appear that he is reacting to two of Müntzer's letters written to secular authority—one to Prince Frederick written in 1523 and one to Herzog Johann in 1524. In both one finds references to Luther's teaching on the state and the magistrate, which very likely is triggered by the destruction of buildings and property. It is probable that Luther here is reacting to events in Allstedt and not necessarily Müntzer's teaching or preaching per se.[29] At bottom, Luther is left to conclude, "the spirit of Allstedt annihilates itself" (*der Geist zu Allstedt rottet sich selbst*).[30]

Aside from their differing understanding of political authority, a second disagreement between the two reformers concerns human nature, the nature of sin, the cross, and the relationship between grace and law. Because of human depravity, as Luther understands it, we are incapable of doing what is good and right; we must, therefore, fall on God's mercy and grace. By means of Christ's sin offering on the cross, satisfaction has been made for the human predicament—a satisfaction that is not obtainable through works of the law or human effort. Faith alone procures the experience of divine grace, and this is the essence of the "new covenant." Müntzer, however, rejects Luther's law-grace contrast. For him, grace and law stand in a sort of dialectic; they are correlates of one another. Punishment by the law is the will of Christ, and to ignore grace is to warrant punishment in the present scheme of things.

Moreover, the law "in the heart," for Müntzer, is not the natural law—something that is transcendent, objective, and conceived of in Pauline terms. Rather, it is subjective and immanent, the very instrument of temporal punishment. Thus, to reject what Müntzer understands as "the call of God" requires that "the judgment of God" be manifest. And what does God? He wills righteousness, obedience, and punishment of the wicked. As it is, Müntzer rejects the Lutheran doctrine of thorough-going universal sin. And, just as important, whereas Luther does not reject a universal Christendom, but rather wishes to renew it, Müntzer rejects it out of hand, wishing to start anew following a total destruction of the ungodly.

29. Hinrichs, *Luther und Müntzer*, 163.
30. Luther, *WA* 15:220.

Retrospectively, in light of criticism of his role in the peasant uprisings, Luther spoke of "two fears." He worried about either the peasants' tyranny or that of the lords, anarchy or tyranny as typically understood. If forced to choose, and given human depravity, he seemed to prefer the latter. One of Luther's responses came in the form of *An Open Letter Concerning the Hard Book Against the Peasants*, penned in July of 1525.[31] Shortly after Müntzer's execution in 1525, Luther would publish a didactic tract under the title *The Horrible History and Judgment of God upon Thomas Müntzer*. Surely, Luther had reason to lament, for it is estimated that between 70,000 and 100,000 peasants were killed in Germany during the year of 1525.[32]

## Conclusion

In April of 1525, Müntzer will leave Allstedt and go to Mühlhausen, a large city in the province of Thuringia. From Mühlhausen he writes to his followers in Allstedt, from which he had fled; he exhorts them:

> Now go at them, and at them, and at them! It is time. The scoundrels are as dispirited as dogs. . . . It is very, very necessary, beyond measure necessary. . . . Take no notice of the lamentations of the godless! They will beg you in such a friendly way, and whine and cry like children. Don't be moved by pity. . . . Stir people up in the villages and town, and most of all the miners and other good fellows who will be good at the job. We must sleep no more! . . . Get this letter to the miners! . . . At them, at them, while the fire is hot! Don't let your sword get cold! Don't let it go lame! Hammer cling-clang on Nimrod's anvil! Throw their tower to the ground! . . . At them, at them, while you have day light! God goes ahead of you, so follow, follow![33]

Soldiers under the command of Prince Philip of Hesse and Duke George of Saxony would march to Mühlhausen, which was viewed as the source of insurrection in the region, and then on to nearby Frankenhausen, where they would encounter an army of between 8,000 and 9,000 peasants carrying farm tools. Of this number, roughly 5,000 would be slaughtered, with only six soldiers being reported as casualties. Müntzer would manage to escape the massacre and go into hiding.

31. Luther reproduced in Ozment, *Age of Reform*, 286–87.
32. Ozment, *Age of Reform*, 284.
33. Müntzer cited in Cohn, *Pursuit of the Millennium*, 247–48.

On the day after the battle of Frankenhausen following his capture, Müntzer was interrogated under torture and confessed that "all things are held in common" (*omnia sunt communia*) and that any prince or lord who was unwilling to permit that himself deserved death[34]—a confession that has understandably received much currency in Marxist interpretation.[35] Anabaptist historian James M. Stayer and German historian Carl Hinrichs both question whether this particular confession was forced or extorted out of Müntzer.[36] Whether the reformer was authentically concerned for the poor and the "common man," Marxist interpretation notwithstanding, remains very much in question. After all, unlike Luther, who himself came from peasant stock and thus sympathized with common people, Müntzer seems not to have come from a lineage of poverty himself,[37] having studied at both the university of Leipzig and the university of Frankfurt (though with no discernible academic focus). It is true that Müntzer did mirror an anti-materialist thrust in two polemical tracts dating ca. 1524, *Ausgedrückte Entblossung* ("Manifest Exposé") and *Hochverursachte Schutzrede* ("Highly-Provoked Vindication").[38] The intriguing question is whether indeed he was genuinely concerned about the plight of the "commoner" or whether he sought to exploit socio-economics and material inequity of his day for the purposes of social revolution. The evidence would seem to point toward the latter.[39] Martin Brecht, the esteemed German biographer of Luther, argues that the social need of the "commoner" was only peripheral to Müntzer's vision, based on the radical reformer's aggressiveness, bombast, and ability to engender conflict, in addition to the overall fruit of his brief life.[40] And indeed it is difficult to argue with Brecht.

34. Müntzer cited in Stayer, *German Peasants' War*, 107.

35. The periodic resurrection in the last 150 years of Müntzer's reputation—from Engels to Marx, from Russian to German radicals—is grounded chiefly in his supposedly being a symbol of "class warfare."

36. Stayer, *German Peasants' War*, 107–8; Hinrichs, *Luther und Müntzer*, 20–22.

37. In fact, Cohn, *Pursuit of the Millennium*, 234–35, rejects any notion of Müntzer knowing poverty, arguing that the dissenter actually came from "modest comfort," and that when he comes into full view in his early 30's, he appears neither as a victim nor as an enemy of social injustice but rather as a student.

38. Both of these tracts are reproduced in Matheson, *Collected Works of Thomas Müntzer*.

39. For a bibliography of general works on the radical Reformation and the Peasants' War, see Baylor, *Radical Reformation*, xxxiii–iv.

40. Brecht, *Martin Luther*, 2:155.

Doubts might legitimately be cast on Müntzer's motivations as a revolutionary. According to a friend of Luther who wrote of Müntzer's capture, Müntzer was hiding in someone's bed before being taken into the custody of Duke George. In response to the Duke's demand to know why he had beheaded four people in the previous week, Müntzer retorted that divine law, not he, had done it.[41] Within hours "divine law" once again would enact itself: Müntzer himself would be beheaded.

Most commentators of the early-sixteenth century are in fundamental agreement that Müntzer inspired either great sympathy or remarkable hatred, either "magnetic attraction or shuddering aversion."[42] In his masterful 1989 work on Thomas Müntzer,[43] historian Eric W. Gritsch argues that Müntzer fell victim to "a tragedy of errors"—both his own and those of his enemies.[44] German historian Hans-Jürgen Goertz is perhaps a degree less sparing, describing the radical reformer as "the first enemy of Luther's who was able seriously to imperil the Reformation."[45] On May 27, 1525, Müntzer was executed as the ringleader of peasants in Saxony.[46] This "ringleader,"[47] whom Luther had previously dubbed the "Enthusiast" (Schwärmer) par excellence,[48] was the one whom both Catholics and magisterial Protestants were convinced was reaping what he sowed. Despite Müntzer's relatively

41. Gritsch, *Thomas Müntzer*, 107; Merx et al., *Akten zur Geschichte*, 2:378–79.

42. Goertz, *Profiles of Radical Reformers*, 30.

43. In a fascinating development, Müntzer research experienced a notable increase during the 1970s, 1980s, and 1990s. For an overview of this research, see Stayer, "Thomas Müntzer on 1989"; Baylor, *Revelation and Revolution*; Bradstock, "Thomas Müntzer"; Rowland, "Thomas Müntzer."

44. Gritsch, *Thomas Müntzer*, xi.

45. Goertz, *Profiles of Radical Reformers*, 31.

46. Pamphleteers for the Peasants' Revolt defended the right of the people to violently overthrow the tyrant or the unchristian leader. Hereon see in particular Hoyer and Rüdiger, *An die Versammlung gemeiner Bauernschaft*.

47. In addition to the early radicals among the Swiss Brethren, radical visionary Hans Römer, who wished to continue the Peasants' War, called Müntzer his "father." See Wappler, *Die Täuferbewegung in Thuringen*, 363–64.

48. Massive revolts occurred in the German territories of Swabia, Franconia, and Thuringia, causing Luther to pen "Against the Robbing and Murdering Peasants," which would go through no less than 21 editions (Ozment, *Age of Reform*, 283–84). Luther's exhortation to the peasants in the aforementioned tract, on the one hand, and his argument in "Whether Soldiers, Too, Can Be Saved," on the other hand, should not be viewed as contradictory. There is a difference between mischievous and rebellion and defending the social order (be they external *or* internal threats). Violence requires severe justification, and contrary to the peasants, Thomas Müntzer, and other revolutionary types, social rebellion and maintaining the social order are not the same.

short life-span and active period of radicalism, we have fairly abundant evidence from the writings of Müntzer himself to observe the manner in which his convictions and behavior developed. Müntzer was a "driven and restless spirit" seeking a faith that with prophetic vengeance would "transform the world"—this in an era of great reform.[49] While it is certainly the case that Müntzer's nomadic pattern renders it difficult to evaluate him as a person, or even his relationship to Luther, his fundamental beliefs, as mirrored in his preaching and his writings, are open to investigation. Gritsch refers to him, with good reason, as "the first Protestant theocrat."[50] Viewed in theological terms, Müntzer's beliefs might be seen as a product of a dialectic between a particular reading of Scripture and charismatic experience, inasmuch as he believed that the Spirit should speak in his day as the Spirit spoke in the apostolic era. Regarding the first of these two elements, it is reasonable to assume that some consequences of the Lutheran Reformation were inevitable. That is to say, once people begin reading the Bible for themselves, they begin interpreting it for themselves, and no particular interpretation can be guaranteed. The "priesthood of every believer," alas, facilitates, at least to some extent, dissenting or "prophetic" views, and liberation can indeed lead to disorientation and misperception.[51]

Whatever the difficulties in assessing Müntzer as a person, what is without question is that his convictions were developed in such a way that led to a violent end. While, on the one hand, his activity discredited the magisterial Reformation, one may reasonably argue, on the other hand, that it helped birth—and refine, in reaction—the primary expression of the radical Reformation, namely, Anabaptism.[52]

---

49. Gritsch, *Thomas Müntzer*, 111.

50. Gritsch, *Thomas Müntzer*, 111.

51. Cohn, *Pursuit of the Millennium*, 252.

52. While most Anabaptists would contest this conclusion because of their commitment to ideological pacifism, mainstream Anabaptism was refined in reaction to the excesses of Müntzer as well as the failed "New Jerusalem" project a decade later in the city of Münster. Müntzer's views were more or less carried on by the community founded by the radical leader Hans Hut, who, like Müntzer was a native of Thuringia and who, like Müntzer, claimed "prophetic" inspiration. One of Hut's professions was that "Christ will give the sword and revenge to them . . . to punish all sins, stamp out all governments, communize all property and slay those who do not permit themselves to be rebaptized" (Hut cited in Cohn, *Pursuit of the Millennium*, 255). The Hutterite community lived with the conviction that Müntzer's mission constituted the beginning of the three-and-a-half year "tribulation," culminating in Christ's return that was projected to occur in the year 1528. Hut would die two years after Müntzer, in 1527.

## CHAPTER 13

# Menno Simons (1496–1561)

## Introduction

IN THE AFTERMATH OF the peasant uprisings of 1524–1525 and the failed "New Jerusalem" in Münster a decade later, it became unavoidable for radical reformers of the sixteenth century to try to make sense out of the lack of success of their cause. What were the lessons to be learned? And how were they to proceed in their cause?

While "Anabaptism" arose in the cradle of Zwinglian reformation in Zürich, it would need to be refined and mature through a full generation of testing, persecution, and refinement before it would achieve its enduring form. Anabaptists tended to be clustered in three primary regions: Switzerland and south Germany, the Netherlands and north Germany, and Austria and Moravia.[1] In Germany, key events in the 1520s and the 1530s confirmed the fears of both secular rulers and magisterial reformers; lodged at the center of these developments was the disruption of law and civil disorder. In the central-northern city of Münster, the "Anabaptists" acquired unprecedented influence. The city had already become officially Lutheran in 1532, aided by conflict between the Catholic bishop and the city council, and what ensued was a veritable "three-cornered struggle" over religion between Catholics, Lutherans and Anabaptists.[2] Münster was one of the few cities in which Anabaptists were tolerated. The radicals were strategically placed to build upon this fissure, and in short order they would attempt to usher in the "New Jerusalem." Not even a Lutheran-Catholic coalition led by the Bishop of Münster could dislodge the radicals—until June of 1535.

1. Depperman et al., "From Monogenesis to Polygenesis," 83–102.

2. Stayer, *Anabaptists and the Sword,* 254–55.

The apocalyptic crusade of Münster had only one parallel previously, and that consisted of the latter years of Thomas Müntzer's activity during the mid-1520s. The animating vision in Müntzer's program, reduced to its essence, was the destruction of the godless. Anabaptists in Münster had had the conviction that defense required a sword, and it is likely that Anabaptist leaders there had read Müntzer's *Sermon to the Princes*. The sword of justice, in Münster, would become a sword for holy war.[3] In fact, one respected Anabaptist historian has furthered the argument that Menno Simons's brother Peter, who happened to be one of the "twelve elders" of the radical Anabaptist community in Münster, would be killed in the fighting that would lead to the community's downfall in 1535.[4] If this was in fact the case, then Menno bore a heavy load as he sought to make sense of a purified Anabaptist community in the Netherlands.

The tragic Münster episode, quite understandably, would reflect negatively on all Anabaptists, especially those in northern Germany and the Netherlands. In the years following Münster, Dutch Anabaptists would gather around the non-violent vision of both Menno Simons and Dirk Philips. Simons's movement away from the Catholic Church and priesthood toward evangelical faith would be gradual; he did not leave the Church at once. Over time, two features in particular would form the heart of Menno's strategy during the 1540s when he would assume leadership among purified Anabaptist communities: (1) combining a non-violent vision with the ban and shunning, which would have the effect of excluding those from the community who could not accept non-violence, and (2) a community orientation or communalism that was distinct from mere spiritualism or mysticism.[5] While Menno Simons did not found the Anabaptist movement in the Netherlands, he had the heart of a founder, combining this vision with a pursuit of godliness that would have lasting results. Menno's greatness, to be sure, was not eloquence, nor was it literary craftsmanship or being a theologian in the technical sense. Rather, it was lodged in the fact that he was a champion of "practical Christianity," stressing a faith-life of purity, charity and good works.[6]

---

3. Stayer, *Anabaptists and the Sword*, 255. According to radical Anabaptist thinking in Münster, before the wicked could be punished, 144,000 saints needed to be found and gathered. Hence, there were attempts to draw sympathetic Anabaptist types from other parts of Germany and the Netherlands to Münster.

4. Stayer, *Anabaptists and the Sword*, 273.

5. McLaughlin, "Radical Reformation," 37–55.

6. Bender, "Brief Biography of Menno Simons," 3–29. Cornelius Krahn writes:

# The Making of Menno Simons

At age 28, Menno Simons was ordained in the priesthood and served in his native West Friesland in the Netherlands. In time, however, doubts would develop regarding both baptism and the Lord's Supper. Just as significant was the debacle at Münster, which had a profound effect on emergent "Anabaptism," moving it away from fanaticism and in the direction of inner renewal and holiness. This was especially the case for Menno, for whom the phenomenon of apocalyptic crusading discredited any attempts to bring about true evangelical reform. Menno's emergence in the first decade after the uprisings in Münster, which left their effect as well in the Netherlands, mirrored a period of deep reflection on the resultant suppression of revolt, executions, and disillusionment among "Anabaptist" types. Was it necessary to break entirely with the existing order? What is the relationship between inward piety and outer social responsibilities? Radical reformers differed on these questions, and their differences, it goes without saying, were profound. No clear, unifying answer was to be found.

As a Catholic priest, by 1531 Menno had come to reject infant baptism and the real presence in the mass, based on personal study of the Bible. He served seven years in the priesthood before writing, "I examined the scriptures diligently and pondered them earnestly, but could find no report of infant baptism."[7] Being a parish priest made the break with the established Church far from easy, yet at this point Menno would take upon himself the yoke of Christ's cross—an important theme in his early writings. During this time, he acknowledges Luther's influence and assistance—particularly in finding confidence in the testimony of Scripture[8]—while disavowing the "erring sects" —embodied, for example, in the militant Anabaptists of Münster—which had become radicalized. He acknowledges his two biggest obstacles to the faith: the matter of baptism and the debacle in Münster with its fanatical blasphemies. Issuing out of these dilemmas are several primary burdens that will surface in his writings—among these: brotherhood (i.e., community), non-violence, separation from the world, and living under

---

"Menno Simons was a Biblicist in the truest and best meaning of the word; he turned away from tradition and became Bible-centered in all his beliefs and practices" (Krahn, "Menno Simons," 582).

7. Simons in Wenger, *Complete Writings of Menno Simons*, 668.

8. Wenger, *Complete Writings of Menno Simons*, 668.

the cross.[9] Regarding Münster, he is deeply saddened that so many Dutch brethren were deceived—as sheep utterly without a shepherd.[10]

Following his baptism, Menno committed himself to public dissent in the form of separation and a disciplined community of believers, much in the tradition of the Swiss Brethren, whose Schleitheim Confession of 1527, with its seven articles of faith and practice, would be normative.[11] In his conversion reflections, not published until the year 1554 and appearing under the title "My Conversion, Call, and Testimony,"[12] Menno lists important steps in his search for truth. Among the most important,

- He sought out a "God-fearing, pious hero" named Sicke Snijder.[13]

- He consulted Martin Luther.

- He consulted Martin Bucer.

- He consulted Heinrich Bullinger.[14]

- He concluded that the magisterial reformers had it wrong concerning baptism.

- He then began to preach publicly.

- He then renounced all things and submitted to Christ's cross.

- And, he continued to anguish over Münster.

In January of 1536, literally weeks after the authorities had quashed the radical "Anabaptist" attempt at instituting the "New Jerusalem" in Münster, Menno would leave his parish priesthood to join the Anabaptist cause. From 1536 onward, he would itinerate in the Netherlands and in northern Germany, emphasizing *inter alia* the nature of true repentance and the "narrow way," separation from "the world," the efficacy of the scriptures, the Lord's Supper, and true baptism while denouncing sin, idolatry and false worship, and, of course, disavowing Munster as well as the use of the sword and coercive force.

9. Goertz, *Profiles of Radical Reformers*, 209–10.

10. Wenger, *Complete Writings of Menno Simons*, 670–71.

11. For English translations of the text of the Confession, see Sattler, "Schleitheim Articles," 172–80; Wenger, "Schleitheim Confession of Faith," 247–53.

12. Wenger, *Complete Writings of Menno Simons*, 668–74.

13. Snijder was martyred in 1531 following his re-baptism.

14. Menno's consultation with both Bucer and Bullinger concerned the matter of baptism.

As suggested thus far, it is impossible to appreciate the evolution of Menno's views without taking into account the role that the Münster tragedy played in his thinking. The relationship between the city, which was overwhelmingly Lutheran, and the Catholic bishop had been strained for years. In July of 1532 Charles V had demanded that evangelical ministers in the city be removed, which the city refused to do, ensuring that religious controversy would simmer. Anabaptist sympathizers from various parts of Germany and from the Netherland then began to move to Münster, in the awareness that the city served as something of a refuge for persecuted Christians. Emergent leaders of the radical Anabaptist community in the city would take on "prophetic" authority and proclaim that Münster was to become "the city of the Lord" and a "New Jerusalem." By Spring of 1535 the collapse of the city, which had been under siege for a year following the radicals' refusal to negotiate with authorities, had begun; in July of that year it would be complete. The "spirit of Münster" would disappear; Anabaptists, however, would remain, though dispersed and purged greatly as a result of religious persecution.[15]

Following the Münster tragedy, an awareness in Menno Simons of the need for godly shepherds who might guard the flock against false shepherds was clearly present. Upon serious reflection on the damage that the failed Münster project had caused, he decided to publish *A Reply to False Accusations*,[16] which was intended to repudiate violence and insist on personal holiness. *A Reply* consists of formal replies by Menno to eight common accusations: being Münsterites, not obeying magistrates, being seditionists or communists, being polygamists, being unwilling to forgive the penitent, claiming sinlessness, holding to a works-righteousness, being demon-possessed and truth-fearing.

Menno frames the common charge leveled by many against the Anabaptist movement in general: "They say that we are seditionists and that we would take cities and countries if we had the power."[17] His response: "This prophecy is false and will ever remain so, and by the grace of God, time and experience will prove that." Further: "We would say [in sum] this much in defense of all of us . . . that we consider the doctrine and practice of those in Münster in regard to King, sword, rebellion, retaliation, vengeance,

15. For a helpful over view of the development of the Münster project as well as its demise, see Krahn, *Dutch Anabaptism*, 135–69.

16. Wenger, *Complete Writings of Menno Simons*, 543–77.

17. Wenger, *Complete Writings of Menno Simons*, 554.

polygamy, and the visible kingdom of Christ on earth a new Judaism and a seductive error, doctrine, and abomination, far removed from the Spirit, Word, and example of Christ."[18]

Moreover, Menno asserts:

> I can fearlessly challenge anybody that none under heaven can truthfully show that I ever agreed with the Münsterites in regard to those points. From the beginning until the present moment I have opposed them diligently and earnestly, both privately and publicly, with mouth and pen, for over 17 years, ever since according too my ability I confessed the Word of the Lord and knew and sought His holy name. I also according to my small talent have faithfully warned everybody against their error and abomination, just as I would want other people to do for my soul. And, in passing, I have pointed and returned several of them to the true way by the grace, assistance, and power of the Lord.[19]

Menno wishes to reassure his readers:

> I have never seen Münster nor have I been in their fellowship. And I trust that by the grace of God, I shall never eat nor drink with such if there should be any left, even as the Scripture teaches me, unless they sincerely acknowledge their abomination, and truly repent, and follow the truth and the Gospel in a genuine way. . . . In short, we herewith and confess before God, before you, and before the whole world that we from our inmost hearts detest the errors of the Münsterites, as well as every other sect which is at variance with the Spirit, Word, and ordinance of the Lord.[20]

The basis for Menno's rebuttal to any accusations that might link him, with his sympathizers, to Münster, is Scripture. Scripture teaches of two opposing princes and kingdoms: the "prince of peace" and the "prince of strife." The apostle Peter serves as an abiding example in this regard, for he was commanded by our Lord to sheathe the sword. All attempts at sedition are therefore to be renounced. Moreover, Christians are commanded to love their enemies and do good to those persecuting. How then, Menno reasons, can a Christian defend war, rebellion, retaliation, slaying and plundering? In the end, our weapons are not swords and spears but patience, silence, and hope, and the word of God. True Christians do not know vengeance, and

18. Wenger, *Complete Writings of Menno Simons,* 547.

19. Wenger, *Complete Writings of Menno Simons,* 547.

20. Wenger, *Complete Writings of Menno Simons,* 547, 549.

despite the persecution and martyrdom of pious saints in the Netherlands, no power or authority can separate them from the Lord. At the same time, the office of magistrate is "ordained of God" and therefore "we have obeyed them when not contrary to the Word of God." This includes paying taxes and tolls and praying for all in authority.[21]

In addition to the "Münsterite" charge, Menno finds it necessary to answer one other major accusation, namely, that Anabaptists will not obey the magistracy. In similar terms, Menno rejects this charge, insisting that "our writings prove this accusation to be false": we "publicly and unequivocally confess" that the office of a magistrate is "ordained of God." "Taxes and tolls we pay," he notes, "as Christ taught and practiced." In addition, "we pray for all in authority." And yet "a public outcry of agitation" continues, he laments, which prompts "the bloody sword against us." Menno adduces scriptural evidence of the legitimacy of the magistrate's office and his sword. This includes Moses, who appointed rulers and judgers, and the apostle Paul, whose teaching in Romans 13 affirms the use of the magistrate's sword against evil, though not against the good. Rulers must use their office wisely, Menno counsels. They should not be deceived; rather, they should seek God and his Christ and embrace the truth, in accordance with their office.[22]

This anguish and the need to disavow Münster deepen within Menno a commitment to ideological pacifism. A central error of Münsterites, he believes, was their preference for the Old Testament over the New, which had immense ethical repercussions. As Menno points out in *The Blasphemy of John of Leiden*,[23] "Now we should not imagine that the figure of the Old Testament [for example, a Moses or David] is so applied to the truth of the New Testament . . . for the figure must reflect the reality . . . and the letter, the Spirit."[24] Correlatively, Menno criticizes the apocalyptic view that God will shortly punish and destroy Babylon and the wicked, and that Christians must be His agents. To believe such is to be deceived, Menno insists; "therefore we will oppose this view with Scriptures."[25] Not by Christians will the

---

21. Wenger, *Complete Writings of Menno Simons*, 549.

22. Wenger, *Complete Writings of Menno Simons*, 549–51.

23. Wenger, *Complete Writings of Menno Simons*, 33–50.

24. Wenger, *Complete Writings of Menno Simons*, 42.

25. Wenger, *Complete Writings of Menno Simons*, 46.

wicked be destroyed, he reminds his readers; rather, it is "the Lord Himself" who "will destroy at His coming all His enemies."[26]

Therefore, a re-reading of Scripture and particularly a certain reading of the "Sermon on the Mount" become central in Menno's thinking to Christian discipleship and Christian non-violence. Moreover, Christ did not defend himself with Peter's sword; rather, he chose to suffer, "And in the same way all Christians must be minded [i.e., to suffer]."[27] For these reasons and more, then, it is not permitted that Christians to fight with the sword.

## Foundations of Anabaptist Theology: Christ and the World in Antithesis

Although Anabaptists—including many Anabaptist historians—have been inclined to speak of Anabaptism as a way of life or a pattern of Christian discipleship and not as a theological system, Anabaptism most assuredly, from its beginning, was predicated on certain theological assumptions and a particular reading of the Old and New Testaments.[28] While it is true that the average sixteenth-century Anabaptist was not conversant with Protestant thought, most radical reformers were. In fact, many of the early radical reformers—examples being Thomas Müntzer and Andreas Karlstadt—either sat under Luther's teaching or were mentored by magisterial reformers, as was the case with the earliest Anabaptist leaders in Zürich such as Conrad Grebel and Felix Mantz, who had been devotees of Huldrych Zwingli. Karlstadt and Müntzer would end up using the very presuppositions that sprang from Luther's evangelical teaching to work against the Wittenberg reformer. In contrast, the Swiss radical reformers, while they shared the reformers' initial dissent in reaction to the mass, the sacraments, and perceived ecclesiastical corruption, in time, particularly after the Münster debacle, they became grounded in the principles of separation and non-violence.

---

26. Wenger, *Complete Writings of Menno Simons*, 47.

27. Wenger, *Complete Writings of Menno Simons*, 45.

28. What is intriguing is that these very Anabaptist historians almost all take the position that Anabaptism alone overcame the perversions of the church of Rome in a way that Luther, Zwingli, Calvin and company did not. This supposition can be seen, for example, in the title of Walter Klaassen's work *Anabaptism: Neither Catholic Nor Protestant*, as if the "radical Reformation" was not part of the sixteenth-century "protest" in which the primacy of faith, grace, and Scripture was asserted.

Earliest Anabaptism, as represented by the Swiss Brethren and its earliest authoritative document, the Schleitheim Confession of 1527 with its seven articles of faith and practice, placed separation at the center of the "Anabaptist" identity. The notion of separation permeates several of the seven articles and is the particular focus of Article IV. Article III reads: "all those who have fellowship with the dead works of darkness have no part in the light. Therefore all who follow the devil and the world have no part with those who are called unto God out of the world. All who lie in evil have no part in the good."[29] The rationale for separation is clarified in Article IV:

> We are agreed [as follows] on separation: A separation shall be made from the evil and from the wickedness which the devil has planted in the world; in this manner, simply that we shall not have fellowship with them [the wicked] and not run with them in the multitude of their abominations. This is the way it is: Since all who do not walk in the obedience of the faith, and have not united themselves with God so that they wish to do His will, are a great abomination before God, it is not possible for anything to grow or issue from them except abominable things. For truly all creatures are in but two classes, good and bad, believing and unbelieving, darkness and light, the world and those who [have come] out of the world, God's temple and idols, Christ and Belial; and none can have part with the other.[30]

In Anabaptist theology, between the believer and "the world" there exists not merely a tension but an antithesis, a vast chasm of irreconcilable differences, between the kingdom of Christ and the kingdom of this world. "The world" lives according to the flesh, following the ways of the devil. Thus, the believer may never be conformed to the world and its ways; friendship with the world is enmity with God. Rather, the believer is to live according to the Spirit, cognizant of the fact that faith overcomes the world (1 John 5:4). The absolute dualism in Anabaptist thinking between faith and the world, between Christ and Belial, between light and darkness, is reminiscent of the antithesis that characterized late Judaism of the post-exilic era, especially among the members of the Dead Sea Scroll community. And because this dualism is absolute, not drawing any distinctions between "the world" as human culture and "the world" as spiritual conflict, it requires a withdrawal from the world, an isolation, and an intentional

29. Wenger, "Schleitheim Confession of Faith," 249.
30. Wenger, "Schleitheim Confession of Faith," 249.

attempt to build a community of like-minded individuals who are uncompromising in their rejection of "the world."

Particularly important for Menno's realization of the Church as a pure brotherhood of saints was the discipline of the ban, understood to be Christ's "second key" (cf. Matt 16:17–19) and based on Matt 18:15–18; 1 Cor 5:11.[31] We know from the ur-Anabaptist profession, the Schleitheim Confession of 1527, that the ban was predicated on the reasoning laid out in Matt 18:15–20, and the practice of shunning anchored in the Pauline rationale developed in 1 Cor 5:1–13. In *Admonition on Church Discipline* (1541), Menno writes: "For we do not want to expel any, but rather to receive; not to amputate, but rather to heal; not to discard, but rather to win back; not to grieve, but rather to comfort; not to condemn, but rather to save."[32] The ban, however, is said to be a command, not merely "counsel." It should produce change, even among married couples. But it does not mean being unloving, cruel or merciless.[33]

## "Foundation of Christian Doctrine": Post-Münster Anabaptist Reflections on the Magistrate and the Sword

The 1539 treatise *Foundation of Christian Doctrine*, the best known of Menno's writings,[34] was written with three primary aims: (1) to familiarize the world with the beliefs of Dutch Anabaptist Brethren, of which Menno became a bishop; (2) to ease persecution; and (3) to indoctrinate the brethren themselves. *Foundation* devotes an extended discussion to the magistrate and the sword. An important part of his reasoning would seem to stem from Menno's mission to correct erring brethren, many of whom were sympathetic to Münster. War, he was convinced, was the instrument of the anti-Christ, whether Münsterite or Zwinglian or Papist.[35] Menno's views, however, ac-

31. Wenger, *Complete Writings of Menno Simons*, 731. Baptism and the ban constitute in Anabaptist theology "entry to and the exit from" real faith (Williams, *Spiritual and Anabaptist Writers*, 261).

32. *Admonition on Church Discipline* in Wenger, *Complete Works*, 413. On whether to shun a banned spouse, Menno wavers (see, for example, Wenger, *Complete Works*, 732).

33. For a helpful summary of Anabaptist theological distinctions, particularly as they express themselves in the dualism of two worlds, see Friedmann, *Theology of Anabaptism*, 36–48.

34. *Foundation* was begun in 1539 and finished in 1540; it was thoroughly revised in 1554. However, it would not be translated into German until 1575.

35. *Foundation of Christian Doctrine* (1539) in Wenger, *Complete Writings*, 190,

cording to one Anabaptist historian, were not the "radical apoliticism" of the Swiss Brethren,[36] insofar as Menno addresses Princes in their tasks, admonishing them to be wise, just, and God-fearing. In so doing he counsels them to "rightly wield the Sword that God has given you."[37]

The language in one section of *Foundation*, "Request to the Magistracy," is one of pleading and supplication. Following are excerpts from this "Request" that mirror Menno's cry for tolerance and the beleaguered state of Anabaptists:

1. "We humbly intreat the Imperial Majesty, kings, lords, princes, magistrates, and officers, everyone in his calling, dignity, and rank. And all our dear and gracious rulers by the crimson blood and wounds of our blessed Lord Jesus Christ, that you would at long last lay aside all ill will and bad opinion concerning us. With proper pity be at least somewhat concerned about the inhuman and heavy oppression, misery, distress, cross, and torture of your sad and innocent subjects."

2. "Therefore condescend to read our writings diligently and ponder them, and that with a God-fearing and unbiased heart, so that you may know with certainty why you are unable to frighten us from our doctrine, faith, and practice by coercion, poverty, misery, persecution, and death."

3. "Therefore humble yourselves in the name of Jesus, that your poor souls may be excused. Examine, I say, our doctrine, and you will find through the grace of God that it is the pure and unadulterated doctrine of Christ."

4. "O dear sirs, sheathe your sword. For as the Lord liveth you do not fight against flesh and blood, but against Him whose eyes are as a flame of fire; who judgeth and contends in righteousness; who is crowned with many crowns. . . . O illustrious lords and princes, it is against Him that you in this manner contend with your counsel and sword and weapon."[38]

In at least three other places, Menno entreats rulers and magistrates toward mercy and understanding, adjuring them to ease Anabaptist

---

although the wider argument is laid out on Wenger, *Complete Writings*, 190–206.

36. Stayer, *Anabaptists and the Sword*, 314.

37. Wenger, *Complete Writings*, 200.

38. Wenger, *Complete Writings*, 117–18.

persecution and eschew unjust use of the sword. Elsewhere in *Foundation*, in a section titled "Appeals for Toleration," he affirms civil authority to the extent that it does not violate Scripture:

> But as to the flesh, we teach and exhort to obedience to the emperor, king, lords, magistrates, yea, to all in authority in all temporary affairs, and civil regulations in so far as they are not contrary to the Word of God. Rom 13:1–3 . . . We teach and acknowledge no other sword, nor tumult in the kingdom or church of Christ than the sharp sword of the Spirit, God's Word, as has been made quite plain in this and our other writings: a sword which is sharp and more penetrating than any sword, two-edged, and proceeding from the mouth of the Lord. . . . But the civil sword we leave to those to whom it is committed. Let everyone be careful lest he transgress in the matter of the sword, lest he perish with the sword. Matt 26:52.[39]

In his 1552 treatise *A Pathetic Supplication to All Magistrates*, Menno continues his appeal to those in authority. Therein he distances the Anabaptists from heretical sects in the church's past and reaffirms Anabaptist commitment to the authority of Scripture, all the while exhorting leaders to rule in the fear of God and cease from the persecution of the godly.[40]

During the sixteenth century, both Catholics and Protestants were of the conviction that government was obligated to "protect the faith." Thus, heresy—on either side of the Reformational aisle—was central to sixteenth-century thinking regarding the relationship between church and state. Relatedly, up until approximately 1530, it was generally the role of governing authorities, not the church, to determine the process for recanting.[41] While various penalties—ranging from fines, imprisonment or banishment to execution—were enforced in the case of sects that were judged to be "heretical," the type of penalty assessed often depended on the geographical region in which heretical views were found.[42] Executions, where the death penalty

39. Wenger, *Complete Writings,* 200.

40. Simons, *Pathetic Supplication to All Magistrates* (1552), in Wenger, *Complete Writings,* 525–30.

41. Clasen, *Anabaptism,* 368.

42. Although a new imperial law was enacted in April of 1529 which ordered all rebaptized men and women to be executed, it was individual cities and territories that in fact did the prosecuting. It is worthy of note that Luther and Melanchthon grew increasingly concerned about civil unrest that claimed inspiration from the evangelical message. Luther would come to support the death penalty for Anabaptists, although over time he gravitated toward banishment rather than the death penalty (Clasen, *Anabaptism,* 382).

was enacted, were usually carried out by princes. The mode of execution was often either burning at the stake (the typical medieval punishment for heretics), beheading, or drowning. The rationale for execution was essentially threefold: violation of civil laws, rebellion, and heresy.[43] It needs reiterating that the great fear of medieval and late medieval society was civil strife or unrest leading to uprisings.

It goes without saying that the general environment of the sixteenth and early seventeenth century was not conducive to religious tolerance, as the Thirty Years' War would abundantly indicate. While Catholic reaction to radical reformers was generally harsher than that of Protestants, this difference consisted only of degrees. It would be unrealistic to expect that religious intolerance of the medieval period would suddenly give way to tolerance in the sixteenth century. Heresy would continue to be viewed as a serious matter, if for no other reason that it was often correlated with civil unrest.

We might summarize the political views and general political orientation of Anabaptists, and "Mennonites" as the enduring expression of Anabaptism, as follows:

- a refusal to participate in the magistracy
- a refusal to take the oath (which typically was to ensure political loyalty)
- a refusal to participate in violence
- an insistence on religious freedom
- a "new economics" (in protest of the neglect of the poor)[44]

Anabaptist and Mennonite refusal to engage in violence or war follows directly from the Anabaptist view of the state and the disciple's separation from the world, not a refusal to serve as a soldier per se. Here we need to remember that there was no conscription; European armies were a mixture of volunteers and mercenaries. In addition, European wars often were religious wars; hence, Anabaptists types viewed this as a denial of the

---

For himself, Melanchthon distinguished between three types of Anabaptists: those who were considered instigators (deserving execution), those who rejected both government and oaths as unchristian (deserving execution), and those who were "simple-minded" and follow error (banishment if they do not recant). See in this regard Oyer, *Lutheran Reformers against Anabaptists*; Blanke, *Brothers in Christ*, 43–71.

43. Clasen, *Anabaptism*, 374.

44. Klassen, *Anabaptism*, 49–62.

Christian faith and the Prince of Peace. Menno Simons summarizes the Anabaptist and Mennonite view of war and coercive force:

> All Christians are commanded to love their enemies; to do good unto those who abuse and persecute them; to give the mantle when the cloak is taken, the other cheek when one is struck. Tell me, how can a Christian defend scripturally retaliation, rebellion, war, striking, slaying, torturing, stealing, robbing and plundering and burning cities and conquering countries?[45]

## Concluding Reflections on the Anabaptist Hermeneutic: The Primacy of Separation and "Non-Violence"

In his *Epistle to Martin Micron* (1556), addressed to a Reformed theologian with whom he had exchanges, Menno mirrors something of a shift on the use of the sword. Up to this point he was ambiguous on its use in a "police function." This ambiguity, for example, can be seen in his 1552 tract *A Pathetic Supplication to All Magistrates*, noted earlier, wherein he writes, "Execute judgment and justice. Assist, against the violent, him that is robbed," while in the very same tract he admonishes, "Do violence to no man."[46] By 1558, in a later edition of *Foundation*, he writes that "Christ is our fortress; patience our weapon of defense; the word of God our sword . . . and iron and metal spears and swords we leave to those who, alas, regard human blood and swine's blood about alike."[47]

But already by 1530, right around the time of Menno's conversion, separatist and pacifist themes among Anabaptists had begun to congeal. Concurrent with this development was a growing theological controversy with non-Anabaptist Protestant reformers, who viewed the Anabaptists' radicalism as being rooted in a theologically deficient understanding of the relationship of the Old Testament to the New. Some of the Reformed leaders, such as Calvin and Bullinger, believed that this deficiency constituted the fulcrum of the debate. Not only a rejection of infant baptism but a cluster of important and related issues hinged on how to interpret the Old and New Testaments, including the Christian's view of the magistrate, the use of the sword, and the public sphere in general. John Roth has perceptively written:

45. Wenger, *Complete Writings*, 555.
46. Wenger, *Complete Writings*, 526.
47. Wenger, *Complete Writings*, 198.

> At stake in the minds of the Reformers was not an abstract schol-
> arly quibble over allegorical or tropological readings of Old Testa-
> ment passages, but rather basic understandings of the sovereignty
> of God, the meaning of the Incarnation, the foundation of Chris-
> tian ethics and the principles of order and authority essential to a
> stable society. Indeed, as subsequent debates would show, virtually
> every distinctive Anabaptist argument—on baptism, the sword,
> the oath, the Christian magistracy, and so on—hinged on their
> insistence that the New Testament was more authoritative than the
> Old in matters of Christian ethics.[48]

The early sixteenth century constitutes something of a remarkable new chapter in reflection on war and coercive force. While Protestant thinkers maintain a dependence on the Augustinian theory that seeks to mediate the tension between two citizenships—the earthly and the heavenly—new developments begin to alter the landscape in dramatic ways. Rethinking the church's relationship to the sword gives rise to an emerging break with medieval life and tradition. In addition, the discovery of the Americas as well as an increasingly fragmented Europe called for attention.

The magisterial reformers held to the conviction that while retribution does not belong to the church, it is not only permitted but commanded of rulers. Thus, two differentiated spheres of authority were understood to co-exist in tension. How that tension was navigated differed considerably from Luther to Calvin and other magisterial reformers; at the same time, a tension was maintained nonetheless. From virtually the beginning, Anabaptists understood these two spheres to be staunchly oppositional; therefore, a Christian could not be a magistrate or punish with the sword. This position was more or less affirmed by the second generation of Anabaptists, the "Mennonites." The Reformed-Anabaptist debate in this regard would come to a head in May and June of 1571 at the Frankenthal Disputation.[49] The Reformed position seemed to expose a weak spot in the general Anabaptist/Mennonite argument: if a Christian could not be permitted to serve in any sort of ruling capacity, the implication is that the office qua office is not of God but of the devil and therefore intrinsically evil. A further inconsistency needed clarification, based on Article VI of the Schleitheim Confession: three times in the opening paragraph of this article the confession states that the sword is "ordained." It is (1) "ordained of God" even when existing "outside the perfection of Christ"; according to the Law (2) the sword was "ordained" for

48. Roth, "Harmonizing the Scriptures," 36.
49. See Yoder, "Frankenthal Debate," 14–35; "Frankenthal Disputation," 116–42.

the purpose of punishment; and the (3) same sword is presently "ordained" and "to be used by the worldly magistrates."[50]

By the end of the sixteenth century Anabaptist types would maintain the stark polarity between Christ and "the world," resulting in an enduring form of separatism and pacifism that, at least in their practical expression, would necessitate a withdrawal from "the world" and be characterized by a narrow sectarianism. Both of these elements, to a large extent, remain 500 years later.

50. This inconsistency, which fails to see the God-ordained necessity of political order due to human nature, largely remains to the present day, as evidenced by one representative Anabaptist historian: "Men will not come to the truth by violence and killing. Only patience and love and gentleness can accomplish that. Violence and killing are rejected in obedience to Christ because they are not the means to be used to achieve Christian ends" (Klaassen, *Anabaptism*, 57).

# Part 4

# Scottish and English Reformers

# Background

THERE WERE POLITICAL ASPECTS of the Protestant Reformation. Resistance as a theo-political doctrine, as set forth by the Protestant reformers, linked with later political thought, which in turn impacted the war for independence in the American colonies. The trajectory of ideas as set forth by John Knox, John Ponet, and Christopher Goodman can be directly traced. For these men, civil disobedience and the responsibility to resist arose in part because of the reign of Mary Tudor, a Roman Catholic monarch. Under her Counter-Reformation measures, many Protestants left England and Scotland for places such as Geneva and Strasbourg where Protestant Reformed teaching was put into practice. Here they interacted with Continental Calvinists and articulated theo-political ideas in response to what they considered to be the lawless rule of the English Queen.[1]

Christian ideas of resistance during the Reformation were closely tied to the varied political circumstances in which the Reformers and their Protestant leaders found themselves. Thus, while all looked to the Bible and their theology for guidance, the immediate political environment, often hostile, in which they lived and wrote, also affected their views. Although there are similarities in core ideas, there are also differences. German Lutherans, Swiss Calvinists (and others), French Huguenots, and Marian exiles all built their political ideas by both drawing from common theology and the diverse political realities of the geographic regions in which they lived. Additionally, there was a maturing of political ideas among groups and individuals as writings were shared, letters exchanged, and political events unfolded. There was growth and development of the idea of resistance.

The idea of resistance was not new in the Reformation era. Reflection on and discussion of the idea had a long medieval heritage wherein

1. For an overview, see Danner, "Resistance and the Ungodly Magistrate," 471–81.

resistance was understood to be a rare exception to the political order and did not extend to the right to reorganize a political and social structure.[2]

What does a mature theory of political resistance entail? It should answer five questions:

- May people ever justly resist established political authority?
- If so, when may they resist?
- By whom shall action be taken?
- How is such resistance to be carried out?
- If the resistance is successful, are the victors then free to reorganize the society after a new image?[3]

These five questions—justification, standard, agent, method, and outcome—were all addressed by the Reformers throughout the sixteenth century and would be expanded in the seventeenth and eighteenth centuries by Christian and non-Christian political theorists.[4]

---

2. Shoenberger, "Development of the Lutheran Theory," 62–63.

3. Shoenberger, "Development of the Lutheran Theory," 61.

4. Among the numerous works available on the subject of the political legacy of the Protestant Reformation, see Witte, *Reformation of Rights; God's Joust, God's Justice.* See also, Berman, *Law and Revolution;* Forster, *Contested Square.*

## CHAPTER 14

# John Knox (1514–1572)

JOHN KNOX, THE SCOTTISH reformer, was born at Haddington, near Edinburgh, around the year 1514. He studied at St. Andrews University and later came under the influence of the Protestant preacher George Wishart, who may have been instrumental in his conversion. He served in his early years as Wishart's bodyguard, bearing a two-handed sword in order to defend him. Following the martyrdom of Wishart, Knox spent nineteen months as a French galley slave. In subsequent years he served as a chaplain to Edward VI and later wrote his *First Blast of the Trumpet against the Monstrous Regiment of Women*, directing it at the queen of England, Mary Tudor, in which he expressed his opposition to women rulers.[1] In his reform program for the Scottish church he presented himself not only as a pastor but also a prophet of God.[2] He wrote with the help of others the foundational documents of the Church of Scotland—the *Scots Confession* (1560), the *Book of Discipline* (1561), and the *Book of Common Order* (1564).

Knox's writings fill six volumes. His political thought in several senses stood in continuity with elements of medieval teaching and with perspectives set forth by Lutheran and Reformed theologians of his time.[3] He embraced radical views, however, in his commitment to private war and tyrannicide on the part of the common man.

Knox presented his reforming agenda for the church in Scotland in his *Letter to the Commonalty* (1558), written to the common people of Scotland

1. de Abreu, "John Knox," 169, draws attention to the fact that it was a commonplace position in the sixteenth century that "women were unfit and ineligible to bear rule over kingdoms."

2. Kyle, "Prophet of God," 85–101; Johnson and McGoldrick, "Prophet in Scotland," 76–86.

3. Greaves, "John Knox," 1–36.

from Geneva. Knox drew attention to the problems that existed in Scotland, namely false religion and the tyranny of political and church leaders.[4] He captured both of these concerns in this assertion: "Your princes and rulers are criminal with your bishops of all idolatry committed, and of all the innocent blood that is shed for the testimony of Christ's truth."[5]

The letter went on to maintain that both the magistrate and the common man had an obligation to seek the reformation of the church. The king along with "lords, rulers and powers" were to provide "true preachers" and "expel such as under the names of pastors devour and destroy the flock."[6] If the magistrates refused to do this, the people were to take action. "You may provide true teachers for yourselves," Knox wrote, "be it in your cities, towns, or villages." He then added, "Them you may maintain and defend against all that shall persecute them."[7]

Knox here asserted that the common people were not only able to support the clergy that they had selected for themselves, but they could also take up arms and defend them against government persecution. In a sense, Knox was advocating the role that he had once had as the sword-wielding bodyguard of the minister George Wishart. It was certainly counsel that many would find problematic in light of Jesus' statement regarding the sword-swinging activity of Peter who as a private individual was seeking to defend Jesus from his enemies in the Garden of Gethsemane: "Put your sword back into its place; for all those who take up the sword shall perish by the sword" (Matt 26:52).

With respect to the issue of idolatry, Knox stood in continuity with medieval perspectives on the crime of heresy.[8] The sword, he believed, is committed to the magistrate to execute judicial punishment upon those who are guilty of religious criminality. Scotland in his view was in a covenant relationship with God, just as ancient Israel had been. Idolaters were to be put to death in Israel, and the same thing was to be done in

---

4. Kyle, "Knox, John," 209, asserts, "His greatest anxiety was idolatry, which he equated with Catholicism; to be a Catholic was to be an idolater. The fight against the 'idolatrous' Mass so dominated his thinking that virtually no major area of his thought was free from it. Increasingly, Knox developed his anti-idolatry theme in a political context and as a spring-board to resistance against political authority."

5. Knox, *On Rebellion*, 124–25.

6. Knox, *On Rebellion*, 123.

7. Knox, *On Rebellion*, 123.

8. See, for example, Aquinas's *Summa Theologica* 2a2ae.11.3.

sixteenth-century Scotland.[9] In *An Admonition or Warning* (1554), Knox called on the civil magistrates to slay idolaters. On this issue, Knox was very much a man of his time. Calvin, Beza, Bullinger, and others in the Reformed community held similar views.[10]

Knox, in continuity with the Lutheran Magdeburg Confession (1550) and Reformed thinking as well, affirmed that inferior magistrates had the right to engage in a defensive war against monarchical tyranny. They were authorized to take up arms against the armies of the prince who would seek to exterminate them. Knox considered the Scottish nobility to be the magistrates who were responsible for resisting a tyrannical monarch. The Scottish nobles had private armies and within their own areas they had rights of jurisdiction. In his letter to the nobility of Scotland in 1557, Knox wrote about the oppression of their subjects. He declared, "You ought to hazard your own lives, be it against kings or emperors for their deliverance." He added, "Your office and duty" is "to deliver your subjects . . . from all violence and oppression."[11]

Knox even contended that inferior magistrates had the responsibility of removing a tyrannical sovereign. In *The First Blast of the Trumpet against the Monstrous Regiment of Women* (1558), Knox maintained that inferior magistrates were to depose and execute a tyrannical monarch. In the thinking of Theodore Beza, Calvin's successor in Geneva, inferior magistrates could only wage a defensive war, endeavoring to protect their people from harm at the hands of the tyrant. Knox stood more in line with the Strasbourg theologian Martin Bucer who argued in his *Explication of the Four Gospels* that inferior magistrates (self-governing city authorities and territorial princes) held the power of the sword not only to defend their people against a godless tyrant who might fall upon them, but also had the right to remove him by force of arms.

Knox then believed that the inferior magistrates provided an institutional remedy for tyranny. He also espoused the doctrine of the servant avenger. He agreed with Calvin that there are men who are "sent by God's

9. Chadwick, "John Knox and Revolution," 258, refers to Knox's view that "idolaters should be liable to . . . execution." Knox affirmed that this "was a commandment of God, whatever his feelings."

10. The doctrine that the crime of heresy merited capital punishment was imbedded in the Justinian Code, which had been part of the civil law of Europe for one thousand years.

11. Knox, *Works of John Knox*, 1:272.

lawful calling to carry out such acts, in taking up arms against kings."[12] Knox expressed the same sentiment in his *Faithful Admonition* (1554). He blasted Mary Tudor as a false and deceitful monarch and called upon God to provide a servant avenger—a Phinehas, Elijah, or Jehu—to overthrow the Catholic regime.[13]

Knox went beyond the theological mainstream in his private resistance theory, differing from Calvin, Bullinger, and Vermigli on this issue. The private person, according to Calvin, is not allowed to initiate active resistance by taking up arms against the tyrant. Calvin issued this warning to private individuals: "If the correction of unbridled despotism is the Lord's to avenge, let us not at once think that it is entrusted to us, to whom no command has been given except to obey and suffer."[14] Calvin added, "A private individual who lays his hand upon a tyrant is openly condemned by the heavenly judge."[15] Heinrich Bullinger likewise forbade the killing of a tyrant by a private person. Appealing to the Old Testament historical narrative of Saul in 1 Samuel, Bullinger called attention to the fact that David "spared the tyrant."[16] Peter Martyr Vermigli took the same position and provided no loophole for private resistance: "Though also it may be lawful to resist tyrants which assail a kingdom, yet when they have obtained the same and also do bear rule, it seems not to belong unto private men to put them down."[17]

Knox dissented from the teaching of Calvin, Bullinger, and Vermigli and accepted the idea that any private individual may use violence and take up arms against a tyrannical government. He believed that the punishment of tyranny is a duty that is required of the whole people—of even the common man, the private individual.[18]

This position fits in with the events of 1546 in which a group of Protestants assassinated Cardinal David Beaton of St. Andrews in retaliation for his execution of George Wishart on the charge of heresy. Knox did not participate in the assassination, but he joined the conspirators in the castle of St. Andrews, the previous residence of the Cardinal. Knox, in other words,

---

12. John Calvin made this statement in *Institutes* 4.20.30.

13. Knox, *Works of John Knox*, 3:293–300, 309, 312, 325–26.

14. Calvin, *Institutes* 4.20.31.

15. Calvin, *Institutes* 3.10.6.

16. Bullinger, *Decades of Henry Bullinger*, 316.

17. I have provided contemporary spelling for this quotation in Vermigli, *Common Places*, 319.

18. Kelly, *Emergence of Liberty*, 56.

had no problem in associating himself with individuals who had eliminated an ecclesiastical tyrant. Knox, in fact, condoned the cardinal's murder as God's vengeance. It appears that Knox justified the action of the conspirators, regarding it as similar to tyrannicide.[19]

Knox's teaching at this point was radical not only in relationship to the views of his Reformed colleagues, but also in terms of the doctrine of the medieval church, which limited the right of war to sovereign princes.[20] Knox's view was also extreme in comparison to the ancient feudal right of private war. In that arrangement, any person of military status had the right to levy war upon his enemies for a just cause.[21] It should be noted that Knox was not merely reverting back to the old feudal principle of legitimate private war. For Knox, the right of private war became the duty of private war for all men against the tyrant—not only the nobility, but the common man as well.

Medieval political thought, along with Lutheran and Reformed ideas, informed Knox's thinking on war. The most influential source for his ideas, however, was the Old Testament. He saw little distinction between Old and New Testaments. For him, the Old Testament history of Israel was being played out once again in Scotland. He was a prophet of God, and Scotland was Israel. This principle of interpretation helps to explain the points in his political theory that move in a radical direction.

## John Knox, "Letter to the Commonalty."

In *On Rebellion*, edited by Roger A. Mason, 124–26. Cambridge Texts in the History of Political Thought. Cambridge: Cambridge University Press, 1994. Used by permission.

It will not excuse you (dear Brethren) in the presence of God, neither yet will it avail you in the day of His visitation, to say: 'We were but simple subjects; we could not redress the faults and crimes of our rulers, bishops and clergy.

---

19. Klempa, "Patrick Hamilton and John Knox," 41.

20. Wormwald, "Knox, John," 380, affirms that Knox set forth "resistance theory at its most radical, for it looked beyond the nobility . . . to the commonalty." She adds, "Only Christopher Goodman, in his *Superior Powers Ought to Be Obeyed*, came anywhere close to Knox in advancing such theory."

21. The medieval church opposed this principle with some success. Over time, the right of private war ceased to operate. Continual opposition and censure by the church had had an effect.

We called for reformation, and wished for the same, but lords' brethren were bishops, their sons were abbots, and the friends of great men had the possession of the church, and so were we compelled to give obedience to all that they demanded. These vain excuses, I say, will nothing avail you in the presence of God who requireth no less of the subjects than of the rulers, that they decline from evil and that they do good, that they abstain from idolatry, superstition, blasphemy, murder and other such horrible crimes which His law forbiddeth and yet nonetheless are openly committed and maliciously defended in that miserable realm.

And if ye think that ye are innocent because ye are not the chief authors of such iniquity, ye are utterly deceived. For God doth not only punish the chief offenders, but with them doth He damn the consenters to iniquity; and all are judged to consent that knowing impiety committed give no testimony that the same displeaseth them. To speak this matter more plain, as your princes and rulers are criminal with your bishops of all idolatry committed, and of all the innocent blood that is shed for the testimony of Christ's truth, and that because they maintain them in their tyranny, so are you (I mean so many of you as give no plain confession to the contrary) criminal and guilty with your princes and rulers of the same crimes, because ye assist and maintain your princes in their blind rage and give no declaration that their tyranny displeaseth you.

This doctrine I know is strange to the blind world, but the verity of it hath been declared in all notable punishments from the beginning. When the original world perished by water, when Sodom and Gomorrah were consumed by fire, and finally when Jerusalem was horribly destroyed, doth any man think that all were alike wicked before the world? Evident it is that they were not if they shall be judged according to their external facts. For some were young and could not be oppressors, neither yet could defile themselves with unnatural and beastly lusts; some were pitiful and gentle of nature and did not thirst for the blood of Christ nor of His Apostles. But did any escape the plagues and vengeance which did apprehend the multitude? Let the Scriptures witness and the histories be considered, which plainly do testify that by the waters all flesh in earth at that time did perish (Noah and his family reserved), that none escaped in Sodom and in the other cities adjacent except Lot and his two daughters. And evident it is that in that famous city Jerusalem, in that last and horrible destruction of the same, none escaped God's vengeance except so many as before were dispersed. And what is the cause of this severity, seeing that all were not alike offenders?

Let flesh cease to dispute with God and let all man by these examples learn betimes to flee and avoid the society and company of the proud contemners of God if that they list not to be partakers of their plagues.

The cause is evident if we can be subject without grudging to God's judgments which in themselves are most holy and just. For in the original world none was found that either did resist tyranny and oppression that universally was used either yet that earnestly reprehended the same. In Sodom was none found that did againstand that furious and beastly multitude that did compass about and besiege the house of Lot. None would believe Lot that the city should be destroyed. And finally in Jerusalem was none found that studied to repress the tyranny of the priests who were conjured against Christ and His Evangel, but all fainted (I except ever such as gave witness with their blood or their flying that such impiety displeased them), all kept silence, by the which all approved iniquity and joined hands with the tyrants, and so were all arrayed and set as it had been in one battle against the Omnipotent and against His Son Christ Jesus. For whosoever gathereth not with Christ in the day of His harvest is judged to scatter. And therefore of one vengeance temporal were they all partakers.

Which thing, as before I have touched, ought to move you to the deep consideration of your duties in these last and most perilous times. The iniquity of your bishops is more than manifest; their filthy lives infect the air; the innocent blood which they shed crieth vengeance in the ears of God; the idolatry and abomination which openly they commit and without punishment maintain doth corrupt and defile the whole land; and none amongst you doth unfeignedly study for any redress of such enormities. Will God in this behalf hold you as innocents? Be not deceived, dear Brethren. God hath punished not only proud tyrants, filthy persons and cruel murderers, but also such as with them did draw the yoke of iniquity, was it by flattering their offences, obeying their injust commandments or in winking at their manifest iniquity. All such, I say, hath God once punished with the chief offenders. Be ye assured, Brethren, that as He is immutable of nature, so will He not pardon in you that which so severely He hath punished in others; and now the less, because He hath plainly admonished you of the dangers to come and hath offered you His mercy before He pour forth His wrath and displeasure upon the inobedient.

## CHAPTER 15

# John Ponet (1514–1556)

JOHN PONET WAS A Cambridge-educated minister who became the Bishop of Winchester and also the Bishop of Rochester, as well as a chaplain to Thomas Cranmer, Archbishop of Canterbury. When Mary I came to the throne in England, Ponet became one of the Marian exiles and fled England. He returned briefly to participate in an uprising known as "Wyatt's Rebellion," and then escaped again going to Strasbourg.[1] There, in 1556, he published *A Shorte Treatise on Politike Power,* in which he argued for resistance, including tyrannicide by private persons, to blasphemous tyrants in both the church and the commonwealth. "No other English dignitary of the time, ecclesiastical or non-ecclesiastical, so blatantly repudiated the absolute right of the king and the absolute wrong of civil rebellion."[2] Conscience, guided by natural law and the Bible, was to be the source for determining political action when there was political and religious oppression.[3] For Ponet, absolute political authority rests not in the hereditary monarch, the collective will of the people, or parliamentary law, but, rather, in the conscience of the individual seeking to follow God's commandments and Scripture. Although some Protestants during Ponet's era argued the right of the nobility to remove an unfaithful tryant, Ponet pushes this right down to the common people and even the individual commoner.

There is little evidence for personal ties between Knox and Ponet, but they shared ideas and distress after the death of Edward VI and the rise of

1. See Thorp, "Religion and the Wyatt Rebellion," 363–80.

2. O'Donovan, *Theology of Law and Authority,* 96.

3. On natural law and resistance during this era, see VanDrunen, "Use of Natural Law," 143–67.

Mary I. However, there is no indication that Knox either relied on or read Ponet's work, although he was probably aware of Ponet's views.[4]

## Christopher Goodman (1520–1603)

A leading member of John Knox's Geneva congregation and a contributor to the Geneva Bible while exiled under Queen Mary, English Puritan and Oxford professor Christopher Goodman was one of the most important proponents of the idea that if rulers were oppressive then they were no longer legitimate rulers.[5] In January 1558, Goodman published *How Superior Powers Ought to be Obeyed*, a work stemming from a sermon he preached on Acts 5:29. In this work he praised the efforts of Sir Thomas Wyatt who had led "Wyatt's Rebellion" in England and argued that if effective resistance cannot be mustered against a tyrant, then exile is the only option for the Christian.[6] Richard Greaves notes of Goodman's ideas, "Tyrants forfeited their right to rule by oppressing their subjects and blaspheming God. By acting in this manner, a tyrant dissolved the contractual bonds with the people, who thereupon no longer owed him political submission. In fact, to submit to an ungodly sovereign was tantamount to rebellion against God himself."[7]

Like Knox and others, Goodman appealed to Old Testament scripture and history to advocate rebellion, resistance, or exile to ungodly or idolatrous monarchs. He also found grounds for revolution in natural law.

While in exile, Goodman first went to Basel and then Strasbourg, where he became friends with Peter Martyr Vermigli (1499–1562), an Italian theologian and reformer who had fled Italy because of his preaching and views. Shortly thereafter, Goodman went to Geneva where his ideas on civil disobedience matured as he ministered alongside John Knox.

Much of Goodman's thought on disobedience and resistance was tied to his understanding of the Ten Commandments and its ongoing applicability. Witte summarizes these ideas as follows:

> This was Goodman's rights formula: the rights and liberties that God gives to each person as his or her "inalienable" "possession" are set out in the Decalogue. Nothing that God requires in the

4. Greaves, *Theology and Revolution*, 152.

5. On the Geneva Bible and the political environment of the day, see Craig, "Geneva Bible," 40–49; Greaves, "Traditionalism," 94–109.

6. Danner, "Christopher Goodman," 64.

7. Greaves, "Concepts of Political Obedience," 25–26.

Decalogue may the magistrate forbid. Nothing that God forbids in the Decalogue may the magistrate require. A person thus has the inalienable right to "observe the Sabbath Day and keep it holy" and "to labor six days and to rest on the Sabbath." A person has the inalienable right to "honor [his or her] father and mother so that [their] days may be long in the land the Lord your God has given [them]." A person has the inalienable right to proper religious worship and speech—to be free from laws commanding him to worship false gods, to maintain graven images, to swear false oaths, or otherwise take the name of God in vain. A person has the inalienable right to life (freedom from killing), to property (freedom from stealing), to marital integrity (freedom from adultery), and to reputation and fair process (freedom from false testimony). A person has the right to be free from having his family, household, and possessions coveted by others. If the magistrate requires or condones conduct contrary to this formula, the magistrate is violating each subject's rights and liberties. To do so is to practice tyranny and to invite resistance for God's sake. This was a considerably more expansive notion of liberties and rights than either Calvin or [Theodore] Beza had countenanced to date.[8]

Goodman's influential thought shows that Reformers were considering many aspects of law and politics, including rights and responsibilities of both those who govern and those who are governed. In the thought of these men and throughout the Reformation we can see development of the idea of resistance from an abnormal to a normal circumstance. The idea shifts from an action that, in the midst of tyranny, is permitted for a few (nobility) to an action that is required of any Christian. It moves from that which is optional to that which is mandatory.

Both Goodman and Knox appealed to natural law, the Old Testament, and the New Testament, but Goodman's ideas and publications predated those of Knox.[9] Although both men knew and consulted with each other, Goodman's ideas were earlier and showed more independence from other reformers such as John Calvin and Henirich Bullinger.

Throughout the mid-sixteenth century religious and political dissent in Scotland, England, and Europe was fueled by the writings and sermons of leaders such as Knox, Ponet, and Goodman. They drew from each other as well as earlier Christian writers and other contemporaries like the

8. Witte, *Reformation of Rights,* 121–22.

9. On the reliance on the Old Testament in both Ponet and Goodman, see Wollman, "Biblical Justification for Resistance," 29–41.

Swiss-born theologian Pierre Viret (1511–1571), whose influence among Protestants in France was enormous.[10]

In France, political and religious circumstances were quite different than in England. Political theory followed a separate history that included the rise of the Huguenots, the French Wars of Religion (1562–1598), the St. Bartholomew's Day Massacre (August 23, 1572), and the Edict of Nantes (1598) in which Protestants were granted substantial civil rights. Also included in the Edict was the famous phrase *cuius regio, eius religio* ("Whose realm, his religion").[11] The Edict was a step toward religious toleration of some Protestants, but it was only a beginning that would not be finalized for French Calvinists until the 1648 Treaty of Westphalia.

## Elizabethan England and Political Disobedience

After the death of Mary Tudor, her half-sister Elizabeth I (1533–1603, r. 1558–1603) ascended to the throne of England and ruled forty-five years as a very popular monarch, returning the country to Protestant rule and overseeing the rise of England as one of the most powerful and prosperous countries of the age. Richard Greaves writes concerning ideas of disobedience during this era:

> In the Elizabethan era there was a striking reversal of political theory with respect to the concept of active resistance. Protestant writers retreated from the radical new theory of tyrannicide and returned to the more quiescent position worked out in the early Tudor period. Neither the Calvinist doctrine of the right of lesser magistrates to overthrow tyranny and idolatry nor the assertion of this right by the common people (as espoused by Knox, John Ponet, and Christopher Goodman) was openly advocated by English Protestants, though it is possible that some of them found the Calvinist position acceptable. For their part, the English Catholics who accepted the validity of active resistance did not look for their inspiration to the Marian exiles but reflected a medieval tradition that included such theorists as Manegold of

10. See Kingdon, "Political Resistance of the Calvinists," 220–33; Linder, "Pierre Viret," 125–37.

11. On the many political and religious issues in France in this period, see Gray, *French Huguenots*. For an overview of religious conflict throughout Europe during these years, see Kaplan, *Divided by Faith*.

Lautenbach, John of Salisbury, William of Ockham, Marsilius of Padua, and Jean Gerson.[12]

Ideas of disobedience, resistance, and tyrannicide receded after Elizabeth started to reign. The next centuries brought new political tensions and conflict to the British Isles, but some of the ideas of the Marian exiles remained and the teachings of these men set the stage for other religious and non-religious thinkers. Danner observes:

> It should be clear that the English Protestant tradition was unique in advocating revolution by civil resistance and tyrannicide and that Christopher Goodman was a leading exponent of this ethos. Perhaps the significance and uniqueness of the English political scene during the Tudor period called for extraordinary and unique responses by Puritans radicalized by exile. Upon Elizabeth's accession, however, radicals like Goodman acquiesced to the system and sought legal, parliamentary revolution. Violent revolution lost its significance in Elizabeth's via media, and Puritans waited for openings, some of which came; more were created by persistent divines who no longer worried about Spanish invasion. Elizabeth sailed a solid political ship; Puritans found her vulnerable where they operated best—in preaching, organizing, pamphleteering, and prophesying. Unlike the chaotic times during Mary's reign, which produced radical political theories, during the reign of Elizabeth revolution would first be a change of heart.[13]

After Elizabeth's reign, things were different. In 1641, during the reign of Charles I, civil war erupted between parliamentarians and royalists, lasting until 1649 when Oliver Cromwell became Lord Protector (1653–1658). Ultimately, in 1689 (the "Glorious Revolution") there arose the British parliamentary democracy wherein the concept of sovereignty passed from power that was held by the monarch to power held in Parliament.

In the ensuing years a much stronger England would face the challenge of independence from its colonies in the New World. However, the strands of the ideology for that revolution were to be found in concepts espoused in the preceding years—much of it during the Reformation. Religious and non-religious ideas, such as those of Samuel Rutherford and John Locke (and others) coalesced into the political philosophy of American colonists, igniting the American Revolution.

---

12. Greaves, "Concepts of Political Obedience," 23.

13. Danner, "Christopher Goodman," 73.

# Bibliography

Aquinas, Thomas. *Summa Theologica.* 5 vols. Allen, TX: Christian Classics, 1948.

Augustine. "Reply to Faustus the Manichaean." In *Nicene and Post-Nicene Fathers, Series 1,* edited by Philip Schaff, 155–345. Vol. 4. Peabody, MA: Hendrickson, 1994.

Bailyn, Bernard. *The Ideological Origins of the American Revolution.* Enlarged ed. Cambridge, MA: Harvard University Press, 1992.

Bainton, Roland. "The Left Wing of the Reformation." *Journal of Religion* 21.2 (1947) 124–34.

Bak, Janos. *The German Peasant's War of 1525.* New York: Routledge, 1976.

Baker, A. G., ed. *A Short History of Christianity.* Chicago: University of Chicago Press, 1940.

Baker, J. Wayne. "Church, State, and Dissent: The Crisis of the Swiss Reformation, 1531–1536." *Church History* 57 (1988) 135–52.

———. "The Covenantal Basis for the Development of Swiss Political Federalism: 1291–1848." *Publius* 23 (1993) 19–41.

———. "Covenant and Community in the Thought of Heinrich Bullinger." In *The Covenant Connection: From Federal Theology to Modern Federalism,* edited by Daniel J. Elazar and John Kincaid, 15–29. London, MD: Lexington, 2000.

———. "Erastianism in England: The Zürich Connection." In *Die Zürcher Reformation: Ausstrahlunger und Rückwirkungen,* 327–49. Bern: Peter Lang, 2001.

Bardolph, Richard. "Some Reflections on Civil Disobedience." *Concordia Theological Monthly* 38.6 (1967) 381.

Baschera, Luca. "Independent Yet Harmonious: Some Remarks on the Relationship between the Theology of Peter Martyr Vermigli (1499–1562) and John Calvin." *Church History and Religious Culture* 91 (2011) 43–57.

Baumgartner, Frederic J. *France in the Sixteenth Century.* New York: St. Martin's, 1995.

———. *Henry II: King of France, 1547–1559.* Durham, NC: Duke University Press, 1988.

Baylor, Michael G., ed. *The Radical Reformation.* Cambridge Texts in the History of Political Thought. Cambridge, UK: Cambridge University Press, 1991.

———. *Revelation and Revolution: Basic Writings of Thomas Müntzer.* Bethlehem, PA: Lehigh University Press, 1993.

Bender, Harold S. "A Brief Biography of Menno Simons." In *The Complete Writings of Menno Simons,* edited by John C. Wenger, 3–29. Scottdale, PA: Mennonite Publishing House, 1956.

———. "Conrad Grebel." In *The Mennonite Encyclopedia: A Comprehensive Reference Work on the Anabaptist-Mennonite Movement*, edited by Harold S. Bender, et al., 566–75. Vol. 2. Scottdale, PA: Mennonite Publishing House, 1952.

———. "Conrad Grebel, the Founder of Swiss Anabaptism." *Church History* 7.2 (1938) 157–58.

———. "Swiss Brethren." In *The Mennonite Encyclopedia: A Comprehensive Reference Work on the Anabaptist-Mennonite Movement*, edited by Harold S. Bender, et al., 669–71. Vol. 4. Scottdale, PA: Mennonite Publishing House, 1969.

Bender, Harold S., et al., eds. *The Mennonite Encyclopedia: A Comprehensive Reference Work on the Anabaptist-Mennonite Movement*. Vol. 3. Scottdale, PA: Mennonite Publishing House, 1957.

Berman, Harold J. "Conscience and Law: The Lutheran Reformation and the Western Legal Tradition." *Journal of Law and Religion* 5.1 (1987) 177–202.

———. *Faith and Order: The Reconciliation of Law and Religion*. Grand Rapids: Eerdmans, 1993.

———. *Law and Revolution: The Formation of the Western Legal Tradition*. Cambridge, MA: Harvard University Press, 1983.

———. *Law and Revolution II: The Impact of the Protestant Reformations on the Western Legal Tradition*. Cambridge, MA: Havard University Press, 2003.

Betts, R. R. "Some Political Ideas of the Early Czech Reformers." *The Slavonic and East European Review* 31.76 (1952) 20–35.

Beza, Theodore. *Concerning the Rights of Rulers over Their Subjects and the Duty of Subjects towards Their Rulers*. Translated by Henri-Louis Gonin. Capetown and Pretoria: HAUM, 1956.

———. "Right of Magistrates." In *Constitutionalism and Resistance in the Sixteenth Century*. Translated by Julian H. Franklin. New York: Pegasus, 1969.

———. *Du droit des magistrat*. Edited by Robert M. Kingdon. Les classiques de la pensée politique 7. Geneva: Librairie Droz, 1970.

Biel, Pamela. "Heinrich Bullinger's Death and Testament: A Well-Planned Departure." *Sixteenth Century Journal* 22 (1991) 3–14.

Biesecker-Mast, Gerald. "Anabaptist Separation and Arguments Against the Sword in the Schleitheim Brotherly Union." *Mennonite Quarterly Review* 74 (2000) 381–402.

Birnbaum, Norman. "The Zwinglian Reformation in Zurich." *Archives de sociologie des religions* 8 (1959) 15–30.

Blanke, Fritz. *Brothers in Christ*. Scottdale, PA: Herald, 1961.

Blickle, Peter. *The Revolution of 1525: The German Peasants' War from a New Perspective*. Translated by Thomas A. Brady. Baltimore: John Hopkins University Press, 1985.

Bowman, Glen. "Early Calvinist Resistance Theory: New Perspectives on an Old Label." *Journal of Law and Religion* 23.1 (2008) 309–19.

Bradstock, Andrew. "Thomas Müntzer: Mystic and Apocalyptic Revolutionary?" *Reformation Journal* 5.1 (2000) 27–53.

Brauer, Jerald C. "The Rule of the Saints in American Politics." *Church History* 27 (1958) 240–55.

Brecht, Martin. *Ordnung und Abgrenzung der Reformation 1521–1532*. Vol. 2 of *Martin Luther*. Stuttgart: Calwer Verlag, 1986.

Britz, Dolf. "Politics and Social Life." In *The Calvin Handbook*, edited by Herman J. Selderhuis, 437–48. Grand Rapids: Eerdmans, 2009.

Bubenheimer, Ulrich. "Thomas Müntzer's Wittenberger Studienzeit." *Zeitschrift für Kirchengeschichte* 99 (1988) 168–211.

Bullinger, Heinrich. *The Decades of Henry Bullinger*. Edited by Thomas Harding. 1849. Reprint, New York: Johnson Reprint, 1968.

———. "Sermon 6 of the Second Decade." In *The Decades of Henry Bullinger*, edited by Thomas Harding, 298–322. 1849. Reprint, New York: Johnson Reprint, 1968.

———. "Sermon 9 of the Second Decade." In *The Decades of Henry Bullinger*, edited by Thomas Harding, 370–93. 1849. Reprint, New York: Johnson Reprint, 1968.

Burns, J. H., with Mark Goldie, eds. *The Cambridge History of Political Thought, 1450–1700*. Cambridge, UK: Cambridge University Press, 1991.

Calvin, John. *Commentaries*. 22 vols. Grand Rapids: Baker, 1979.

———. *Institutes of the Christian Religion*. translated by Ford Lewis Battles. Philadelphia: Westminster, 1960.

———. *The Register of the Company of Pastors in the Time of Calvin*. Translated by Philip E. Hughes. Grand Rapids: Eerdmans, 1966.

———. *Sermons on 2 Samuel*. Translated by Douglas F. Kelly. Edinburgh: Banner of Truth, 1992.

———. *Sermons on Deuteronomy*. Translated by Arthur Golding. Edinburgh: Banner of Truth, 1987.

Carty, Jarrett A. *God and Government: Martin Luther's Political Thought*. Montreal: McGill-Queens University Press, 2017.

Chadwick, W. Owen. "John Knox and Revolution." *Andover Newton Quarterly* 15 (1975) 258.

Charles, J. Daryl, and Timothy J. Demy. *War, Peace, and Christianity: Questions and Answers from a Just-War Perspective*. Westchester, IL: Crossway, 2010.

Chenevière, Marc. "Did Calvin Advocate Theocracy?" *Evangelical Quarterly* 9 (1937) 108–15.

Clasen, Claus-Peter. *Anabaptism: A Social History, 1525–1618*. Ithaca/London: Cornell University Press, 1972.

Coffey, John. *Political Religion and the British Revolutions: The Mind of Samuel Rutherford*. Cambridge, UK: Cambridge University Press, 1997.

Cohn, Henry J. "Anticlericalism in the German Peasants' War 1525." *Past & Present* 83 (1979) 3–31.

Cohn, Norman. *The Pursuit of the Millennium: Revolutionary Millenarians and Mystical Anarchists of the Middle Ages*. Rev. ed. New York: Oxford University Press, 1970.

Colish, Marcia L. *Medieval Foundations of the Western Intellectual Tradition 400–1400*. New Haven: Yale University Press, 1997.

Corey, David D. "Luther and the Just War Tradition." *Political Theology* 12 (2011) 305–28.

Craig, Hardin, Jr. "The Geneva Bible as a Political Document." *The Pacific Historical Review* 7.1 (1938) 40–49.

Danner, Dan G. "Christopher Goodman and the English Protestant Tradition of Civil Disobedience." *Sixteenth Century Journal* 8.3 (1977) 61–73.

———. "Resistance and the Ungodly Magistrate in the Sixteenth Century: The Marian Exiles." *Journal of the American Academy of Religion* 49.3 (1981) 471–81.

Davies, Norman. *Europe*. Oxford: Oxford University Press, 1996.

Davis, Paul K. *Encyclopedia of Invasions and Conquests from Ancient Times to the Present*. London: W. W. Norton and Co., 1996.

de Abreu, Maria Zina Gonçalves. "John Knox: Gynaecocracy, 'The Monstrous Empire of Women.'" *Reformation and Renaissance Review* 5.2 (2003) 166–87.

de Bonnechose, Émile. *Letters of John Huss, Written During His Exile and Imprisonment, with Martin Luther's Preface.* Translated by Campbell Mackenzie. Edinburgh: William Whyte & Co. 1846.

de Kroon, Marjin. "Martin Bucer and the Problem of Tolerance." *Sixteenth Century Journal* 19.2 (1988) 157–68.

Depperman, Klaus et al. "From Monogenesis to Polygenesis: The Historical Discussion of Anabaptist Origins." *Mennonite Quarterly Review* 49 (1975) 83–102.

Dickens, A. G., and John M. Tonkin. *The Reformation in Historical Thought.* Cambridge, MA: Harvard University Press, 1985.

Donnelly, John Patrick. *Calvinism and Scholasticism in Vermigli's Doctrine of Man and Grace.* Leiden: Brill, 1976.

———. "Italian Influences on the Development of Calvinist Scholasticism." *Sixteenth Century Journal* 7 (1976) 81–101.

———. "Peter Martyr Vermigli's Political Ethics." In *Peter Martyr Vermigli: Humanism, Republicanism, Reformation,* edited by Emidio Campi, 59–66. Geneva: Droz, 2002.

Edwards, Mark U. *Luther's Last Battles: Politics and Polemics, 1531–1546.* Leiden: Brill, 1983.

Eijnatten, Joris van. "'Religionis Causa': Moral Theology and the Concept of Holy War in the Dutch Republic." *Journal of Religious Ethics* 34 (2006) 609–35.

Eire, Carlos M. N. *Reformations: The Early-Modern World, 1450–1650.* New Haven/ London: Yale University Press, 2016.

Fast, Heinold. "Conrad Grebel: The Covenant on the Cross." In *Profiles of Radical Reformers: Biographical Sketches from Thomas Müntzer to Paracelsus,* edited by Hans-Jürgen Goertz, 118–31. Scottdale/Kitchener, ONT: Herald, 1982.

———, ed. *Der linke Flügel der Reformation.* Bremen: Schünemann, 1962.

Fernandez, Jose A. "Erasmus on the Just War." *Journal of the History of Ideas* 2 (1973) 209–26.

Forster, Greg. *The Contested Square: The Crisis of Christianity and Politics.* Downers Grove, IL: InterVarsity, 2008.

Foster, Herbert D. "International Calvinism through Locke and the Revolution of 1688." *American Historical Review* 32.3 (1927) 475–99.

Franz, Günther. *Der deutsche Bauernkrieg.* 10th ed. Darmstadt: Wissenschaftliche Buchgesellschaft, 1975.

Friedmann, Robert. *The Theology of Anabaptism: An Interpretation.* Scottsdale/Kitchener, ONT: Herald, 1973.

Fuchs, Walter Peter. *Akten zur Geschichte des Bauernkriegs in Mitteldeutschland II.* Jena: Scientia Verlag, 1964.

Fudge, Thomas A. "Hus, Jan." In *The Oxford Encyclopedia of the Reformation,* edited by Hans J. Hillerbrand, 277. Vol. 2. New York: Oxford University Press, 1996.

———. *The Memory and Motivation of Jan Hus, Medieval Priest and Martyr.* Turnhout: Brepols, 2013.

Gäbler, Ulrich. "Huldrych Zwingli and His City of Zurich." *Andrews University Seminary Studies* 23.2 (1985) 143–60.

Goertz, Hans-Jürgen. *The Anabaptists.* Translated by Trevor Johnson. Christianity and Society in the Modern World. New York: Routledge, 1996.

————. *Pfaffenhaus und gross Geschrei: Die reformatorischen Bewegungen in Deutschland 1517–1529*. Munich: Beck, 1987.

————, ed. *Profiles of Radical Reformers: Biographical Sketches from Thomas Müntzer to Paracelsus*. Scottdale/Kitchener, ONT: Herald, 1982.

————. *Thomas Müntzer; Apocaplyptic Mystic and Revolutionary*. Translated by Jocelyn Jacquiery. Edited by Peter Matheson. Edinburgh: T&T Clark, 1993.

Gonçalves de Abreu, Maria Zina. "John Knox: Gynaecocracy, 'The Monstrous Empire of Women.'" *Reformation and Renaissance Review* 5 (2003) 166–87.

Gordon, Bruce. *The Swiss Reformation*. Manchester, UK: Manchester University Press, 2002.

Gosselin, Edward A. "David in *Tempore Belli*: Beza's David in the Service of the Huguenots." *Sixteenth Century Journal* 7 (1976) 31–54.

Gray, Janet Glenn. *The French Huguenots: Anatomy of Courage*. Grand Rapids: Baker, 1981.

Greaves, Richard L. "Concepts of Political Obedience in Late Tudor England: Conflicting Perspectives." *Journal of British Studies* 22.1 (1982) xx.

————. "John Knox, the Reformed Tradition, and the Development of Resistance Theory." *Journal of Modern History* 48.3 (1976) 1–36.

————. "Radicals, Rights, and Revolution: British Nonconformity and Roots of the American Experience." *Church History* 61.2 (1992) 151–68.

————. *Theology and Revolution in the Scottish Reformation*. Washington, DC: Christian University Press, 1980.

————. "Traditionalism and the Seeds of Revolution in the Social Principles of the Geneva Bible." *Sixteenth Century Journal* 7.2 (1976) 94–109.

Greenawalt, Kent. "Conscientious Objection, Civil Disobedience, and Resistance." In *Christianity and Law: An Introduction*, edited by John Witte Jr. and Frank S. Alexander, 105–24. Cambridge, UK: Cambridge University Press, 2008.

Grendler, Paul F. "In Praise of Erasmus." *Wilson Quarterly* 7 (1983) 88–101.

Greschat, Martin. *Martin Bucer: A Reformer and His Times*. Translated by Stephen E. Buckwalter. Louisville: Westminster John Knox, 2004.

Gritsch, Eric W. *Thomas Müntzer: A Tragedy of Errors*. Minneapolis: Fortress, 1989.

Haberkern, Phillip N. *Patron Saint and Prophet: Jan Hus in the Bohemian and German Reformations*. Oxford: Oxford University Press, 2016.

Hantsch, Hugo. "Zum ungarisch-türkischen Problem in der allgemeinen Politik Karls V." In *Festschrift Karl Eder zum Siebzigsten Geburtstag*, edited by Helmut J. Mezler-Andelberg, 57–69. Innsbruck: Universitätsverlag Wagner, 1959.

Hendrix, Scott. "Luther." In *The Cambridge Companion to Reformation Theology*, edited by David Bagchi and David C. Steinmetz, 41. Cambridge, UK: Cambridge University Press, 2004.

Hillerbrand, Hans J., ed. *The Oxford Encyclopedia of the Reformation*. New York: Oxford University Press, 1996.

————. *The Reformation: A Narrative History Related by Contemporary Observers and Participants*. Reprint, Grand Rapids: Baker, 1979.

Hinrichs, Carl. *Luther und Müntzer: Ihre Auseinandersetzung über Obrigkeit und Widerstandsrecht*. Arbeiten zur Kirchengeschichte 29. Berlin: de Gruyter, 1952.

Holt, Mack P. *The French Wars of Religion, 1562–1629*. Cambridge, UK: Cambridge University Press, 1995.

Hostetler, Beulah S. *American Mennonites and Protestant Movements.* Scottdale, PA: Herald, 1987.

Housley, Norman. *Religious Warfare in Europe 1400–1536.* New York: Oxford University Press, 2002.

Hoyer, Siegfried and Bernd Rüdiger. *An die Versammlung gemeiner Bauernschaft: Eine revolutionäre Flugschrift aus dem Deutschen Bauernkrieg (1525).* Leipzig: Bibliographisches Institut, 1975.

Hsia, R. Po-Chia, ed. *Reform and Expansion 1500–1660.* Vol. 6 of *The Cambridge History of Christianity.* Cambridge, UK: Cambridge University Press, 2007.

Hudson, Anne. "From Oxford to Prague: The Writings of John Wyclif and His English Followers in Bohemia." *The Slavonic and East European Review* 75.4 (1997) 642–57.

Huizinga, Johan. *Erasmus and the Age of Reformation.* New York: Harper & Row, 1957.

Hunt, George L., ed. *Calvinism and the Political Order.* Philadelphia: Westminster, 1965.

Hyman, Elizabeth Hannan. "A Church Militant: Scotland, 1661–1690." *Sixteenth Century Journal* 26.1 (1995) 49–74.

James, Frank A. "Peter Martyr Vermigli: At the Crossroads of Late Medieval Scholasticism, Christian Humanism and Resurgent Augustinianism." In *Protestant Scholasticism: Essays in Reassessment,* edited by Carl R. Trueman and R. Scott Clark, 62–78. Carlisle: Paternoster, 1999.

Jenkins, Gary W. *Calvin's Tormentors: Understanding the Conflicts That Shaped the Reformer.* Grand Rapids: Baker Academic, 2018.

Jeon, Jeong Koo. "Calvin and the Two Kingdoms: Calvin's Political Philosophy in Light of Contemporary Discussion." *Westminster Theological Journal* 72 (2010) 299–320.

Johnson, Dale W., and James E. McGoldrick. "Prophet in Scotland: The Self-Image of John Knox." *Calvin Theological Journal* 33.1 (1998) 76–86.

Johnson, James Turner. *The Holy War Idea in Western and Islamic Traditions.* University Park, PA: Pennsylvania State University Press, 1997.

———. *Just War Tradition and the Restraint of War: A Moral and Historical Inquiry.* Princeton: Princeton University Press, 1981.

———. *The Quest for Peace: Three Moral Traditions in Western Cultural History.* Princeton: Princeton University Press, 1987.

Josipovic, Mario, and William McNeil. "Thomas Müntzer as 'Disturber of the Godless': A Reassessment of His Revolutionary Nature." *Mennonite Quarterly Review* 70 (1996) 431–47.

Kaplan, Benjamin J. *Divided by Faith: Religious Conflict and the Practice of Toleration in Early Modern Europe.* Cambridge, MA: Harvard University Press, 2007.

Kaufman, Peter Iver. "Social History, Pyschohistory, and the Prehistory of Swiss Anabaptism." *Journal of Religion* 68.4 (1988) 527–55.

Kelley, Donald R. "Martyrs, Myths, and the Massacre: The Background of St. Bartholomew." *American Historical Review* 77.5 (1972) 1323–42.

Kelly, Douglas F. *The Emergence of Liberty in the Modern World: The Influence of Calvin on Five Governments from the Sixteenth through Eighteenth Centuries.* Phillipsburg, NJ: P & R, 1992.

Kessler, Johannes. *Johannes Kesslers Sabbata, mit kleineren und Briefen.* St. Gallen: Fehr, 1902.

Kingdon, Robert M. *Adultery and Divorce in Calvin's Geneva.* Cambridge, MA/London: Harvard University Press, 1995.

————. "Church and State." *The Calvin Handbook*, edited by Herman J. Selderhuis, 355–61. Grand Rapids: Eerdmans, 2009.

————. "The First Expression of Theodore Beza's Political Ideas." *Archiv für Reformationgeschichte* 46 (1955) 88–100.

————. "The Function of Law in the Political Thought of Peter Martyr Vermigli." In *Reformatio Perrennis: Essays on Calvin and the Reformation*, edited by B. A. Gerrish, 159–72. Pittsburgh: Pickwick, 1981.

————. *Myths about the St. Bartholomew's Day Massacres, 1572–1576.* Cambridge, MA/London: Harvard University Press, 1988.

————. "Peter Martyr Vermigli and the Marks of the True Church." In *Continuity and Discontinuity in Church History*, edited by F. Forrester Church and Timothy George, 198–214. Leiden: Brill, 1979.

————. "The Political Resistance of the Calvinists in France and the Low Countries." *Church History* 27.3 (1958) 220–33.

————. "The Political Thought of Peter Martyr Vermigli." In *Peter Martyr Vermigli and Italian Reform*, edited by Joseph C. McClelland, 121–39. Waterloo, ONT: Wilfrid Laurier, 1980.

————. "Reactions to the St. Bartholomew Massacres in Geneva and Rome." In *Church and Society in Reformation Europe*, edited by Robert M. Kingdon, 88–99. London: Variorum Reports, 1985.

Kirby, Torrance. "Political Theology: The Godly Prince." In *Companion to Peter Martyr Vermigli*, edited by Torrance Kirby, et al., 401–21. Leiden/Boston: Brill, 2009.

Kirchner, Herbert. *Luther and the Peasants' War.* Minneapolis: Fortress, 1972.

Klaassen, Walter. *Anabaptism: Neither Catholic Nor Protestant.* Waterloo, ONT: Conrad, 1973.

Klempa, William. "Patrick Hamilton and John Knox on 'The Pith of All Divinity.'" *Touchstone* 24 (2006) 34–46.

Knox, John. "Letter to the Commonalty." In *On Rebellion*, edited by Roger A. Mason, 115–127. Cambridge Texts in the History of Political Thought. Cambridge, UK: Cambridge University Press, 1994.

————. *On Rebellion.* Cambridge Texts in the History of Political Thought. Cambridge, UK: Cambridge University Press, 1984.

————. *The Works of John Knox*, ed. David Laing. Edinburgh: Wodrow Society, 1864.

Kolb, Robert. "Luther on the Peasants and Princes." *Lutheran Quarterly* 23 (2009) 125–46.

————. *Luther's Wittenberg World: The Reformer's Family, Friends, Followers, and Foes.* Minneapolis: Fortress, 2018.

Krahn, Cornelius. *Dutch Anabaptism: Origin, Spread, Life and Thought.* 1981. Reprint, Eugene, OR: Wipf & Stock, 2004.

————. "Menno Simons." In *The Mennonite Encyclopedia: A Comprehensive Reference Work on the Anabaptist-Mennonite Movement*, edited by Harold S. Bender, et al., 577–84. Vol. 3. Scottdale, PA: Mennonite Publishing House, 1957.

Kusukawa, Sachiko. "Melanchthon." In *The Cambridge Companion to Reformation Theology*, edited by David Bagchi and David C. Steinmetz, 57–67. Cambridge, UK: Cambridge University Press, 2004.

Kyle, Richard G. "Knox, John (c. 1514–1571)." In *Encyclopedia of the Reformed Faith*, edited by Donald K. McKim, 208–209. Louisville: Westminster John Knox, 1992.

————. "Prophet of God: John Knox's Self Awareness." *Reformed Theological Review* 61.2 (2002) 85–101.

Larson, Mark J. *Calvin's Doctrine of the State: A Reformed Doctrine and Its American Trajectory, the Revolutionary War, and the Founding of the Republic.* Eugene, OR: Wipf & Stock, 2009.

———. "The Holy War Trajectory among the Reformed: From Zurich to England." *Reformation & Renaissance Review* 8.1 (2006) 7–27.

Laing, David, ed. *The Works of John Knox*, Edinburgh: Wodrow Society, 1864.

Lindberg, Carter. *The European Reformations.* 2nd ed. New York: John Wiley & Sons, 2010.

Linder, Robert D. "Forgotten Reformer." *Christian History Magazine* 71 (2001) 35–37.

———. "Pierre Viret and the Sixteenth-Century French Protestant Revolutionary Tradition." *Journal of Modern History* 38.2 (1966) 125–37.

———."Pierre Viret's Concept of a Just War." *Andrews University Seminary Studies* 22 (1984) 213–30.

———. *The Political Ideas of Pierre Viret. Travaux D'Humanisme et Renaissance LXIV.* Geneva: Librairie Droz, 1964.

Luther, Martin. "Against the Robbing and Murdering Hordes of Peasants." In *Luther's Works*, edited by Jaroslav Pelikan et al., 49–55. Vol. 46. St. Louis: Concordia, 1967.

———. "Letter to the Princes of Saxony Concerning the Rebellious Spirit (1524)." In *Luther's Works*, edited by Conrad Bergendoff, 49–59. Vol. 40. Philadelphia: Fortress, 1955.

———. "Preliminary Notice." In *Letters of John Huss, Written During His Exile and Imprisonment, with Martin Luther's Preface*, edited by Émile de Bonnechose, 1–12. Translated by Campbell Mackenzie. Edinburgh: William Whyte & Co., 1846.

———. "On War against the Turk." In *Luther's Works*, edited by Jaroslav Pelikan et al., 161–205. Vol. 46. St. Louis: Concordia, 1967

———. "Temporal Authority: To What Extent It Should Be Obeyed (1523)." In *Luther's Works*, edited by Walther I. Brandt, 81–129. Vol. 45. Philadelphia: Fortress, 1955.

———. "Whether Soldiers, Too, Can Be Saved." In *Luther's Works*, edited by Jaroslav Pelikan et al., 93–137. Vol. 46. St. Louis: Concordia, 1967.

McDonald, Forrest. "Eighteenth-Century Warfare As a Cultural Ritual." In *Requiem: Variations on Eighteenth-Century Themes*, edited by Forrest McDonald and Ellen Shapiro McDonald, 39–58. Lawrence, KS: University Press of Kansas, 1988.

McGrath, Alister. *Christianity's Dangerous Idea: The Protestant Revolution—A History for the Sixteenth Century to the Twenty.* New York: HarperOne, 2007.

McKim, Donald K., ed. *Major Themes in the Reformed Tradition.* Grand Rapids: Eerdmans, 1992.

McLaughlin, R. Emmet. "The Radical Reformation." In *Reform and Expansion 1500-1660*, edited by R. Po-Chia Hsia, 37–55. Vol. 6 of *The Cambridge History of Christianity.* Cambridge, UK: Cambridge University Press, 2007.

McNeill, John T. "The Democratic Element in Calvin's Thought." *Church History* 18 (1949) 153–71.

———. "Left-Wing Religious Movements." In *A Short History of Christianity*, edited by A.G. Baker, 127–32. Chicago: University of Chicago Press, 1940.

Manetsch, Scott. *Theodore Beza and the Quest for Peace in France, 1572–1598.* Leiden: Brill, 2000.

Mansfield, Harvey C., Jr. "The Right of Revolution." *Daedalus* 105.4 (1976) 151–62.

Matheson, Peter, ed. *The Collected Works of Thomas Müntzer.* Edinburgh: T&T Clark, 1988.

Melanchthon, Philip. "1521 *Loci Communes.*" In *Melanchthon and Bucer*, edited and translated by Wilhelm Pauck, 148–50. Philadelphia: Westminster, 1969.

———. 1543 *Loci Communes.* Translated by J. A. O. Preus. St. Louis: Concordia, 1992.

———. *Commentary on Romans.* Translated by Fred Kramer. St. Louis: Concordia, 1992.

Merx, Otto, et al. *Akten zur Geschichte des Bauernkriegs in Mitteldeutschland.* Vol. 2. Jena: Scientia Verlag, 1964.

Mezler-Andelberg, Helmut J., ed. *Festschrift Karl Eder zum Siebzigsten Geburtstag,* Innsbruck: Universitätsverlag Wagner, 1959.

Miller, Gregory J. "Fighting Like a Christian: The Ottoman Advance and the Development of Luther's Doctrine of Just War." In *Caritas Et Reformatio*, edited by David M. Whitford, 41–57. St. Louis: Concordia, 2002.

———. "Luther on the Turks and Islam." In *Harvesting Martin Luther's Reflections on Theology, Ethics, and the Church*, edited by Timothy J. Wengert, 185–203. Minneapolis: Fortress, 2017.

———. *The Turks and Islam in Reformation Germany.* New York: Routledge, 2017.

Monter, E. William. *Calvin's Geneva.* New York: Wiley and Sons, 1967.

Mühling, Andreas. "Calvin and the Swiss Confederation." In *The Calvin Handbook*, edited by Herman J. Selderhuis, 63–74. Grand Rapids: Eerdmans, 2009.

Mundry, Paul. "John Calvin and Anabaptists on War." *Brethren Life and Thought* 23 (1978) 239–47.

Naphy, William G. "Church and State in Calvin's Geneva." In *Calvin and the Church*, edited by David Foxgrover, 13–28. Grand Rapids: CRC Product Services, 2002.

Niebuhr, H. Richard. *The Social Sources of Denominationalism.* Cleveland/New York: World, 1957.

Oberman, Heiko A. "Europa afflicta: The Reformation of the Refugees." *Archiv für Reformationsgeschichte* 83 (1992) 91–111.

———. "The Gospel of Social Unrest: 450 Years After the So-Called 'German Peasants' War' of 1525." *Harvard Theological Review* 69 (1976) 103–29.

———. *The Reformation: Roots and Ramifications.* Translated by A. C. Gow. London/ New York: T&T Clark, 2004.

O'Donovan, Joan Lockwood. *Theology of Law and Authority in the English Reformation.* Grand Rapids: Eerdmans, 1991.

O'Donovan, Oliver, and Joan Lockwood O'Donovan, eds. *From Irenaeus to Grotius: A Sourcebook in Christian Political Thought.* Grand Rapids: Eerdmans, 1999.

Olin, John C., ed. *Desiderius Erasmus: Christian Humanism and the Reformation.* New York: Harper & Row, 1965.

Olson, Jeannine E. "Calvin and Social-Ethical Issues." In *The Cambridge Companion to John Calvin*, edited by Donald K. McKim, 153–72. Cambridge, UK: Cambridge University Press, 2004.

———. "Church and Society in Calvin's Theology and Its Early Reception." In *Calvin's Theology and Its Reception*, edited by J. Todd Billings and I. John Hesselink, 193–215. Louisville: Westminster John Knox, 2012.

Olson, Oliver K. "The Theology of Revolution: Magdeburg, 1550–1551." *Sixteenth Century Journal* 3.1 (1972) 56–79.

Opitz, Peter. "Bullinger's *Decades*: Instruction in Faith and Conduct." In *Architect of Reformation: An Introduction to Heinrich Bullinger, 1504–1575*, edited by Bruce Gordon and Emidio Campi, 101–16. Grand Rapids: Baker Academic, 2004.

Oyer, John Stanley. *Lutheran Reformers against Anabaptists: Luther, Melanchthon and Menius and the Anabaptists of Central Germany*. The Hague: M. Nijhoff, 1964.

Ozment, Steven E. *The Age of Reform, 1250–1550*. New Haven: Yale University Press, 1980.

———. *Mysticism and Dissent: Religious Ideology and Social Protest in the Sixteenth Century*. New Haven/London: Yale University Press, 1973.

Packull, Werner O., and Geoffrey L. Dipple, eds. *Radical Reformation Studies*. Aldershot, UK: Ashgate, 1999.

Paquin, René. "Calvin and Theocracy in Geneva: Church and World in Ordered Tasks." *Arc: The Journal of the Faculty of Religious Studies, McGill University* 28 (2000) 91–113.

Patterson, Eric, and Timothy J. Demy, eds. *Philosophers on War*. Newport, RI: Stone Tower, 2017.

Peardon, Barbara. "The Politics of Polemic: John Ponet's Short Treatise of Politic Power and Contemporary Circumstance 1553–1556." *Journal of British Studies* 22.1 (1982) 35–49.

Pellerin, Daniel. "Calvin: Militant or Man of Peace?" *Review of Politics* 65.1 (2003) 35–59.

Pfeffer, Leo. *Church, State, and Freedom*. Boston: Beacon, 1967.

Porter, J. M., ed. *Luther: Selected Political Writings*. Lanham, MD: University Press of America, 1974.

Preus, James S. "Political Function of Luther's *Doctrina*." *Concordia Theological Monthly* 43 (1972) 591–99.

Raath, Andries. "Covenant and the Christian Community: Bullinger and the Relationship between Church and Magistracy in Early Cape Settlement (1652–1708)." *Sixteenth Century Journal* 33.4 (2002) 999–1019.

Raath, Andries, and Shaun de Freitas. "Rebellion, Resistance, and a Swiss Brutus?" *Historical Journal* 48 (2005) 1–26.

Reid, W. Stanford. "John Knox's Theology of Political Government." *Sixteenth Century Journal* 19.4 (1988) 529–40.

———, ed. *The Reformation: Revival or Revolution?* New York: Rinehart and Winston, 1968.

Roth, John D. "Harmonizing the Scriptures: Swiss Brethren Understandings of the Relationship between the Old and New Testament during the Last Half of the Sixteenth Century." In *Radical Reformation Studies: Essays Presented to James M. Stayer*, edited by Werner O. Packull and Geoffrey L. Dipple, 35–52. Aldershot, UK: Ashgate, 1999.

Rowland, Christopher. "Thomas Müntzer (c. 1489–1525)." *The Expository Times* 126.9 (2015) 417–24.

Sattler, Michael. "The Schleitheim Articles." In *The Radical Reformation*, edited by Michael G. Baylor, 172–80. Cambridge Texts in the History of Political Thought. Cambridge, UK: Cambridge University Press, 1991.

Schaff, Harold H. "The Anabaptists, the Reformers, and Civil Government." *Church History* 1.1 (1932) 27–46.

Schaff, Philip. *Modern Christianity: The Swiss Reformation*. Vol. 8 of *History of the Christian Church*. Grand Rapids: Christian Classics Ethereal, 1882.

Scott, Tom. *Thomas Müntzer: Theology and Revolution in the German Reformation*. London: Macmillan, 1989.

Shoenberger, Cynthia Grant. "The Development of the Lutheran Theory of Resistance: 1523–1530." *Sixteenth Century Journal* 8 (1977) 61–76.

Simons, Menno. "Foundation of Christian Doctrine (1539)." In *The Complete Writings of Menno Simons*, edited by John C. Wenger, 105–226. Scottdale, PA: Mennonite Publishing House, 1956.

———. "My Conversion, Call, and Testimony (1554)." In *The Complete Writings of Menno Simons*, edited by John C. Wenger, 668–74. Scottdale, PA: Mennonite Publishing House, 1956.

———. "A Pathetic Supplication to All Magistrates (1552)." In *The Complete Writings of Menno Simons*, edited by John C. Wenger, 525–30. Scottdale, PA: Mennonite Publishing House, 1956.

———. "A Reply to False Accusations (1552)." In *The Complete Writings of Menno Simons*, edited by John C. Wenger, 543–77. Scottdale, PA: Mennonite Publishing House, 1956.

———. "A Reply to Gellius Faber (1554)." In *The Complete Writings of Menno Simons*, edited by John C. Wenger, 717–23. Scottdale, PA: Mennonite Publishing House, 1956.

Smahel, Frantisěk, and Ota Pavlicek, ed. *A Companion to Jan Hus.* Leiden: Brill, 2015.

Smither, James R. "The St. Bartholomew's Day Massacre and Images of Kingship in France: 1572–1574." *Sixteenth Century Journal* 22 (1999) 27–46.

Smith, Robert O. "Luther, the Turks, and Islam." *Currents in Theology and Mission* 34.5 (2007) 351–64.

Snavely, Iren L. "Huldrych Zwingli and the Preaching Office in German Switzerland." *Fides et Historia* 25.3 (1993) 33–45.

Snyder, Arnold. "The Influence of the Schleitheim Articles on the Anabaptist Movement: An Historical Evaluation." *Mennonite Quarterly Review* 63 (1989) 323–44.

Solt, Leo F. "Revolutionary Calvinist Parties in England under Elizabeth I and Charles I." *Church History* 27.3 (1958) 234–39.

Stayer, James M. *Anabaptists and the Sword.* Lawrence, KS: Coronado, 1972.

———. *The German Peasants' War and Anabaptist Community of Goods.* McGill-Queen's Studies in the History of Religion. Montreal/Kingston: McGill-Queen's University Press, 1991.

———. "Thomas Müntzer on 1989: A Review Article." *Sixteenth Century Journal* 21.4 (1990) 655–70.

Stayer, James M., et al. "From Monogenesis to Polygenesis: The Historical Discussion of Anabaptist Origins." *Mennonite Quarterly Review* 42.2 (1975) 83–121.

Stephens, W. Peter. "The Authority of the Bible in Heinrich Bullinger's Early Works." *Reformation and Renaissance Review* 10 (2008) 37–58.

———. "Huldrych Zwingli: The Swiss Reformer." *Scottish Journal of Theology* 41 (1988) 27–47.

———. "The Theology of Zwingli." In *The Cambridge Companion to Reformation Theology*, edited by David Bagchi and David C. Steinmetz, 80–99. Cambridge, UK: Cambridge University Press, 2004.

Sterry, Peter. *The Comings Forth of Christ in the Power of His Death.* London: Matth. Simmons, 1650.

Stevenson, William R. "Calvin and Political Issues." In *The Cambridge Companion to John Calvin*, edited by Donald K. McKim, 173–87. Cambridge, UK: Cambridge University Press, 2004.

Tallett, Frank. *War and Society in Early-Modern Europe 1495–1715.* London: Routledge, 1992.

Thompson, John L. "Patriarchs, Polygamy, and Private Resistance: John Calvin and Others on Breaking God's Rules." *Sixteenth Century Journal* 25.1 (1994) 3–27.

Thorp, Malcolm R. "Religion and the Wyatt Rebellion of 1554." *Church History* 47.4 (1978) 363–80.

Treasure, Geoffrey. *The Huguenots.* New Haven: Yale University Press, 2013.

Treesh, Susanna K. "The Waldensian Recourse to Violence." *Church History* 55.3 (1986) 294–306.

Turnbull, Stephen. *The Hussite Wars 1419–36.* Oxford: Osprey, 2006.

"The Twelve Articles of Upper Swabia." In *The German Peasants' War: A History in Documents*, edited and translated by Tom Scott and Robert W. Scribner, 252–57. Atlantic Highlands, NJ: Humanities, 1991.

VanDrunen, David. "The Use of Natural Law in Early Calvinist Resistance Theory." *Journal of Law and Religion* 32.1 (2006) 143–67.

Van Dussen, Michael. *From England to Bohemia: Heresy and Communication in the Later Middle Ages.* Cambridge, UK: Cambridge University Press, 2012.

Vermigli, Peter Martyr. *The Common Places.* Translated by Anthony Marten. London: Denham and Middleton, 1583.

———. "Of Warre or Battell." In *The Political Thought of Peter Martyr Vermigli: Selected Texts and Commentary*, edited by Robert M. Kingdon, 61–86. Geneva: Droz, 1980.

Walton, Robert C. "The Institutionalization of the Reformation at Zürich." *Zwingliana* 13 (1972) 497–515.

———. "Zwingli: Founding Father of the Reformed Churches." In *Leaders of the Reformation*, edited by Richard L. DeMolen, 69–98. Selinsgrove, PA: Susquehanna University Press, 1984.

———. *Zwingli's Theocracy.* Toronto: University of Toronto Press, 1967.

Walzer, Michael. *The Revolution of the Saints: A Study in the Origins of Radical Politics.* Cambridge, MA: Harvard, 1965.

Wappler, Paul. *Die Täuferbewegung in Thuringen von 1526–1584.* Jena: Gustav Fischer, 1913.

———. *Thomas Müntzer und die "Zwickauer Propheten."* 2nd ed. Gütersloh: Mohn, 1966.

Wartenberg, Günther. "Philip Melanchthon, the Wittenberg Reformer Alongside Luther." *Lutheran Quarterly* 12 (1998) 373–82.

Wenger, John C., ed. *The Complete Writings of Menno Simons.* Scottdale, PA: Mennonite, 1956.

———. "The Schleitheim Confession of Faith." *Mennonite Quarterly Review* 19.4 (1945) 243–53.

Wengert, Timothy J., ed. *Harvesting Martin Luther's Reflections on Theology, Ethics, and the Church.* Grand Rapids: Eerdmans, 2003.

———. "Philip Melanchthon and Augustine of Hippo." *Lutheran Quarterly* 22 (2008) 249–67.

———. "Philip Melanchthon and a Christian Politics." *Lutheran Quarterly* 17 (2003) 29–62.

Whitford, David M. "Luther's Political Encounters." In *The Cambridge Companion to Martin Luther*, edited by Donald K. McKim, 178–92. Cambridge, UK: Cambridge University Press, 2003.

———. *Tyranny and Resistance: The Magdeburg Confession and the Lutheran Tradition.* St. Louis: Concordia, 2001.

Whitney, J. P. "Erasmus." *English Historical Review* 35 (1920) 1–25.

Williams, George Huntston. "Radical Elements in the Reformation." In *The Reformation: Revival or Revolution?*, edited by W. Stanford Reid, 30–36. New York: Rinehart and Winston, 1968.

———. *The Radical Reformation*. Sixteenth Century Essays & Studies 15. 3rd ed. Kirksville, MO: Truman State University Press, 1992.

———, ed. *Spiritual and Anabaptist Writers: Documents Illustrative of the Radical Reformation*. Library of Christian Classics 25. Philadelphia: Westminster, 1957.

Witte, John, Jr. *God's Joust, God's Justice: Law and Religion in the Western Tradition*. Grand Rapids: Eerdmans, 2006.

———. *Law and Protestantism: The Legal Teaching of the Lutheran Reformation*. Cambridge, UK: Cambridge University Press, 2002.

———. *The Reformation of Rights: Law, Religion, and Human Rights in Early Modern Calvinism*. Cambridge, UK: Cambridge University Press, 2007.

———. "Rights, Resistance, and Revolution in the Western Tradition: Early Protestant Foundations." *Law and History Review* 26 (2008) 545–70.

Witte, John, Jr., and Frank S. Alexander, ed. *Christianity and Law: An Introduction*. Cambridge, UK: Cambridge University Press, 2008.

Wollman, David H. "The Biblical Justification for Resistance to Authority in Ponet's and Goodman's Polemics." *Sixteenth Century Journal* 13.4 (1982) 29–41.

Wormwald, Jenny. "Knox, John." In *The Oxford Encyclopedia of the Reformation*, edited by Hans J. Hillerbrand, 380–81. Vol. 2. New York: Oxford University Press, 1996.

Yoder, Jess. "The Frankenthal Debate with the Anabaptists in 1571: Purpose, Procedure, Participants." *Mennonite Quarterly Review* 36 (1962) 14–35.

———. "The Frankenthal Disputation: Part II: Outcome Issues, Debating Methods." *Mennonite Quarterly Review* 36 (1962) 116–42.

Yoder, John Howard. *Anabaptism and Reformation in Switzerland. An Historical and Theological Analysis of the Dialogues between Anabaptists and Reformers*. Edited by C. Arnold Snyder. Kitchener, ONT: Pandora, 2004.

Ziegler, Donald J. "Marpeck versus Butzer: A Sixteenth-Century Debate over the Uses and Limits of Political Authority." *Sixteenth Century Essays and Studies* 2 (1971) 95–107.

Zuck, Lowell H., ed. *Christianity and Revolution: Radical Testimonies 1520–1650*. Philadelphia: Temple University Press, 1975.

Zuidema, Jason. "Peter Martyr: Protestant Monk?" *Reformation and Renaissance Review* 13 (2011) 373–86.

Zwingli, Huldrych. *The Defense of the Reformed Faith*. Translated by E. J. Furch. Allison Park, PA: Pickwick, 1984.

———. "An Exposition of the Faith." In *Zwingli and Bullinger*, translated by G. W. Bromiley, 266–68. Philadelphia: Westminster, 1953.

———. *Huldreich Zwinglis Sämtliche Werke*. Vol. 3. Corpus Reformatorum 90. Leipzig: Heinsius, 1914.

———. *Huldreich Zwinglis Sämtliche Werke*. Vol. 6.1. Corpus Reformatorum 93.1. Zürich: Berichthaus, 1961.

# About the Authors

**Timothy J. Demy, ThD, PhD,** is Professor of Military Ethics at the US Naval War College. He earned the MSt in international relations from the University of Cambridge, a MA in national security and strategic studies from the US Naval War College, a ThM and ThD in historical theology from Dallas Theological Seminary, and a MA and PhD in humanities from Salve Regina University. Among his many books and publications, he is co-author with J. Daryl Charles of *War, Peace, and Christianity: Questions and Answers from a Just-War Perspective* (2010), co-editor of *Philosophers on War* (2017), and co-editor of *War and Religion: An Encyclopedia of Faith and Conflict* (3 vols., 2017).

**Mark J. Larson, PhD,** majored in biblical studies at Cedarville University and Baptist Bible School of Theology. He studied political theory and international relations at Regent University. He earned a ThM in systematic theology at Westminster Theological Seminary and a PhD in historical theology at Calvin Theological Seminary. He is the author of *Abraham Kuyper, Conservatism, and Church and State* (2015); *Calvin's Doctrine of the State: A Reformed Doctrine and Its American Trajectory, the Revolutionary War, and the Founding of the Republic* (2009); and numerous encyclopedia entries and articles.

**J. Daryl Charles, PhD,** is the Acton Institute Affiliate Scholar in Theology and Ethics, a contributing editor of the journal *Providence: A Journal of Christianity and American Foreign Policy* and the journal *Touchstone*, and an affiliated scholar of the John Jay Institute. He is author, co-author, editor or co-editor of eighteen books, including *Natural Law and Religious*

*Freedom* (Routledge, 2017); (with David D. Corey) *The Just War Tradition: An Introduction* (2012); (with David B. Capes) *Thriving in Babylon* (2011); *A Return to Moral First Things: Retrieving the Natural Law* (2008); and most recently, (with Mark David Hall) *America's Wars: A Just War Perspective* (2019). Charles has taught at Taylor University and Union University, served as director of the Bryan Institute for Critical Thought & Practice, was a 2013/14 visiting professor in the honors program at Berry College, and served as a 2007/8 William B. Simon visiting fellow in religion and public life at the James Madison Program, Princeton University, as well as the 2003/4 visiting fellow of the Institute for Faith & Learning, Baylor University. The focus of Charles's research and writing is religion and society, Christian social ethics, the just war tradition, and the natural law. Prior to entering the university classroom, Charles did public policy work in criminal justice in Washington, DC.